MISSING

CLAIR M. POULSON

MISSING

CLAIR M. POULSON

SWEETWATER BOOKS
An imprint of Cedar Fort, Inc.
Springville, Utah

Paperback ISBN 13: 978-1-4621-5046-5
eBook ISBN 13: 978-1-4621-5047-2

Published by Sweetwater Books, an imprint of Cedar Fort, Inc.
2373 W. 700 S., Suite 100, Springville, UT 84663
Distributed by Cedar Fort, Inc., www.cedarfort.com

Library of Congress Cataloging Number:

Cover design by Shawnda Craig

Edited by Ashley Gebert
Typeset by Liz Kazandzhy

Printed in the United States of America

10 9 8 7 6 5 4 3 2 1

Printed on acid-free paper

To my wife and our family for their unfailing support.

CONTENTS

Prologue

Sammy Anders was a small boy for his age. At eight, he was more the size of an average five-year-old. He was a gifted artist and highly intelligent, which was perhaps partly why he preferred to be alone rather than playing with other kids.

He was the only son of a couple who were devoted to him. They had hoped for more children, but it had not happened. The family of three lived in St. George, and Sammy didn't mind the heat. One of his favorite things to do from the age of four was explore in the desert with his father on Saturdays. He saw many animals along the way, which he would draw from memory when he got home. They often explored old mines, and there, again, he found things to draw.

They were very active in The Church of Jesus Christ of Latter-day Saints, and Sammy enjoyed primary. It wasn't being with children his own age that made it fun for him; it was learning about Jesus Christ, the Book of Mormon, and prophets of old. And he loved the primary songs and committed many of them to memory. His parents, Ophelia and Samuel, would smile at each other when they'd hear him singing at the top of his voice in his room.

One Saturday, when he was seven, Ophelia packed them a lunch, and Sammy and Samuel headed to the desert to check out an old mine. They were driving on a dirt road a few miles west of St. George when dust appeared on the road ahead of them.

"From the looks of that dust trail, somebody is in too much of a hurry," Samuel said to Sammy. "This road is rough and narrow. I think I'll pull to the edge of the road and give him room to pass."

Samuel slowed down and was pulling to the edge in his small pickup when the other vehicle, a pickup with large tires, came around a curve ahead of them, sliding as it completed the turn. Samuel had not been able to get entirely off the road when the pickup approached at a terrible speed, accelerating. It hit a hole in the road and lost control.

Sammy screamed as the larger truck careened toward them.

Samuel shouted, "Duck down, son," as he attempted to drive clear of the narrow road.

The large pickup struck Samuel's small one slightly off from head-on. The driver's sides of both trucks came together, flipping the Anders truck off the road and onto its top. The large pickup also rolled, and the two vehicles ended up stuck together, both upside-down.

Sammy's scream stopped abruptly. The driver's side of the small pickup was smashed flat. Sammy's, on the other hand, gave him room to move, though it had been banged up too. He alertly unfastened his seat belt and rolled onto the smashed cab. He looked at his dad, who had been crushed terribly. Sammy instinctively feared that his father was dead. He tried to scream again, to call out to his dad, anything . . . but no sound came out. Tears flowed, but he couldn't even cry properly.

Sammy eventually fell asleep, exhausted from the sorrow and horror and trauma of the crash. He woke up when someone touched him. His rescuer had reached through the little space where the passenger window had been and told Sammy he would be freed from the truck in a short time. He had no idea what was used to pry the cab up enough for him to crawl out until one of the paramedics eventually told him they had used the jaws of life.

Sammy didn't respond to anything his rescuers asked him or said to him, for he had lost his voice. He was put in an ambulance, whisked away from the accident scene, and taken to the hospital in St. George to be examined. He was very aware of all that was occurring around him. He was almost positive that his father was dead, and Sammy's heart was broken.

Sammy eventually fell asleep in a hospital bed. When he awoke, it was to the sound of his mother's voice. "Sammy," she said, "they're going to let me take you home now. Your father was injured much worse than you were, and he will be in the hospital for a few days."

Sammy still couldn't speak, but knowing his father was alive cheered him up. His mother took him to see Samuel in the ICU, where she explained that he was in a medically induced coma. But just seeing his face was a huge comfort to the young boy.

The days ahead were terribly difficult for both Sammy and his mother. He had not been able to utter a single word. She took him to a doctor, but nothing seemed to help.

A seventeen-year-old cousin named Gina Rogers and her family visited from their home in Duchesne a few days after Samuel was released from the hospital. The second evening of their visit, Gina was alone with Sammy in his room.

"Sammy," Gina said to him, "what happened to you is very hard. I'm so sorry. I just wish you could talk to me and tell me how you're feeling."

Sammy looked Gina in the eyes. Something about her touched his heart—perhaps the fact that she looked very much like his mother. He'd told her that before. He opened his mouth, and the words, "I'm sad that my dad has been hurt so badly," came out. That was the beginning. Gina's presence had done what no one else, including doctors, had been able to do; she had somehow enabled him to talk.

She stayed with him for nearly an hour, and by the time she and Sammy left his room to join the others in the living room, they had talked together about his dad's injuries and how much his mother needed him. "You are the man of the house until your dad is better," she told him.

As they entered the living room, Sammy ran to his mother, crying. "I love you, Mom, and I love Dad, and I love Gina. She helped me talk." A miracle had occurred in the midst of so much suffering. The two families prayed together and thanked Heavenly Father for restoring Sammy's ability to talk.

Even though he recovered the ability to speak, he became very quiet and lost himself in his drawing. He could sketch anything from memory, and the subject was always easily recognized by anyone who saw his work.

Sammy was a boy who absorbed everything going on around him. One of which was his mother's declining health. Something was seriously wrong. She told him it was nothing to worry about, that she was just tired from having to work so hard at her job to provide a decent living for the three of them.

However, one day when he was eight, while studying in his room, he heard his mother cry out, and then there was a thud. Sammy raced from his room to find his mother lying face down on the kitchen floor. He dropped beside her, crying out. "Mom, are you okay?"

Ophelia was not okay. Sammy dialed 911 on his mother's phone, which had fallen from her hand. But before he could say anything to the dispatcher, his voice failed him. He tried and tried to speak, but he couldn't get a sound out. For the next several minutes, he sat beside his mother on the floor, one hand clutching the phone, which was still unlocked, and one holding his mother's very still hand.

He was aware of a voice on the phone asking him to identify himself over and over again. He tried to respond but still couldn't do it. Then the voice said something to the effect that a police officer was coming to the address the operator had identified. Only then did Sammy close the phone and dial another number that was stored in his memory.

His cousin Gina answered the phone. "Hi, Ophelia. My friend and I are just walking home from school. How are you doing?" Gina heard no words over the phone, just a siren somewhere in the background, and her heart skipped a beat. Then the call ended abruptly, and a moment later, a text pinged on Ophelia's phone. It read: "It's me, Sammy. Mommy has fallen to the floor. I can't wake her up. And I can't talk. A policeman is coming."

***

Gina, heart now pounding, said to her best friend, Maya Warwick, "Something has happened to my aunt Ophelia. And Sammy can't talk. He texted me when he couldn't tell me what had happened over the phone."

"Oh no, Gina. I hope she'll be okay," Maya responded.

"Yes, I hope so too," Gina said. "Sammy and I talk on the phone occasionally. The last time he called me, it was on their house phone, and he told me that he was sure something was wrong with his mother but that she told him she was just overworked and tired. There must have been something more than that going on with her."

The two girls, with their schoolbooks in backpacks, began to jog. They bypassed Maya's house, which was the closer of their two homes. They lived three blocks apart. They were about halfway between their houses when Gina's phone rang again. She answered it, hoping it was Ophelia this time. But that was not to be. It was a police officer telling Gina that Mrs. Anders was being taken to the hospital and that her little boy couldn't talk. He explained that the boy had just dialed the phone again and handed it to the officer. Gina and the officer had a short discussion, during which she explained her relationship to Sammy and his parents and that there were no other relatives in the St. George area. She told the officer that she was sure a neighbor would watch the boy until her family could get there. Then she asked to speak with Sammy, who still couldn't talk.

Knowing that Sammy's father was in the hospital and would be for quite some time yet, eighteen-year-old Gina reassured Sammy that the officer would help find a neighbor to watch him until her family could get down there. "We'll fly down in Dad's airplane," she said. "So we won't be too long. Sammy, keep your mother's phone with you so I can reach you. I have your bishop's number. I'll call him, and he might have a better place for you to stay than the neighbors'."

Gina kept hoping that her voice would help him recover his own, like it had when his father had been injured. However, she had a feeling it wasn't her voice but the fact that she looked so much like his mother that had helped him to talk following the injury of his father. She didn't hear a sound. She ended the call. By then, the girls had reached Gina's family's house. They both went in, and Gina found her mother cooking in the kitchen.

The moment she saw her mother, Sue, she began to sob. When she cried, so did her best friend, Maya. Concern covered Sue's face, and she stopped what she was doing and ran to Gina. "Honey, what is the matter?"

"Aunt Ophelia is in the hospital," she managed to say through her sobs.

Her mother was shocked, and tears also flowed from her eyes.

"Mom, Sammy lost his voice again. I talked to a police officer and asked him to see if a neighbor could take care of Sammy until we can get there. Or maybe we should call their bishop, and he can find a better place for him to stay."

"I'll call him," Sue said as she rubbed her eyes. "His number is in my phone from when Samuel was first hospitalized. I'll also call your dad and have him get the plane and bring it to Duchesne. We'll all go. Sammy will need all the support we can give him."

An hour later, the Rogers family was on its way to St. George in their airplane. They had communicated with Sammy several times by text. He was no longer with a neighbor; the bishop and his wife had picked him up and taken him home with them.

Sammy got his voice back after spending some time with Gina. "Can I come live with your family while Dad and Mom get well?" he asked. "I would rather be with you than with the bishop's family."

That had already been decided, as Gina and her family had discussed it over their flight to St. George. Sammy's face brightened when he was told he would be living with them in Duchesne until his parents recovered. He hugged Gina tightly.

The next day, they flew back to Duchesne. Sammy, thanks to Gina and her fourteen-year-old brother, Peyton, was once again a moderately happy boy. He did speak often of how much he missed his parents. It seemed, though, that he was going to be fine living with the Rogers family for a while. He had even become friends with eight-year-old Bradly Warwick, Maya's brother and the son of Dale and Natalie Warwick. But he was closest to Gina. She reminded him very much of his mother, and she treated him with love and compassion.

Chapter 1

CARTER KEEFE HAD BEEN HOME FROM HIS MISSION TO ENGLAND FOR over a year. He'd considered going to college but had become acquainted with Bentley Radford, Bentley's wife, Kamryn, and Bentley's nephew, Cedric Skeed, a month following his return to Duchesne, Utah. Cedric was the brother of Bentley's first wife, who had died in an automobile accident. Cedric's parents had also been killed earlier in an accident, leaving Bentley as the only person who could care for the teenage boy. Bentley was a private investigator and an author of suspense novels. They lived on a small homestead in the hills west of Duchesne.

Kamryn invited Carter to dinner at the Radfords' cabin one Sunday afternoon. He was fascinated by the work Bentley did as a PI—with the occasional help of his fourteen-year-old nephew and his wife. As they'd visited that afternoon, Bentley had mentioned that he'd never expected to be so busy with the investigations that came his way. He wanted to spend more time writing novels.

"Have you considered hiring someone to help you with your cases?" Carter asked.

"I've thought about it," Bentley responded. "Would you be interested in helping me?"

"Are you serious?" A shiver of excitement raced down Carter's spine.

Bentley looked at his wife, and she smiled and nodded but didn't say anything.

Cedric grinned. "We could take on a few more cases if Carter worked with us, and you could still write more."

Bentley looked at Kamryn again. This time, she spoke. "I agree with Cedric," she said. "You've had to turn down some interesting cases because you didn't feel like you had enough time to devote to them."

"What do you think, Carter? Would you be interested in becoming a private investigator?"

Carter jumped at the opportunity, nodding vigorously. "If you're sure, I'd love to work for you."

"It's not always exciting work. In fact, at times, it's very dull," Bentley stressed. "And there are lots of reports to write. Lots of time spent on the phone too."

"If you're trying to make me change my mind, it's not working. If you really mean it, I'm in." Carter grinned broadly.

"Then you're hired," Bentley said.

Within a couple months, Carter Keefe was licensed as a private investigator and assisted Bentley in his work. It turned out that he liked it very much. So instead of going off to college like he'd been planning, he was able to stay in Duchesne, the town he'd grown up in and loved very much. He lived in an apartment in the same ward as the Radfords. He'd started taking a couple of online classes about investigating.

Carter felt good about his decision, and he very much enjoyed working with Bentley and his wife and nephew. One of the reasons he was glad to be able to stay in Duchesne was that he had his eye on a couple of young ladies. More specifically, one of the two, but the two seemed to always be together.

Both women lived in the same ward as Carter, and he became friends with them. They were seniors in high school, soon to graduate. Their families were active members of The Church of Jesus Christ of Latter-day Saints. Both women adhered to high standards in language and dress. They honored their parents and respected their siblings.

Gina Rogers and Maya Warwick had been close friends since kindergarten. Both were eighteen, two of the oldest in their class. Neither of them had a serious boyfriend, but both were very popular and had plenty of dates.

Carter eventually asked Gina Rogers to go out with him. Maya was certainly beautiful, but his eye had been on Gina, the pretty blonde girl, since the first time he saw her after returning from his mission.

Gina had blues eyes and a winning smile. She was about five eight and took good care of herself. Even though she was four years younger than him, they found that they enjoyed one another's company and began to date regularly. Maya Warwick and another young man occasionally double-dated with Gina and Carter. Both girls also occasionally dated other guys. After all, they were popular girls and very involved in sports and other activities at Duchesne High School.

After the first date, Carter had no strong desire to date anyone other than Gina, but he was fine with her going out with other guys for now. He simply concentrated on learning to become a good investigator. Gina and Maya were working hard on their studies and looking forward to their graduation. Carter also became close to Cedric Skeed after he was called to work with him and other boys his age in the young men's program in the ward.

Cedric liked to talk to Carter about his interest in the cases Bentley worked on. They also talked about the classes they were taking online. Cedric was homeschooled by the Radfords, but much of his education came from online classes. Carter, meanwhile, took classes to learn all he could about investigating. He spent quite a bit of time at the small Radford homestead. He enjoyed the animals Bentley raised. He liked to help with them when he could. Life for Carter Keefe was good.

***

Gina and Maya talked often about boys.

"You like Carter a lot, don't you?" Maya said to Gina one day as they were walking home from school.

"Yes, I do. He's fun to be with, he's cute, and he has a strong testimony of the gospel. What's not to like about him?" Gina responded with a grin.

"If he asked you to date him and no other guys, would you?" Maya asked.

Gina thought for a moment. "Yes, I would. I don't really enjoy spending time with any of the other guys. Not as much as spending time with him."

The two close friends had talked about going to Snow College, in Ephraim, for a year. They would be roommates there. Then when they turned nineteen, they both believed that they would serve missions. Gina was thinking about that now, and she was quite certain that Maya was thinking about it too.

The two walked in silence for three or four minutes. Maya finally broke the silence. "If you and Carter become exclusive, what would that do to your plans to go to Snow College? There will be lots of cute guys there."

Gina stopped walking. Maya did the same.

"Well, what are you thinking?" Maya pressed.

"I'm thinking that I like Carter a lot, and like I said, I don't really care about any other guys," Gina said.

"That's what I thought," Maya said with a serious look on her face.

"But I don't know if Carter likes me all that much," Gina said, even though in her heart she didn't believe that. She was quite certain that he was developing strong feelings for her, and she liked the idea very much. "Anyway, Maya, I don't think he will ask me to be exclusive."

Maya shook her head and grinned. "You don't really believe that, do you? Be honest with me."

"Maya, you're right. I really don't want to go with anyone but him. I know I'm young and probably shouldn't be feeling this strongly about Carter. But I really care about him."

"Do you love him?" Maya asked.

"I'm not sure," Gina said, but in her heart, she realized that her feelings for him were something close to love. For the life of her, she didn't know how that had happened. She felt eighteen was too young for her to develop such feelings for a guy. She changed the subject by saying, "I hope we can win our softball game tomorrow."

Both girls were very athletic and loved to play softball. They were having a winning season and hoped to reach the state championship game. "I'm ready, I think," Maya said. "You have a lot of pressure on you as the pitcher, though. Are you ready?"

"My arm feels really good. Yes, I'm ready."

The girls then talked softball the rest of the way to Maya's house, where they parted, and Gina went on to her house just three blocks farther.

Chapter 2

Duchesne, Utah, is a small town in Eastern Utah. It's not a crime-free community, but it is safer than most places. Folks were not afraid to go on walks at night without looking over their shoulders. Serious violent crime was rare, but when cases arose, the sheriff often called on Bentley to assist in the investigations. When Bentley became involved, so did his young partner, Carter Keefe.

There were problems with drug abuse and distribution, but it was not as rampant as in the larger cities. The sheriff and his deputies had a good idea who the more serious drug offenders were, and they kept a close eye on them. Occasionally someone would go missing, usually a teen, but they were never missing for long. In those rare cases when young people disappeared, it was usually because they had been troubled over a family problem or a disagreement with other kids and simply ran away. But they were soon found. More times than not, they returned on their own. In all cases, the community was concerned and took the matter seriously until the young person was home and safe.

Carter had been thinking about Gina all day, and he had decided to pay her a visit. He dropped in unannounced at Gina's to ask her if she would go to dinner and a movie with him that coming Friday evening. He liked her a lot and enjoyed the time they spent together. He was seriously thinking about asking her to date him exclusively. He wasn't sure how she would react to that, but it was all he could think about over the past few weeks. He had developed some deep feelings for Gina. He wasn't sure, but he suspected she had similar feelings for him. He was pretty sure that she hadn't accepted dates with anyone else for a while now. And he certainly had no intention of asking anyone else out.

He rang the doorbell and waited only a moment before the door opened. Gina's fourteen-year-old brother, Peyton, stood there grinning. "Hi, Carter," he said. "Come in. Gina talks about you all the time, you know."

Peyton was a member of Carter's teacher's quorum and best friends with Cedric Skeed. Carter was very fond of the boys, and they liked him a great deal too. He stepped in and stood just inside the door.

"You are looking for Gina, aren't you?" Peyton asked, still grinning broadly.

"Yes. Would you mind telling her I'm here?" Carter asked as he processed the news that Gina talked about him to her family a lot.

"Are you going to ask her for another date?" Peyton asked. "I don't want her to go out with Elliot Jones. He's such a creep, and his father is scary." The grin vanished as Peyton offered that information.

Carter was surprised. He knew about the Jones guy and his father. They were not good people. Elliot was at least two or three years older than Carter. "Did Gina go out with him?" he asked, pretty sure that she hadn't gone out with him or anyone else lately, but especially not Jones.

"No! She would never do that. She says she doesn't want to go out with anyone but you. But he keeps asking. He's called her three times now, and she told Mom and Dad and me that the last time he told her that he would keep asking until he convinced her, that he knew she wanted to. When she told him she didn't want him to call her again, he said, 'Oh, Gina, I will keep asking until you say yes. We are made for each other.' Or something like that." Peyton's grin reappeared. "Gina hung up on him. That was a week ago. Gina was so angry. He hasn't called since then. She doesn't think he will. I hope he doesn't, and so do Dad and Mom."

"I hope he doesn't call her again. I know about him, Peyton. He lives with his dad in Ballard. Detective Parker told Bentley and me about those two," Carter said. "He's been in trouble in both Uintah and Duchesne County. He's bad news. I wonder how he even knows who Gina is." Carter's concern grew and for good cause.

"I think he's seen her picture in the paper. The last time he called her, she said he told her he'd watched the last softball game she was in," Peyton revealed. "He complimented her on her pitching and on winning the game."

Carter felt a twist in his gut. He'd been at that game and hadn't noticed Elliot. Was the man stalking Gina? The very thought scared him for her. He decided right then to caution her about the guy. He looked at Peyton, whose face had a worried look on it. The grin was gone.

"Again, would you mind telling Gina I'm here?" he asked Peyton.

"I would, but she's over at Maya's. They're studying for a test tomorrow."

"Shucks, I'm sorry I missed her."

"Just go over to Maya's. I've heard them talking about you."

That made Carter smile. "Maybe I'll do that."

"Or you could call her cell phone," Peyton suggested.

"No, I want to ask her in person. I'll go over to Maya's," Carter responded. "I don't think she would mind. Do you think she would?"

Peyton grinned again. "I know she wouldn't."

Carter felt good about that.

Just then, he noticed that Gina's cousin, Sammy Anders, was watching him talk with Peyton. He had gotten to know the boy after the health issues with his parents. Gina's family were the only relatives he had. Or at least that's what they believed, and he was quite sure they must be right.

Sammy was very bright and was an amazing artist. He stepped up beside Peyton but was looking at Carter. "May I go over to Maya's house with you? I drew a picture for Bradley. I would like to give it to him, you know, if it's okay with you."

Sammy then looked at Peyton. "I'll ask Uncle Jim or Aunt Sue. Will you wait for me, Carter?"

"Sure, I'll stay right here."

Sammy was back in less than a minute. "Aunt Sue says I can go with you."

"Good, then let's get in my truck."

"Let me grab the picture," Sammy said. Once again, he was back in a minute, smiling and holding the paper in his hand.

Moments later, Carter parked his pickup on the curb in front of the Warwick house. He was having second thoughts about interrupting the girls' studies, despite what Peyton had said. He sat in his new red Chevy Silverado for a moment. Then he finally decided that since he was here and Sammy was holding the drawing he'd made for Maya's little brother, he might as well go to the door. He really wanted to see Gina. The worst that could happen would be her turning him down. He honestly didn't think that would happen. She hadn't turned him down yet. He looked for the little green Subaru that Gina drove but didn't see it. Then he recalled seeing it parked beside her house. That was the reason he'd knocked; he'd thought that if her car was there, she would be too. She must have walked to Maya's house. It was a mild evening, after all, and it was only a three-block walk.

Maya answered the door. "Hey, Carter and Sammy. Come in. You must be looking for Gina. She told me she had a feeling you would visit her sometime tonight." Maya grinned mischievously. "Maybe you can help us with our studies."

Sammy stood quietly beside Carter, holding the drawing he'd created for Bradley. Just then Bradley appeared, and Sammy handed him the drawing that he'd created.

"Hey, that's me. You drew me," Bradley said. "Look, Maya. It looks just like me."

"It sure does," Maya said with a smile, and then she turned back to Carter.

"Why would Gina think I'd visit?" Carter asked.

Maya grinned. "She has a sixth sense when it comes to you. I can't explain it, and I won't try, but she honestly told me she thought you'd come see her tonight. I'm sure you tried her house first."

"I did, and Peyton told me to come over here," he said.

Just then Gina walked into the hallway. She smiled when she saw Carter. "Hi," she said brightly. "What are you doing? Did you and Sammy come to help us with our studies?"

"I probably wouldn't be much help," he said as she approached him and gave him a quick hug. Wow! He hadn't expected that, but he liked it.

"You could quiz us while Sammy and Bradley play. We've been quizzing each other. Would you mind?" Gina asked as she fluttered her long eyelashes at him.

"On one condition," he said with a grin as the two boys skipped happily to another room.

"Okay, what's the condition?" Gina asked as she put her hands on her hips and gazed sternly into his eyes.

"Would you go to a movie and dinner in Roosevelt with me on Friday night?" Carter asked.

"I would like that a lot," Gina said. "Come into the kitchen with us. We have some questions that you can read to us. If you have time, that is."

"I have time. So, let's do it."

"Thanks, Carter. Maya and I just baked some cookies. We'll share with you and the little guys."

"How can I turn cookies down?" Carter laughed.

"If we didn't have cookies, would you tell us that you wouldn't help us?" Gina asked with a fake frown on her pretty face.

"Of course I would help you anyway," he said. "And remember, I said I would if you accepted a date with me for Friday evening. That has nothing to do with cookies."

"I'm glad. What time will you pick me up on Friday?" Gina asked with a slight blush on her face.

"Will five work for you?" he asked.

"Yes, I can't wait. Thanks for asking me out again. You know, I would rather spend time with you than any other guys," Gina said with a deeper blush as she ducked her eyes.

Carter felt his heart flutter.

"I would rather spend time with you than any other girls," he said, and he meant it. Gina was becoming very important to him. She was more important than he'd realized until this evening. She was someone he loved to be with, and he wanted nothing more than to spend time with her.

For the next thirty minutes, he helped them while the three of them munched on cookies and drank pop. Maya rewarded Carter, Sammy, and Bradley with chocolate ice cream and more oatmeal-raisin cookies when they had finished. When Carter went to leave a few minutes later, he said, "Gina, I could give you and Sammy a ride home if you would like."

"I would like that, but we need to study some more on another subject. It's only three blocks, and I don't mind walking. I do it all the time. Maya and I both do. It's nice out there tonight," she said. "Thanks for bringing Sammy over. And thanks for offering. I'll see you Friday evening."

"Sounds great," he said. "Thanks for agreeing to be my date for Friday."

"I'll be your date anytime you ask me."

Wow! He liked that a lot. She was special. She followed him out to his truck. They talked for a minute, and then she said, "Good night, Carter. Thanks for helping me or, rather, for helping us tonight." He got another hug. Wow again!

"Thanks for the cookies and ice cream. Good night and stay safe," Carter said. He watched her until she was back in Maya's house. That girl sure did have a way of making him feel good. He just then remembered that he was going to warn her about Elliot, but he'd forgotten. Oh well, he would do that Friday on their date. He was quite certain that she would never have anything to with Elliot or anyone like him.

As he drove home, for some reason he could not explain, he had a bad feeling about Gina and Sammy walking home. But he attempted to shrug it off. This was a good town, and she lived in a nice neighborhood. He was just feeling overprotective. He shoved the worry from his mind. Or at least he tried to, but he couldn't shake it completely.

***

Gina and Maya spent about another hour studying. Finally, Gina said, "Sammy and I had better get home. I don't want Dad and Mom to worry about us."

They walked to the door. Maya opened it and grinned at Gina. "He's a great guy, you know."

"Who are you talking about?" Gina asked, knowing full well who Maya was referring to.

"You know who. Carter has a huge crush on you."

"Do you think so?" Gina asked as she felt a pleasant tingle in her stomach.

"Oh yes," Maya said. "I do think so. In fact, it's more than a crush. I also think you have more than a crush on him."

Despite herself, Gina blushed. "Maybe I do," she agreed.

"Just don't let that creepy guy from Ballard talk you into going out with him."

"Believe me, Maya, I would never date a guy like that. He's creepy." Gina walked out the door and headed to the sidewalk. She couldn't help smiling at herself. Carter Keefe was a great guy. And yes, she admitted she had some very deep feelings for him. A crush didn't come close to describing how she felt about Carter.

She turned and looked back. Maya was still standing at her door. The two girls waved at each other as the two boys did the same. Maya called out, "See you in the morning."

When Gina was halfway home, she noticed something in the shadows beside the sidewalk a short way ahead.

Chapter 3

Gina had been gone for only fifteen minutes when Maya remembered something she'd forgotten to ask Gina. She knew she wouldn't be in bed yet, so she dialed Gina's cell phone. It rang several times. Then it went to voicemail. *She must be in the shower*, Maya decided. So she waited and called again fifteen minutes later. Once again, the call went to voicemail. A wave of worry crashed over her. It wasn't like her best friend not to answer her phone.

She decided to try again in about ten minutes. So she began to get ready for bed. She put her phone down on her dresser when it began to ring. She assumed it would be Gina calling her back, but it wasn't. It was Gina's mother. The second Maya answered, Sue said, "Hi, Maya. It's Sue Rogers. Will you tell Gina and Sammy that they need to get home now? It's late, so I think I'll have her father drive over and give them a ride."

A chill settled over Maya. "They left over a half hour ago. I've been trying to call her, but she isn't answering."

"They aren't home yet. Jim and I will go out and check. I hope neither of them fell and hurt themselves. But this is not like Gina at all," Sue said. "If one of them is hurt, she would have called."

Maya could feel the fear in Sue's voice. She was scared too. Her dad, Dale Warwick, was watching the TV in the family room. She hurried to him as the call from Sue ended. "Dad, Gina and Sammy left over a half hour ago, and they aren't home yet. I'm worried."

"Didn't I hear Carter Keefe's voice earlier? Maybe they're with him."

"No, Dad. Carter went home over an hour ago. Gina's parents are going out to look and see if one of them fell and got hurt or something. She isn't answering her phone," Maya said as the worry intensified.

"Call Carter and make sure they aren't with him. I'll go out and walk toward the Rogers's house. I'm sure she's okay," Maya's father said. He clicked off the TV and got to his feet.

Maya was already calling Carter, and he answered on the second ring. "Hi, Maya. What's up?"

"Carter, are Gina and Sammy with you?" Maya said.

"No. What's going on?" Carter asked.

"We can't find them," Maya said, and she choked up. "They left here nearly forty-five minutes ago. Her parents and my dad are going out to look for them. I'm scared, Carter. I'm really scared."

"I'll come over right now. Have you called the cops?" Carter asked as worry leaked from his voice and over the phone.

"No, should I?"

"Let me. I'll call Hank Parker. We'll find them, Maya."

"Her mother thinks one of them may have stumbled and got hurt or knocked out or something."

"I'm heading for my truck right now. I'll be there in a couple minutes," Carter said.

***

Carter called Detective Sergeant Hank Parker. "Hank," he began, "Gina Rogers and Sammy Anders headed home from Maya Warwick's house about forty-five minutes ago. But they never showed up at home."

"That's not good," Hank said. "I'll head that way right now."

"I'll be there in a minute. I'm going to go to Maya's house first," Carter told his detective friend.

"Do you have any idea what Gina and Sammy were wearing?" Hank asked.

"I do. I was with the girls at Maya's house for a little while earlier. I think Sammy was wearing a brown shirt and brown shorts. He was carrying a drawing pad. Gina was wearing blue jeans, a green blouse, and white tennis shoes. She had a small blue backpack and had her black leather purse with her. Her long blonde hair was in a ponytail. She had worn her pink-framed glasses instead of contacts," Carter reported.

"That's a good description. You obviously paid attention to how she was dressed," Hank said perceptively. "That's good."

Yes, Carter had paid attention. How could he not? Gina was a very attractive young lady.

"You've been dating Gina lately, haven't you?" Hank asked.

"Yes, and when I was with them, I had asked her out for a date on Friday night," Carter said.

"She accepted, I'm sure. I've noticed how she looks at you," Hank said, and with that, the call ended.

A minute later, Carter pulled up in front of Maya's home. She came out of the house as Carter got out of his truck. She ran to him, tears streaming down her face. "I can't believe Gina and Sammy didn't make it home. I watched them for a minute after they left. I know Gina would never run away in a million years, and she would do anything for Sammy," Maya said through her tears. "You've got to find them."

"We'll find them, Maya," Carter said in a much calmer voice than he was feeling. "Did you see any cars come down the street here by chance?"

"No, but one could have come from another street that way." She pointed in the direction of the Rogers's home three long blocks away.

Just then Detective Sergeant Hank Parker pulled up and hurriedly exited his gray sheriff pickup. For the next couple minutes, Carter and Maya told him what little they knew—the direction Gina and Sammy had gone—and Maya confirmed what Carter had told him regarding what Gina was wearing.

"Maya, you'd better stay in the house and lock your doors. Carter and I will walk toward Gina's house," Hank said.

"My dad's already gone that way, and Gina's parents are coming this way," Maya said.

"That's good, but Carter and I are trained to look for clues that others might miss. Keep your phone on you," Hank instructed.

"Okay. You guys have got to find them," Maya said in a broken voice and then walked slowly into her house with her head drooping and tears streaming down her cheeks.

Hank and Carter had very bright flashlights, and they slowly walked along the sidewalk. They shined their lights to both sides of the sidewalk as they walked slowly and deliberately, concentrating on the search for something, anything that might give them a clue as to where Gina and Sammy were at or what might have happened to them.

"Hey, look over there, Hank," Carter said as someone with a flashlight came toward them.

"That's probably Dale Warwick. I wonder if he's found anything," Hank said.

"No, I mean look right there in those weeds," Carter said as he shined his light onto what he'd seen at the edge of the sidewalk.

They were in the middle of the second block from Maya's house, an area with two vacant houses. The yards had gone to weeds with trash scattered about. There were realtor signs in front of them.

"Glasses," Carter said.

"Yes, I see them now," Hank agreed. Both detectives leaned down and looked closer without leaving the sidewalk. The glasses were about a yard into the weeds and trash from the sidewalk. "Someone must have lost them."

"Hank, they're pink. Gina was wearing pink glasses tonight," Carter said. "Those are her glasses. I'm positive."

"Carter is right," Dale Warwick said as he stepped up beside them. "Those are the ones Gina was wearing tonight."

Carter's phone rang. He pulled it from his pocket and looked at the screen. Then he answered. "Hi, Bentley. Gina and Sammy are missing. We think we just found Gina's glasses."

"Maya called me. I'm on my way to town. I'll get there as soon as I can. Where exactly are you at?"

"We're at the middle of the second block east of Dale Warwick's house."

"Is that the spot where there are two empty houses?" Bentley asked. "Halfway between the Rogers's and the Warwicks' houses?"

"Yes, the glasses are in some weeds about a yard from the sidewalk," Carter responded as his gut clenched. "They can't have just fallen off her face that far from where she would have been walking. Someone did something to her."

"I'll see you soon." Bentley let out a frustrated breath. "I'm driving as fast as I dare."

"This is awful," Carter said as his gut clenched and fear for the girl he had deep feelings for intensified.

Carter put the phone back in his pocket and then turned his attention to what Hank was doing. He was leaning forward taking pictures of the glasses without leaving the sidewalk. "I brought the image closer on my phone camera," Hank said. "Look at this."

He held the phone out for Carter to look at.

"The weeds have been trampled in that area," Carter observed as he studied the images on the phone. Hank allowed Dale Warwick to see them too. Then he turned and leaned down toward the edge of the sidewalk. "They are badly trampled right next to the sidewalk now that I look closer. Hank, I think Gina and Sammy were struggling with someone."

Mr. Warwick mumbled an agreement.

As Carter spoke, his stomach became unsettled, and a pain shot through his head and left it throbbing. He also felt himself choking up, unshed tears making his eyes and throat sting. He fought it all off. He had to be strong.

He shined his light beyond where the glasses were sitting atop the weeds. The weeds had been disturbed closer to the vacant house, and there was also a pad of paper on the ground there. This could mean only one thing. Someone had grabbed Gina and Sammy, and one or both of them tried to fight that person off. "Gina fought someone here," he said to Hank, "and Sammy must have been grabbed too. He was drawing something for Maya's little brother when I was at the Warwicks' house."

Hank had drawn the same conclusion. "I agree. And it looks like someone fell just past where Gina's glasses are. I'm going to step around the area that has been disturbed and take a closer look. You men wait here."

Carter watched as Hank looked carefully at the area and snapped some pictures with his camera with the flash on. He continued to move around, and then he walked to the east, staying several feet from the sidewalk. Carter and Mr. Warwick moved in the same direction but stayed on the sidewalk.

Hank took an abrupt turn and was soon back on the sidewalk about forty or fifty feet closer to the Warwicks' house from where the glasses still lay on the weeds. "It appears to me that Gina was dragged in front of this vacant house where she lost her glasses." He pointed with his flashlight and added, "They reached the sidewalk right there. I also spotted what I believe are tracks made by Sammy. I think he was running after Gina and whoever was dragging her. He loves Gina and would do anything to try to save her."

Carter knew what that meant. Gina and Sammy had both been loaded in a car and taken away. "They're gone, aren't they?" he asked as he glanced at Hank in the dark.

"It appears that way," Hank agreed. "But we will find them. I will collect her glasses and Sammy's notebook and put them in a bag."

Carter felt helpless as he watched Hank retrieve the two items a minute later. And he worried about both of them. His helplessness turned to anger and then to determination.

He looked up when he heard a vehicle coming. It was his boss, Detective Bentley Radford. With Hank's and Bentley's help, Carter felt some confidence that Gina and Sammy would be found. But what kind of shape would they be in? They might be badly hurt or . . . no, he didn't want to go there. Gina and Sammy had to survive this terrible thing.

Carter had a thought. "What if Sammy wasn't taken? Maybe he's hiding here somewhere."

"It's possible," Hank said.

They began shouting Sammy's name repeatedly, but there was no response. They also searched around the abandoned house, but there was no sign of him. Finally, they decided that he must have been taken too.

Chapter 4

GINA HAD NOT SEEN THE FACE OF THE MAN WHO GRABBED HER. SHE did, however, smell the awful stench that he carried with him, and it was truly terrible. He'd come out of the darkness behind her and Sammy so suddenly that she'd had no time to try to grab Sammy and get away. The man had put a hand over her mouth when she'd tried to scream. She'd managed to pull him off balance into the weeds beside the sidewalk. Sammy had followed, but she didn't hear a sound from him. The terror of the situation had apparently taken his voice again.

The kidnapper had fallen and dragged her onto him. Then he'd flipped her over as she screamed, wrenching her left arm. He'd shoved Sammy out of the way as the little guy had attempted to hang on to her. He'd put a hand over her mouth again, knocking her glasses off, and stopping her desperate scream for help. He'd jerked her to her feet with one strong hand, but she'd fought hard, kicking him in the shin and then losing her balance and tumbling into the weeds. That time, he'd fallen on her, driving the air from her lungs, leaving her almost unable to breathe as she gasped for air. She was aware of Sammy pounding the evil man with his fists, but once again, the man had swatted him out of the way.

The kidnapper had sworn with words she'd seldom heard and called her a nasty name while still lying on top of her. But then he had managed to get to his feet, losing his hold on her. She'd tried to get to her feet so she could grab Sammy and run. She'd gulped for air and managed to get to her knees. But when she'd tried to stand, he'd kicked her savagely in the side, and over she'd gone again.

Gina had been frightened, but she had also been very angry. She'd kicked him from where she had fallen on her back when he'd leaned over and tried to grab her arm. She'd felt as well as heard a crack that she hoped was his nose breaking, and she thought she might have loosened some of his teeth. She'd kicked again, this time striking one of his hands as he'd again tried to grab her.

Never in her eighteen years had Gina ever heard such horrible language. She'd known he was hurting, because for a moment he'd stood and moaned in pain. She had managed to get some air and scrambled backward, crablike, away from him, and then she'd managed to get to her feet and reach for Sammy. But she'd only carried Sammy two or three steps before the kidnapper had grabbed her long blonde ponytail and jerked her backward. He'd dragged her through the weeds in front of a vacant house. Sammy bravely hit the man, though he didn't make a sound. But again, he got swatted away.

Gina felt pain with every step he took as she'd bounced on the ground. She'd feared that her hair would come out by the roots. It had not, but it had hurt terribly. She'd tried to scream some more, but she'd found herself short of air again as she was dragged.

Her phone rang. *Oh no*, she thought. *I should have put it on silent*, she berated herself. Of course, she couldn't have known why she might need to do that just walking home from Maya's house.

The evil man had dropped her and kicked the side of her head, stunning her. Then she'd felt him feeling for her phone. The feel of his hands had made her tremble with disgust. She'd tried, despite her head spinning, to turn away from him, but it had been a futile effort. He'd found her phone a moment later in the back right pocket of her jeans where she'd stored it as she was leaving Maya's house. Earlier, she'd considered turning the flashlight on, but she hadn't, for she knew the way very well and the stars were bright and had given her just enough light to walk safely. She had kept hold of one of Sammy's hands. She'd found herself enjoying the peacefulness of the night and Sammy's sweet company until . . . she couldn't believe she hadn't heard the man sneaking up on her until the last moment, and by then, it had been too late.

He'd pulled her phone out, kicking her in the side when she tried to get up. She'd recoiled in pain. She'd been certain he'd bruised some of her ribs. Then he'd put her phone on the ground and stomped on it several times before picking it up, kicking her again as she lay curled in the fetal position in the weeds, and then tossing it as far as he could into the cluttered yard. She'd again tried to move, but it was to no avail because of the intense pain she was experiencing. She'd never known such severe pain. Her head hurt terribly, and her side felt like it was on fire. Breathing had brought intense pain, but she'd needed air more than anything.

Sammy stayed right with her, but the man kept swatting him away. A moment later, he'd again grabbed her long ponytail and began to pull her along the ground, through the weeds. She could feel when they crossed the sidewalk and dropped onto the road from the curb. It had caused the pain to increase as she was jarred so much. Shortly after that, he was lifting her and throwing her violently into the back seat of a vehicle.

"Run, Sammy!" she'd screamed, but the boy stayed with her and was continually being pushed away. The man grabbed Sammy and threw him into the vehicle with her. He'd taken a minute to wrap some duct tape around her wrists and legs as she'd tried to punch and kick him. But her efforts had been ineffective as she'd become so weak. He'd fastened a seat belt around her and then taped Sammy's hands and feet. Finally, he slapped her hard on the face before shutting the door, running to the driver's side, and jumping in. A second later, he'd started the engine and drove recklessly away.

That had all occurred about an hour ago, as near as Gina could guess. She no longer had her wristwatch, since her captor had torn it from her wrist and tossed it out the truck door while he was fighting to put the duct tape on her wrists and ankles. She had no idea where she was now. And she was without her phone. She was frightened and suffering from the pain he had inflicted, but she kept her wits about her. She was constantly aware of Sammy right beside her. She was quite certain they'd been thrown into a gray pickup. She hadn't yet figured out the model or who the smelly man was. But as she'd listened to him rant at her for hurting him, she thought he sounded vaguely familiar.

The more she thought about it, the more she wondered if her captor could possibly be somehow related to Elliot Jones. She'd only ever heard Elliot's voice on the phone and one time in person. But the voice sounded a lot like his. She knew it wasn't Elliot because this man sounded a lot older than Elliot.

She knew that she could be way off base in her thinking. Then again, she had turned Elliot down on dates several times, and she was certain he'd been stalking her. Elliot was a scary-looking guy. He had long black hair and dark-brown, evil eyes, and a large scar on the left side of his face. She could imagine him doing something like this because of her refusing to go out with him. But she also knew the driver was not Elliot. So who had kidnapped her and sweet Sammy?

The more she thought about it, the more she believed that the voice did resemble Elliot's. She'd heard it several times when he'd called her asking her to go out with him. She'd heard it too when he'd come to her home one day to ask her out in person. She'd refused as politely as she could, but she had seen his scarred face and his dark, brooding eyes that day.

She repeatedly asked their abductor who he was.

Finally, he relented. "I'm Harry Jones. I'm taking you to be with the man who loves you. My son, Elliot, feels bad that you keep turning him down when he knows you really want to be with him. But you made a bad choice. Now you will enable the two of us to earn some money from your wealthy parents." He was silent for a minute before saying, "They'd better give me what I want in order to buy freedom for you and this little pest that I had to take when he wouldn't run off."

Gina was stunned. This man was Elliot's father! That's why the voice was familiar.

"I wouldn't have had to do this if you had been smart enough to accept a date from a fine young man who is in love with you. But now you two will be together for a while. The only way we will let you go is if your father pays the ransom we'll ask for. You brought this on yourself by refusing to date my son."

This was insane; Harry Jones kidnapped her because she had refused to go out with his disgusting son, Elliot! Her parents were not as rich as this man seemed to think they were. But she knew that her father would spend whatever it took to save her and Sammy. But she swore to herself that she would make every effort to escape before her dad paid a ransom. Her life and Sammy's very likely depended on it. She didn't believe that he would actually release the two of them if her parents paid the ransom

"Please, just let us go, Mr. Jones," she begged.

"I can't do that. You should not have been so rude to my son. He is a good man," Harry said, and he seemed to believe what he was saying, even though Gina knew nothing could be further from the truth. "It is your fault that it has come to this, but since you refused Elliot's offers, your family will pay whatever we ask to get you back. You and that pesky boy."

Harry drove for a long time, much of the journey on very rough roads, before finally stopping and jerking Gina and Sammy from his pickup truck. Despite the darkness of the night, the headlights of his truck enabled her to see an old cabin surrounded by trees.

Elliot cut the tape from her feet and Sammy's with a strict warning not to try to run away. "This is wild country, and if you two were to run into the forest, you would be killed by wild animals. There are bears and cougars and wolves in the forest."

With that warning, he escorted both of them into the old cabin, where he told them to lie down on a bed in a separate room near the back of the cabin. Then, to her horror, he duct-taped her to the bed. He also taped Sammy, whom he had thrown onto the narrow bed beside her. He once again taped their feet. Then he left the two of them there. She listened as Harry left the room and the cabin. She heard his truck start up and drive away. Gina lay there, suffering intense pain, unable to move or see in the darkness of the cabin. She wondered how long they would be forced to lie on the bed.

She couldn't think of a good scenario, and it frightened her terribly. It was clear that Elliot and Elliot's father were convinced that she had brought this on herself by refusing to date him. She and Sammy were in a helpless situation. She spoke to Sammy, who was lying against her. "Sammy, we will get away. We need to have faith. There is one thing we can do. We can pray and ask Heavenly Father to help us get away." She prayed vocally and fervently to her Father in Heaven and asked Him to help them escape with their lives from this evil man. She told God that she would endure the pain if He would allow her and Sammy to live through this abduction.

Sammy didn't say anything. She wondered what it would take for him to be able to speak again. She prayed a second time, asking God to help him speak. Then she did the only thing she could do: try to get loose from the tape.

She didn't know when Harry Jones would show up, but there was no doubt in her mind that he would come along. After a while, she could hear Sammy breathing gently. She assumed he had fallen asleep. At some point, despite the pain and her frightening thoughts, Gina was so exhausted that she also drifted to sleep.

***

Large bright lights had been set up in the area where Gina and Sammy had been abducted—for everyone was convinced that that was what had happened to them. Carter had found her watch. It was in the weeds near the sidewalk.

Hank photographed it and then collected it with gloved hands and placed it in an evidence bag. "We may be able to get fingerprints off it," he explained to Carter.

"Are you suggesting the kidnapper threw it there?" Carter asked. "I thought maybe it had fallen off her wrist."

"No, he threw it there. I would bet on it. It probably happened when he was loading them in his vehicle."

"I wonder where her phone is," Carter said. "We all tried calling it earlier, and it goes to voicemail. Maya said she saw Gina put it in the back pocket of her jeans when she and Sammy were leaving her house."

"I can't imagine the scumbag who took her would have let her keep it," Bentley said.

"We've probably missed it somewhere between here and where he first grabbed her," Carter suggested.

"You're probably right. Or her abductor may have it, and of course, he likely wouldn't answer it. We need to go back over the area again with more lights and see if we can find it," Hank suggested.

No one disagreed, and an intense search for the phone ensued. The detectives had been joined by Sheriff Terry Goldman and a couple other deputies and a highway patrol trooper. Detective Sergeant Hank Parker quickly organized a search grid, and they began to slowly walk back toward where the original scuffle had taken place. They were spaced out about three feet apart and were shining their lights carefully over every square inch of the ground they covered.

They worked their way back on a second pass, farther from the sidewalk and closer to the front of the vacant house than on the first one. And then they did a third, still farther from the sidewalk. It was on that final pass that Carter called out, "I found it! It's smashed."

The others gathered around where the phone lay on a spot of mostly bare dirt. Hank took pictures before picking it up with gloved hands and depositing it in an evidence bag. "Hopefully we'll find the abductor's fingerprints on this," he said.

"Unless he wore gloves," Bentley said.

"I suppose that could be the case, but we can at least try to find prints on both the phone and the watch," Hank said. "I'm guessing he didn't touch the glasses, but we might check them for prints, just in case he tossed them where we found them."

Chapter 5

There was nothing more they could do in the area where Gina and Sammy had been abducted. So they gathered in the Rogers home, where they discussed who might be behind the abduction. Carter had his suspicions, and he voiced them. "She was being stalked by Elliot Jones. She had turned him down several times. I wonder if it was him."

"He was stalking her?" Detective Sergeant Parker asked with a raised eyebrow. "How do you know that?"

Carter took a moment to explain his concerns.

"That sounds serious," Hank agreed after listening carefully to Carter's explanation. "Maybe it would be a good idea to go to his house in Ballard. We could eliminate him as a suspect if he's at home or seriously consider him as the abductor if he isn't."

Hank and the sheriff went in one pickup, and Bentley and Carter rode together in Bentley's truck. A deputy from Uintah County by the name of Cory Storm met them in front of the Jones residence in Ballard. The home was located on a few acres of ground that looked like it hadn't been given any care for a very long time. The yard around the white frame house was also in very poor shape, and the paint peeled from the walls. Junk littered the area.

As was expected at this time in the middle of the night, the house was dark. The bright stars and a half-moon that had risen a few minutes ago made it possible to see without the use of flashlights. Hank recognized the pickup parked in a dirt driveway beside the house as belonging to Elliot Jones. It was a rusty gray Dodge Ram, an older model.

"Just one truck," Deputy Storm said. "That's the one that Elliot drives. I don't see his dad's truck."

"Well, officers, let's see who, if anyone, is home. Elliot could be driving his father's truck," Sheriff Goldman said. "Or they might both be in the other, slightly newer truck. Let's find out."

Deputy Storm and Carter covered the back while Sheriff Goldman and Detective Sergeant Parker went to the front door. Bentley covered a door that was on the north side of the house. The house itself faced the street on the west.

Hank knocked on the front door, and then he and the sheriff stood on either side and waited. After a short time, he knocked again, harder this time. There was no doorbell. "Someone is moving around inside," Hank whispered.

Just then a light came on inside, and then the porch light flooded the area around the two lawmen. Both men stepped farther back from the door and waited, alert, pressed against the wall. A minute passed before Hank heard the doorknob being worked, and then the door opened just a few inches, and the face of Elliot Jones appeared.

"What are you jerks doing at my house in the middle of the night? You are invading my privacy. Leave now unless you want to be sued. And I will sue you," Elliot Jones said angrily.

Hank spoke up. "Is your father at home?"

"None of yer business," Elliot said.

"We just need to speak with you and your father," Hank said. "We aren't here to arrest anyone." To himself, he thought, *unless Gina is in the house.*

"He ain't here," Elliot said and tried to shut the door. But Hank's boot kept it from shutting. "Move yer foot, pig!"

"We need to speak with your father," Hank said as Elliot continued to push on the door, but Hank was not going to move his foot.

"I said he ain't here," Elliot shouted. "Now get!"

"Where is he?" Sheriff Goldman asked.

"Outa town," was the angry reply. "If you weren't blind, you could see that his truck ain't here."

"In that case, we'd like to speak with you for a minute," the sheriff said calmly as Deputy Storm joined them.

"Hey, Elliot. You know me, Deputy Storm," the Uintah County officer said. "We need to come in and have a look around."

"Ain't got no weed or nothing like that," Elliot said.

"It would only take us a couple minutes, and then we'll leave if we don't find what we're looking for," the deputy added.

"What ya looking fer?" Elliot asked as he released the pressure on the door, and Hank was able to push it open a little bit more. "What ya looking fer?" he repeated.

To Hank it seemed that Elliot was getting nervous. "Open the door, and we'll talk for a little while," Hank said in a nonthreatening manner.

Elliot relented. "Okay, but I ain't got nothing to say to you pigs."

When Elliot stepped back, Hank stepped in, followed by the sheriff and Deputy Storm. The deputy went to the back door and opened it as he said to Elliot, "I'm just going to let the other guys know that you are cooperating."

Bentley and Carter stepped in when the back door was opened. Elliot resisted a little, but when Hank assured him that they just wanted to peek in the rooms, that they were not interested in what was in drawers or other small spaces, he grudgingly allowed them to look.

It only took a couple of minutes to determine that Elliot was alone in the house. As the men went to the front door and started to file out, Hank turned back to Elliot and asked, "When do you expect your father to return?"

"I ain't got no idea," Elliot said. "He don't have to tell me what he's doing, just like I don't have to tell him what I'm doing."

With that, Hank followed the others outside. When they got back to where their trucks were parked, they spoke to each other for a moment. "Elliot knows where his father is and what he's doing," Hank said. "I'd hang my hat on that."

They all mumbled their agreement.

"I'm betting that his father is the one who took Gina and Sammy," Carter said next. "Do you think he's hiding somewhere around here and just waiting to bring them into the house?"

"That could be," Sheriff Goldman agreed. "Maybe someone should stay nearby and watch for him."

"I'm the officer on duty in this end of the county tonight, and I've got nothing else going on, so I'll watch for Harry," Deputy Storm volunteered.

"Thanks, Deputy," Sheriff Goldman said. "If you see him, it is very important to try to determine if Gina is with him. But don't confront him by yourself. You should be able to see if he takes her in the house with him. If he does, call for us and another backup and we'll try to arrest him, but we need to do it without harming the victims."

"And one other thing, Deputy," Hank said. "If Elliot takes off, we need to know that too."

Goldman, Hank, Bentley, and Carter all gave Storm their cell phone numbers, and then they headed back to Duchesne.

***

As soon as the cops had all driven away, Elliot got on the phone with his father, who had just returned to the cabin. The signal was weak at the cabin, which was in a remote forest area, but they were able to speak. "Dad, I think the cops suspect you have Gina and that boy. They were just here. I let them look through the house even though they didn't ever tell me what they were looking for. But I know they were looking for Gina and the kid. Did you say his name is Sammy?"

"Yes, Sammy Anders."

"Is Gina okay? I don't want her to be hurt very much, just enough to make her learn to obey if you need to. We don't need trouble from her. What we need is a ransom from her rich father, and that might take a few days."

"She's okay. I had to slap her around a little when she fought me. She's a feisty one. But she's duct-taped to the bed now. She ain't going nowhere," Harry told his son. "And the kid ain't going anywhere either. I made sure he believed there were lions and wolves and bears in the forest. He ain't going anywhere. And I doubt he can get the duct tape off Gina."

"But what if he does?" Elliot asked.

"She's afraid of the forest and the wild animals too. They won't leave. Oh, and there is a problem with the kid. He can't talk. He's mute, but he seems to hear okay."

"I'll meet you tomorrow night like we planned. I think the cops are going to watch me, so I don't dare leave tonight, but by tomorrow night, they will have given up and moved on to someone else. I think they think you are going to bring them here," Elliot said. "They are stupid, like all cops are. Just make sure Gina and the kid are okay."

"I know what I'm doing, Elliot," Harry said. "I told you this before, but you need to take supplies to the cabin and make sure they are staying put. Even if the kid gets the duct tape off her, they'll stay there. I've got them brainwashed. I'm sure that they know that they need us to survive."

"When should we take them to the other place?" Elliot asked. "It's a nice place, and they will like it there after spending time in that junky cabin."

"As soon as I think we should, we'll fly to our other place." He laughed. "And then we'll make the ransom demand."

"But you don't have a plane," Elliot reminded his dad. Harry was a pilot but hadn't flown much in recent years.

"I'll get one," Harry said, and he laughed again.

"Hey, is that Gina screaming? What's going on with her? Is she hurt?"

"No, she's trying to get me to take her to the bathroom. I guess she doesn't know there isn't one. She won't like that, but she'll have to make do."

"At least take her out in the trees and let her do what she must. We've got to make her think we're going to be good to her until we get the money," Elliot said.

"I'll take her out in a few minutes. The kid too," Harry told Elliot. "Oh, there's one more thing that you need to do before you come."

"What's that, Dad?"

"She'll need changes of clothes—underwear and socks as well as pants and shirts. Also, she'll need spare shoes and a jacket. The kid will have to make do with what he's wearing for a while."

"Surely you don't expect me to go in a store and buy those kinds of things, do you?"

"Use your head, Elliot. I boxed up your mom's clothes after she died. They're in the basement. That will be good enough. We won't have her for very many days. But I want her to look good when we demand the ransom, to show that she is being take care of."

"But, Dad, Mom's clothes probably won't fit her," Elliot argued.

"Actually, she's much the same size as your mom was. Get two of everything. And get your mother's newest clothing. We want Gina to feel like we are making sure she is comfortable. Bring some deodorant and a toothbrush and toothpaste. In fact, one of the boxes has your mom's personal hygiene items. Bring that whole box so she can pick out what she needs."

"Okay, I'll see you tomorrow."

Chapter 6

Sammy Anders and Gina Rogers hadn't seen anyone since Harry Jones had left them in the cabin for the second time. Before he left that time, he had taken the tape off them, warning them that if they went outside, the wild animals would kill them. Once Harry was gone, Sammy was able to use his voice again. They had been locked in the dirty cabin with a pile of junk food and bottles of water that they were told they could use until Harry got back. Behind a hanging blanket, there was a bucket they were to use as a toilet.

They had thought about escaping, but the only windows in the cabin had been boarded over, and they had no way to get the boards off. And the door to the outside had been locked from the outside. They pushed on it, but it didn't give. Of course, they didn't really want to go outside because of the bears and wolves and mountain lions that they'd been told were in the forest.

Sammy and Gina believed that, because the very first night, they'd heard wolves howling somewhere nearby. And the very next afternoon, they heard something walking around outside. They'd peeked through a crack between the boards on one of the windows. And what they saw shot terror into them. A bear. *A very large bear.*

"I think we're safer staying in the cabin," Gina said, "even if we could get out."

"I'm afraid of the animals outside," Sammy said, a tremble in his voice. But despite fear, he didn't lose his voice again.

There were a couple of large candles in the cabin, and there were matches beside each of them. Gina used them, grateful that they had some light to see by. Harry had left a notebook and pencil in the cabin. Sammy, encouraged by Gina, used the pencil to make small sketches in the notebook. Gina found a pocketknife in a drawer, and even though it was kind of dull, they were able to keep the pencil sharp enough to draw with.

From his memory, Sammy sketched wolves, mountain lions, bears, and he even sketched a very good likeness of Harry, the bearded man who had kidnapped them. After drawing Harry, Sammy said, “Gina, what if Harry looks at the pictures in the notebook?”

Gina smiled at him. “I don’t think it will matter. When we are rescued, we can show the picture to the police and tell them that this was the man who had kidnapped us.”

Sammy grinned. “Yeah, we can do that.” But then the grin faded. “If we are rescued.”

“We have prayed. Now we must have faith, Sammy. Heavenly Father will help us. We have to keep thinking about that.”

Chapter 7

Carter was discouraged. They had no leads regarding where Gina and Sammy had been taken. Deputy Storm was relieved by another deputy, who took over watching Elliot and Harry's house. He reported that shortly after noon, Elliot had gotten in his truck and driven away. The deputy had followed. Elliot had driven to nearby Roosevelt and went into the nearest grocery store. The deputy had not followed him inside, but when he'd come back out, he carried a small bag of groceries.

Elliot had next stopped at a station and filled his truck before returning to the house. The deputy was called on a family fight early that evening. He handled the call without having to make an arrest. When he hurried back to the Jones residence, Elliot's truck was gone. Even though the officer watched the house for the next hour, Elliot did not come back. Finally, the deputy left. He'd checked with his sergeant, and they both thought it likely that Elliot would not be coming back anytime soon.

***

"Elliot has probably gone somewhere to meet his father, if that is who took Gina and Sammy, and I'm quite sure it is," Carter said upon hearing that Elliot was gone. Carter was in the conference room at the sheriff's department where the sheriff was meeting with him, Bentley, Detective Sergeant Parker, and a couple other deputies.

No one disagreed with him, even though there was a small chance that someone else had kidnapped them. There were no fingerprints on Gina's smashed phone or pink glasses, which led the officers to assume the kidnapper had worn gloves. The phones at the Rogers's home were being monitored constantly in the unlikely event a ransom call was made.

The Rogers family was fairly well off financially, so the kidnapping was considered one where a ransom would most likely be demanded. There was nothing yet. All they could do is wait, and that waiting was torture. Carter hated to go home, but the sheriff insisted that they all needed rest. "If anything develops during the afternoon or evening, everyone will be notified," Sheriff Goldman assured them.

***

Sammy was terribly frightened. It was still light outside, but he thought it might be dark soon and that only increased his frightening thoughts. Gina was frightened too, but she tried not to show it and did all she could to comfort Sammy. The man who'd kidnapped them had not come back since he'd first left them there with a warning about how if they went outside, they would be killed by wild animals.

Despite the warning, they had tried the door, but it apparently locked from the outside. Not that they wanted to see the smelly man who had brought him here, but Sammy worried about wild animals breaking into the cabin.

"I don't think we need to worry about that," Gina told him, But he still worried and clung tightly to her.

They kept one of the candles burning to give them some light, which helped Sammy worry a little less. Even though it was chilly in the cabin at night, there was a small wood stove with a large pile of firewood close to it. Gina made sure the fire was kept burning, and that kept the worst of the chill off them.

They had food and water, so they were not thirsty or hungry, just scared. Gina had pulled the thin mattress from the bed in the second room, a small one that was at the far end of the cabin. She positioned it in front of the stove where they were able to nap from time to time.

The time passed slowly. Sammy spent much of his time drawing pictures in the large notebook they had found in the cabin. Gina encouraged him and was fascinated with how easily the drawing came to him. They didn't have any way of knowing what time it was, but Gina knew it was a long time after it had grown dark that they heard something prowling around outside. But even when she tried to peek through the cracks between the boards, she couldn't see anything.

Sammy clung to Gina. "I think it's a big bear."

"Maybe it's an elk or a deer," Gina said. But she didn't really believe that. She, too, worried that it might be a bear. They sat up on the mattress and listened to the sounds outside.

Sammy grabbed Gina with both hands when something scratched at the door.

"Let's take the mattress back to the bed," she said.

They pulled the mattress back to the bed. There was no door between the big room and the small one. All it accomplished by moving into that room was to make it a little farther from the door that was being scratched at. They could see that locked door from the bed. There was a thump and the door shook. It felt like the whole cabin shook.

They looked around both rooms for anything that they might use as a weapon. The first thing they found was a broom. It had a sturdy handle. But Gina didn't kid herself. She was not very strong. She could never scare a bear away with the broom.

They searched more and found another old pocketknife. It was rusty, but Gina managed to open the single blade. The blade was about four inches long, which was more than the one they'd found earlier. Its blade was only about three inches long. Sammy had been using that one to sharpen the pencil. It wasn't very sharp, but somehow, holding it in his hand comforted him. Gina held the longer one. Though rusty, it was sharper than the little knife.

The scratching and thumping continued. Bears were big. "What if the bear breaks the door down?" Even the knives and the broom handle wouldn't be enough to fight off a bear—if it was a bear. At that point, both of them believed it was. They were in the main room again. Sammy's eyes were glued to the door. He held on to Gina with one hand while he pointed at the door with the other.

Gina looked up, and with the light from the candle, she saw rafters up there below the pitch of the roof. They were quite a long way up. She pointed it out to Sammy and said, "If we can climb up there, the bear may not be able to reach us."

Before they tried that, Gina wanted to try to scare the bear away. They slowly approached the door, their meager weapons in their hands. "Shout, Sammy. Let's make lots of noise."

Sammy opened his mouth to scream at it. They both fearfully approached the wooden door where the scratching and thumping were becoming more pronounced. Sammy was shaking so violently that he could barely hold on to the knife. While Gina shouted, Sammy took a deep breath and tried to scream.

Not a sound came out. His voice had gone again. Gina knew what had happened; terror had robbed him of his voice. She thumped at the door with the broom handle. She hit it several times. It made a reasonably loud noise.

The thumping and scratching from outside stopped. So, Gina stopped hitting the door. She put her ear close to it and listened. Sammy, who was shaking with fear did the same. "I think we scared it away," Gina said hopefully. In fact, she was sure she could hear it moving farther away.

They were mistaken.

A growl came from somewhere near the door. Sammy waited with escalating fear, holding his knife in one hand and clinging to Gina with the other. A minute or two passed, and then the creature hit the door with a hard thump. The whole cabin shook. A moment later, the creature once again began to claw at the door and pound on it.

They backed away from the door. Gina looked around them again. The candle provided a little bit of light. She looked up at the rafters. "We've got to get up there," she said to Sammy.

He looked up and nodded. There was a tall, strong cupboard against one wall of the big room.

"Sammy, if we can climb up that cupboard, we can get on the rafters. It's tall enough. Let's try that." They backed up to the cupboard. Then Gina spotted a place where boards covered the rafters where they met the small room. "Look, Sammy, there's a shelf up there. We can crawl along the rafters and then sit on it. We'll be safe from the bear up there."

She was certain that the creature outside was a bear. Sammy let go of her, put his knife in his pocket, and started to climb. Gina grabbed the unlit candle and tossed it and some matches onto the shelf. She needed to snuff the other candle out. If the bear got inside and knocked the candle over, it would probably set the cabin on fire.

"Sammy, as soon as you are on the shelf, light that candle I just threw up there."

Sammy moved as quickly as he could across the rafters to the shelf. He lit the candle. Gina snuffed out the other one. She looked at the cooler that contained their food and water. She grabbed several bottles of water and threw them up onto the shelf. She also threw some cans of food up there. She'd liked to have thrown everything up there, but she didn't dare take any more time. The dangerous creature was clearly determined to get inside, and she feared that it would probably soon succeed.

She grabbed one of the packages of cookies and threw it up. Then she climbed up and joined Sammy. The continual scratching and thumping and the occasional hard bump against the door and what sounded like boards breaking made the two of them cling to each other.

The shelf was only about five feet deep and five feet long. But it was large enough to hold them both. Sammy had pushed the food and water she'd thrown up there against the wall. They peered down and watched the door across the room from him in the dim light of their candle. The creature had quit clawing at the door, but it continued to make a horrible sound that was as loud as thunder. After a little while, it began again, and within only another minute or two, it succeeded in breaking the door down. Sammy shook in fright. Gina was trembling too, but she held him tight, and they prayed.

As they feared, it was a bear, and it entered the cabin and began walking around, sniffing and exploring every bit of space in there. It looked right up at the shelf where Sammy and Gina sat with their backs to the wall and their knees pulled up to their chins. The bear lumbered over and stood at its full height. Its front paws lightly struck the bottom of the shelf, but it couldn't reach over it. It roared so loud that Gina thought her heart would quit beating. Sammy held tightly to her. The large black bear finally dropped to all four feet again and explored the rest of the cabin.

It found the cooler that had the rest of the food and water in it. It tore the cooler apart and began to bite the cans and bottles and packages. In moments, it had eaten the bread and cookies and other junk-food items from the cooler. Eventually the large creature succeeded in tearing open a can of chili. It ate the contents and then went to work on more cans.

Sammy realized there was going to be nothing left to eat or drink except what was on the shelf with them. His greatest fear was that the bear would once again reach up to the shelf and try to break it down and eat Sammy for dessert. He trembled at the thought. Never in his short life had Sammy Anders known such paralyzing fear.

After a few agonizing minutes, the bear once again lumbered over to where Sammy and Gina were sitting on the shelf. It rose up and scratched the shelf with one paw and then both of them. The rafters shook, but the sturdy shelf was nailed solidly to the rafters, so the only way it was going to fall was if the rafters it spanned broke. Sammy squeezed his eyes shut and prayed like his mother had taught him to. He prayed for safety and for rescue.

Eventually, the bear gave up, wandered around inside the small cabin for a few moments more and then lumbered through the broken doorway. Eventually young Sammy Anders fell asleep, still clinging to Gina.

Chapter 8

Sammy and Gina had both waited to use the bathroom. They had made their way along the rafters and back to the tall cabinet and onto the floor. By then, the bear had been gone for a long time. They hoped that it would never come back, but they couldn't be sure. So they did what they had to do, then Gina emptied the bucket outside just a few feet from the broken door. They found a couple bottles of water that the bear hadn't ruined. They tossed them onto the shelf, and then Sammy tossed his notebook up and stuffed the pencil in his pocket with the knife.

Sammy and Gina kept stopping and listening for any sound of the bear returning. Gina finally tossed a blanket up there. Then they once again climbed back up and settled in for a long wait. They didn't know if the man would ever come back. One thing they knew was that they couldn't last forever with such a small amount of food and water.

They wrapped themselves in the blanket, keeping their hands and arms free. The candle was still burning, and by its light, Sammy began to draw. It wasn't hard to be realistic. Sammy drew the bear as they had seen it below, stretched up on its back legs. He drew it with its mouth open and its eyes focused on where Gina and Sammy sat on the shelf.

"Wow, Sammy, that is really good," Gina said after he'd finished the drawing. "Now what are you going to draw?"

"I'll show you," he said.

Gina was grateful that he had regained his voice. She watched as he drew a picture of the bear coming through the door, a door that had been sturdy before it had busted open.

"The drawings are amazing. You got every detail right," she praised him. He drew from what he remembered, which was very accurate.

Sammy and Gina napped a couple of times throughout the day. They got down only briefly to use the bathroom, then as darkness settled in again, they made themselves as comfortable as they could and prepared for a long and miserable night. They each slept for short periods, but at least they got some rest. As the sun rose outside the cabin and light leaked through cracks and the broken door telling them that another day had begun, they listened more intently for the sound of the bear returning.

About an hour passed when the huge form of the bear again filled the broken doorway. It looked across the room and up right where Sammy and Gina sat wrapped in the blanket. It roared so loud the whole cabin seemed to shake. They feared that the walls might collapse and the shelf tumble to the floor. The bear ceased its terrible roaring, but like before, it reached up high with its front paws, and its mighty palms barely touched the bottom of the shelf. Luckily for Sammy and Gina, the shelf was barely too high for the bear to push up. So the large creature dropped to all fours again. It lumbered around the cabin, but when it found nothing more to eat, it left.

"Gina, I'm not getting down from this shelf place again," Sammy said. "The bear must not live very far from the cabin."

"We can't stay up here forever," Gina reasoned. "As much as we fear Harry, I hope he comes and kills the bear." In the meantime, they had a long and uncomfortable time ahead of them.

Sammy found himself thinking of his mother and father. "I miss being with Mom and Dad," he said softly. "But I'm glad that I can be with you. I love you, Gina."

"I love you too," Gina said as she wiped tears from her eyes.

***

Harry and Elliot each parked in front of the cabin where they were holding Gina and Sammy.

"Did you get the clothing for Gina?" Harry asked as they got out of their respective trucks.

"Of course I did," Elliot responded. "Are you sure Mom's clothes will fit her?"

"I'm pretty sure. She looks about the same size as your mother was. Did you get the nicest clothes?" Harry asked.

"Of course I did, Dad. I got Mom's personal items too. Are you sure they will be everything Gina needs?"

"It was what your mother used, so I'm sure it will be fine for Gina."

"I also got a change of clothes for Sammy. I hope they will fit him," Elliot said.

***

Constant surveillance at the Jones's residence in Ballard was getting discouraging. Neither Elliot nor Harry had shown up. Carter was convinced in his own mind that the two would not be coming back. At least, if they did, it would not be anytime soon.

Work continued as attempts were made to locate the men and the girl and little boy they'd kidnapped. By this time, Carter thought that a ransom demand would have been made, but there had been no communication between the kidnapper and Gina's parents. Detective Parker had found a partial fingerprint on Gina's broken phone after checking more thoroughly. No one was surprised that it matched the right index finger of Harry Jones. There was no doubt in anyone's mind that Harry was the kidnapper, and they assumed that his son, Elliot, was involved in some way.

The sheriff ordered that everything that could be done had to be done to find and arrest the kidnappers and get the two victims home safely. Carter was assigned to go to the county building and check the records in the recorder's office. He was looking for any property that Harry or Elliot might own besides the house in Ballard. He found nothing there, so he drove to Vernal and did a similar check there. When that turned up nothing, he drove to Heber and checked there. He also checked Summit County records.

Carter was elated when he discovered the location of a five-acre parcel of land in a remote area just outside the boundaries of the national forest in Summit County. There was no mention of any structures on the property, but Carter suspected there might be something there. He called Bentley and reported what he'd found. Bentley told him to write down the information and then meet him and Hank, if Hank was available, in Heber. The three detectives then went in search of the location. They set out with high hopes of finding Gina and Sammy there and rescuing them.

Chapter 9

Gina and Sammy heard a vehicle, or possibly two vehicles, arriving in front of the cabin. Elliot began to curse when the two of them approached the cabin. "Dad, look, the front door is broken and awkwardly hanging open," Elliot said.

It was not difficult to hear what the men were saying, since the broken door left the doorway empty. Sounds came into the cabin easily.

"Do you think someone has taken them?" Elliot said. "And if so, who could it be?"

Harry's voice then carried into the cabin. "There is no way that anyone would have any idea this cabin is here."

"But someone broke the door down. Gina and the little boy are probably gone," Elliot said angrily.

Harry sounded closer to the cabin than his son did. "Look at the ground here," Harry said. "There's been a bear here."

"These tracks are huge. So, the bear is very large too. Gina and the boy are probably dead," Elliot said.

"It's a big one, that's for sure," Harry confirmed. "It's tromped all around here. It must have smelled Gina and the boy. I'd say it might have heard him screaming, but the little rat is mute. But Gina may have screamed. Or they may have heard it walking around the cabin."

"I wonder how long it took to break the door," Elliot said.

"That's a strong door. It was obviously very large and determined to get inside," Harry said. "We need to grab our rifles before we look inside. It could still be in there."

Gina and Sammy listened as the men walked to their trucks. A minute later, the kidnappers approached the broken door. "There goes our money," Elliot said. "We need the money Gina's dad would have given us."

The two men stopped before they reached the doorway. "I'm sure the bear killed them. There may be parts of them inside," Harry said.

"Parts of them won't get us the money," Elliot said, and he cursed long and loud, something Gina was totally unaccustomed to. Some of the kids at the school used bad language, but this was in a whole other league. It was vile, horrible language.

"We will kill the bear if it's inside. If it's not, then we will track it and kill it."

"Dad, we're still not going to the get the ransom money. I'm sure Mr. Rogers will demand proof that they are still alive," Elliot said.

"We don't have to give proof that they are alive. Soon I will make the call and demand the money. Rogers will pay even if we don't prove they are alive. Don't worry. We'll get our money."

Gina couldn't believe these guys. They were going to demand a ransom, and she knew her father would pay to get them back. That was her only hope. She silently cried for Sammy and her. All Harry cared about was the money. He was so evil, such a devilish man. Kidnapping was a terrible crime, and these men had done it for the sole purpose of getting money.

The kidnappers stood on the wooden porch that extended about five feet out from the door. A moment later, they entered and started tromping about inside.

"Look at this, Elliot. Every bit of the food and water is gone. But I don't see Gina or the boy here."

"Dad, I don't see any blood. Maybe the bear carried them out and into the trees somewhere," Elliot said as Gina and Sammy watched them from their high shelf. "He must have eaten our food before he dragged them into the forest."

"Surely they didn't manage to get past the bear and out the door. No way could they be fast enough to do that," Harry said. "But either way, they're gone. It's good we have some supplies in the trucks, but we'll need more soon. And we'll have to fix the door as well as we can for now. We will need to stay here for a few days, and we don't want to have that bear bothering us."

"If it comes back, I'll shoot it," Elliot said.

"Yeah, I guess you're right, but it probably won't come back anyway without any food here," Harry said. "Maybe we'll stay here after we get the ransom money. No way could the cops ever find us here."

Chapter 10

THE MEN HAD NOT YET LOOKED UP OR THEY WOULD HAVE SEEN GINA and Sammy huddled against the wall on the shelf.

Gina smiled at Sammy and whispered, "We'll be okay, but we will need to get down. We should have said something to them earlier. My father will pay them, and then we'll be able to go home."

"Elliot," Harry said loudly, "let's look around in the trees. Maybe we'll get lucky and see the bear. Its hide would be worth something."

Harry and Elliot left with their rifles.

"We need to let them know where we are," Gina said. She wondered if, by any chance, there were pistols in the truck. She guessed there might be. If she could just get one, maybe she could turn the tables on them.

After the men had gone, she climbed down and checked both trucks, just in case they had not locked them. Unfortunately, both trucks were locked, and if either of them had pistols, they were stashed where she couldn't see them from outside the trucks.

She went back inside and called up to Sammy where he was anxiously staring down at her. "You can come down now," she said. "I think the best way to let them know we aren't hurt is to clean up the mess the bear made before they come back."

They still had water and cans of food on the shelf. Sammy dropped a bottle of water for Gina to catch.

"Throw the rest of the food down. We'll tell them where we were and show them that the bear didn't get everything."

So he dropped everything down, grinning at her as if to say that they'd outsmarted the bear.

Next, he threw down his large notebook followed by a pencil. Then he scrambled across the rafters and to the cupboard. He climbed down and said, "I hope they won't hurt us when they get back."

"We'll be busy cleaning, and maybe that will keep them from getting mad at us," she said. Sammy rushed to her and held his arms wide. She knelt and held her arms out as well, and when he reached her, he threw himself into her arms and they hugged each other tightly.

"Sammy, you are so brave. I love you. We've prayed, and I believe Heavenly Father will protect us," Gina said. "Let's get busy cleaning up the mess the bear made."

Sammy reached for the notebook and the pencil. He placed them on a shelf of the cupboard. Then the two of them began to clean the cabin.

As they worked side by side, they listened for any sound that might indicate the men were near the cabin again. Gina said softly, "We will find a way to escape. I don't know how, but we will do it, Sammy."

"Yes. But you make me feel brave because you are brave. I've been praying like Mom and Dad taught me to. Can I say a prayer now?"

Gina smiled. "Sammy, when those guys come back, let's make them think you still can't talk. Will you do that for me? We need to fool them. Okay?"

"Okay, Gina," he said.

"If they hear you talk, they might think you were fooling them, and it will make them mad, and they might hurt you. So until you and I find a way to escape, no matter how long that takes, you will only talk to me when we are alone. Will you promise me that you will do that?"

"I promise. We will trick them, Gina. Now let's pray."

"Let me look outside and make sure they aren't back yet. And if they aren't yet, then we'll pray. When they do come, I'll explain how we fooled the bear."

"Okay," he said.

She went to the door, looked out, and then returned to him. "Okay, say your prayer," she said.

He bowed his head, closed his eyes, and said, "Father in Heaven. Thank you for Gina. Help us escape. Bless my mom and dad to get well. Name of Jesus Christ, Amen." He looked up, tears pouring down his cheeks. "Your turn."

Gina wiped the tears from her eyes and made sure she had control of her emotions, and then she gave a short, very sincere prayer. Mostly she asked Heavenly Father to help her and Sammy to be patient and then help them find a way to escape. She closed her prayer and when she did, Sammy said, "Amen."

She would be so grateful to Heavenly Father, because she felt like He would help them get back to her family.

With Sammy's help, Gina set about cleaning and straightening up the cabin. She had a feeling that it would be their home for a while, unless she could somehow get away in one of their trucks, but she knew that was unlikely. But despite that, she would look for an opportunity.

The Jones men had been gone for what felt like an hour or two. Without a watch, she couldn't be sure. She wondered if she'd made a mistake by not taking Sammy and hiking away right then. She supposed they still could, but the men would probably be back soon, so they wouldn't have gotten far. Even if they'd left earlier, she knew that there were dangers they would have had to face. And they would be in the forest without food. That just wouldn't do.

First, and most likely, Harry and Elliot might be able to track them, and if that happened, they would be caught and severely punished. The second danger was getting lost and starving or freezing when it got dark. The final danger was the bear that had broken into the cabin and possibly other dangerous animals. The knives that they had found would give them each a weapon, but not very good ones.

Common sense told her that it was best that they hadn't left and that they still shouldn't. Sammy had gotten tired and lay on the bed in the small room to rest in one of only two small beds in this two-room cabin, which was going to be a problem. She decided to take a short break too. She was very tired and didn't feel very well. She moved to the second bed, which was also in the small room. But as she did, she spotted Sammy's notebook. It was on the bed beside him. He was fast asleep.

She picked up the notebook and opened it. What she saw made her smile. Sammy had drawn more pictures with the pencil. They were amazing. She thumbed through the notebook. He'd drawn animals, the cabin they were in, and his mother and father. She'd watched him as he drew while they were on the shelf and before the bear came to the cabin.

Sammy had also drawn a picture of Harry Jones. It was as accurate as a snapshot with a camera would have been. She didn't see a drawing of Elliot, but that didn't surprise her, because she didn't think he'd seen him until today. The final page he'd drawn on had a picture of a huge bear, standing and reaching in the air. She had been amazed at how fast he drew the pictures.

She closed the notebook just as she heard a rifle shot in the distance. Had they just now found and shot the bear? She hoped so; fear of it returning had been in the back of her mind ever since the kidnappers reached the cabin. A second shot followed. Then there was a third. She wondered if the bear was hard to kill or if they were bad shots and missed it.

Another hour passed. She tried to nap but couldn't fall asleep, which was probably just as well, she decided. She wanted to be awake and busy when the Joneses returned. She had barely begun to clean the empty cupboard that they had used to climb to the rafters when she could hear the men talking a short distance away.

She kept working and heard them drop something on the wooden porch. Then they both turned and walked in the direction of their trucks. She stepped to the door and watched as they locked their rifles in their trucks. Perhaps at some point she could break a window and steal a rifle. As she was having that thought, she looked to the right and there, on the far side of the porch was a dead deer, a small buck. So that was what they'd shot. Not the bear.

She stepped away from the door and back to the cabin. The men entered the cabin through the broken door. "Hey, look at this. The place is clean," Harry said so loudly that it woke Sammy. The boy sat up, his eyes wide with fright. "Well, will you look at that, Elliot? These two must have been hiding outside. At least the bear didn't get them. We'll be able to get the ransom money after all."

Gina instinctively stepped over to the bed Sammy was on and sat beside him. "It's okay," she said. "They aren't going to hurt us." Sammy said nothing. Either he was doing exactly what he had promised Gina and kept silent, or perhaps the fright of seeing them again may have once more stolen his ability to speak. She put a protective arm around him and pulled him close to her.

"When did you two come in the cabin?" Elliot asked, frowning at Gina.

"We were here all the time," she said as she entered the main room. She glanced upward at the shelf. "We were up there where the bear couldn't reach us."

Harry slapped his leg with a grin on his ugly bearded face and said, "Did the bear scare you, Sammy?"

To Gina's relief, the boy remained silent but nodded his answer in the affirmative.

"How did you two get up there?" Elliot asked.

Sammy pointed to the cupboard and Gina said, "We climbed up to the rafters on that cupboard and then crawled across the rafters to the shelf."

"You must have taken food and water up there before the bear broke the door," Harry said. "It looks like you two did a very good job of cleaning up the mess. Well, let's get the deer skinned and cut up. Gina and Sammy, we are going to have roasted venison for our dinner."

"So, you didn't get the bear? Did you even see it?" Gina asked.

"We saw its tracks, but it seems to have left the area. I'm sure we don't need to worry about it anymore. Elliot, hang up the deer and go to skinning. It is going to be mighty tasty.

Gina, you can help us cut it up if you will be careful with the knife we let you borrow."

"I will be very careful," she said seriously. "Sammy, do you want to sleep some more? We didn't get a lot of sleep up there." She was testing him again. To her relief, he shook his head. Then he grabbed his notebook and pencil, sat on the floor with his back against the wall beneath the shelf, and began to draw. His face was scrunched in concentration.

Chapter 11

Elliot spent the night in his truck after they dined on fried venison. It was his job to listen for the bear. He'd pulled his truck close to the cabin. They'd set up a cot for Harry in the main room. Sammy slept in one bed in the small room, and Gina slept in the other bed. It wasn't too cold, as there was a good fire burning in the stove. Gina was glad about that for more than the heat. The stove smoked a little, and that made Harry's and Elliot's bad smell tolerable. Well, at least somewhat disguised.

Gina did not sleep well, because the door was not entirely fixed. It was propped shut, but a moth could knock it open again. That worried her. And having Elliot outside in his truck with a gun was not a great comfort either. She could imagine him shooting at the bear and sending a rifle bullet into the cabin if he missed. She had nightmares during what little time she managed to sleep.

Even though Harry had hung a tarp up in one corner to allow some privacy if anyone needed to use the bathroom during the night, it bothered Gina a lot. But it was still preferable to going outside in the middle of the night for fear the bear might come back. Or worse yet, she could imagine Elliot getting confused and thinking that she was the bear in the darkness and shoot her. Gina also wondered if the bear was only an excuse for Elliot to be out there with a rifle. Nothing about this night appealed to Gina.

Sammy, on the other hand, was sleeping like a log. He'd not slept much up on the shelf, and he was catching up now. Gina just hoped that he would not have a bad dream and call out in his sleep, alerting Harry to the fact that he could use his voice now. Or could he? She honestly wasn't sure whether he'd lost his voice again out of the terror of seeing the two horrible kidnappers.

When morning finally came, Gina volunteered to cook some hotcakes on the stove from a large sack of mix the men had brought in one of their trucks. Harry and Elliot didn't mind, so with little Sammy sticking to her like glue, she went to work on breakfast. When it was done, she was required to clean up. They'd used paper plates and cups, but there was not a lot of water in the five-gallon plastic container they had brought in the cabin, and Harry told her she better not waste it.

When she was through cleaning up, she sat beside Sammy on his bed and watched him draw. To her delight, he drew an excellent picture of her. Smart kid that he was, he made her look like she would with her hair neatly brushed and her face clean. She was totally dedicated to saving him.

He had very little to say, but when he did want to communicate with her, he would write in the notebook and show it to her. She became more convinced than ever that being in the presence of such evil as the kidnappers represented that he honestly had lost his voice again.

Sometime in the mid-morning hours, Harry announced that he needed to drive many miles to the nearest town and buy some supplies for them, mostly food. Before he left, he instructed Gina that she was to wear some of the clothing that Elliot had brought for her. She changed behind the hanging tarp, glad for something clean, but wishing she could have a long hot shower. But that wasn't going to happen. She couldn't even wash her face or her tangled, matted hair.

Elliot made Gina very uncomfortable as he stuck way too close to her all day and constantly leered at her. Of course, the smell that came from him was, if anything, worse. He made her sick. She tried to stay as far from him as she could, often taking Sammy outside where they walked around the parking area. Sammy held her hand each time they went out. Fear of the bear was very real to him, and for that matter, she worried a little about it too.

Harry did not come back that night. Elliot seemed unconcerned, but Gina wondered what he was up to. When Harry returned, it was late the next morning. He did not bring any supplies into the cabin. She asked him where the food was that he was going to get.

"It's in the truck," he said. "We won't be staying here much longer. In fact, we will be leaving for a nicer place."

Gina had to assume that meant they would be going even farther from Duchesne. She wondered where it might be, but of course, neither Harry nor Elliot would say. What surprised her was that they loaded everything from Elliot's truck into Harry's. That made no sense to her. It appeared that they would be leaving Elliot's truck at the cabin.

That turned out to not be correct. Instead, Elliot drove it several miles back the way they had driven when they came here, and then he hid it in some thick trees quite some distance from the road. Then he got in with Harry, in the front seat, thank goodness, leaving Sammy and Gina to occupy the back seat, which was quite crowded with canned and dry food, such as cereal and flour and pancake mix. At least that was what she could see. There were other things in the sacks that she couldn't see.

They drove for a couple hours, or so it seemed. What little Gina could see beyond the truck was unfamiliar to her. That was not surprising. She didn't expect to be closer to home, only farther away. Probably much farther, she thought. Never at any time did her commitment to escape drift far from her mind. And she kept wondering why they hadn't said anything more about a ransom demand from her father. She wanted the ransom call to be made, because she knew her father would pay it to get her and Sammy safely home.

***

Gina's father, Jim Rogers, called the sheriff around ten o'clock that Thursday morning. "One of the men I share ownership of an airplane with just called me. He was planning to fly to Seattle on business this evening, which I knew all about. What he told me, though, is that our plane is not at the airport in Roosevelt where we keep it. He wondered if I'd forgotten that he was going to use the plane that night or if either I or one of the other two owners had forgotten his plans and flown the plane somewhere."

"I'm assuming that since you are calling me, you aren't going anywhere in it," Sheriff Goldman said.

"I'm staying close to home in case I get a call from the kidnapper or even from Gina. I keep hoping she might find a way to get away from him. At any rate, I called our partners just to make sure, but none of us have taken the plane," Jim reported.

"That means it has been stolen," the sheriff said. "Is that what you're thinking?"

"That's exactly what I'm thinking. Someone took our plane. One of the other fellows was going to call the Roosevelt City Police, but I wanted you to know," Jim explained. "I keep expecting a call demanding ransom, but that has not happened."

"Is there a reason you wanted me, specifically, to know?" Sheriff Goldman asked.

"Yes, there is. I don't know if you are aware of this or not, but Harry Jones has a pilot's license."

"I see where you're going with this. You're wondering if Jones stole your plane and is planning to take Gina and Sammy somewhere far away. This makes no sense. I would have thought the kidnappers would have called about a ransom by now."

"I'll pay whatever is demanded, but I can't if I don't get contacted. I'm very worried about what they are up to," Jim said.

"This is very strange. I can't imagine why they're waiting. About your plane, did anyone at the airport see the plane leave?" the sheriff asked.

"According to my partner, the answer is no."

"Do you have any idea when it was last seen there?"

"We've had a little engine problem with it, and a mechanic was supposed to fix it for us before my partner left for Seattle. He was going to take care of it this morning."

"Did the mechanic fix it? That should be easy enough to check on," the sheriff suggested.

"His name is Alec Harmon. We assume he did not, or he would have been there working on it this morning, but we are unable to reach him. If he couldn't get here this morning at eight like he'd told us, he would have let one of us know," Jim said. "He's a good mechanic, and he also has a pilot's license."

"The first thing we need to do is find him and talk to him about why he didn't come this morning. Where does he live?" Sheriff Goldman asked.

"Myton, but he's not answering his phone," Jim said.

"What about his wife, or does he have one?"

"She's dead. She committed suicide two or three years ago. He lives alone."

"Oh yes. I remember that," the sheriff said. "We had some questions about it, but it looked like it was a suicide. I'm still not satisfied, but Hank and I could never prove otherwise. Anyway, it's always sad to see someone take their own life. She'd been despondent and in poor health according to her husband and grown children. I didn't make the connection when you mentioned the mechanic's name."

"He's a good aircraft mechanic. It's not like him to stand us up like this," Jim said.

"Do you have his address?" the sheriff asked.

Jim gave him the address, and then the sheriff said, "I'll have an officer check his house right away. I'll get back with you."

"Sheriff, I'm in my truck and on my way to Roosevelt right now, but I could stop at the mechanic's house on my way. I hope we don't get a call from someone demanding ransom. But my wife is there if a call is made, and I have my cell phone with me."

"You're right. I think it would be a good idea for you to stop at his house. In the meantime, I'll have an officer head that way as well," the sheriff reported.

Jim thanked the sheriff and ended the call. He then called his concerned partner at the airport and told him what he was doing. A few minutes later, he pulled up in front of Alec Harmon's house and stepped out of his truck. The blue Dodge Ram that Alec drove was in the driveway. It didn't make sense that he would be home when he had a job to do. He'd always been very dependable.

Alec did not respond to the doorbell or Jim's repeated knocking. Jim wasn't sure what to do except wait for an officer to arrive. He began to wonder if Alec was ill. Had he experienced a heart attack or a stroke? Jim felt strongly that he should check on him.

Thankfully, it wasn't long before Detective Sergeant Hank Parker pulled up. Jim was glad to see that Sheriff Goldman had sent him. Clearly the sheriff was taking this very seriously.

Hank joined Jim on Alec's porch. "Good morning, Jim. I assume you've knocked."

"I have, but there's no response. His truck is here, so I would assume he's at home," Jim advised Hank. "I'm worried that he may be ill."

"Let's knock and ring the bell some more. If he still doesn't respond, we should probably do a welfare check," Hank suggested. So he knocked hard and rang the bell repeatedly. When there was still no response, Hank suggested they try the back door.

There was no answer from knocking there either. "Let's see if either door happens to be unlocked. Since they were at the back door, Hank tried the doorknob. The door was not locked and opened easily. Hank stepped through the doorway with Jim right behind him and reached for a light switch. When he hit the switch, nothing happened.

"Must be a burned-out light bulb," Hank said.

They entered the house and tried the light switch in Alec's kitchen. The light came on. Curtains were drawn, so it was quite dim in the house without the light. But they could see fine now.

They stood just inside the kitchen as Jim called Alec's name. He didn't respond.

"I don't like the feel of this," Jim said. "I glanced in his truck, and his tool chest is there. So no one else would have given him a ride to the airport. Anyway, we know he didn't show up like he was supposed to this morning. Now that we're in here, let's check the rest of the house." So the two men began to walk from room to room.

Alec Harmon was not at home.

Chapter 12

Alec could not believe what had happened. He was afraid he was going to die. A man he thought was a friend of sorts had betrayed him in a way he would never have believed. Harry Jones was his cousin, and they had always been reasonably friendly with each other. The only trouble they'd ever had was over Alec's wife. She'd been dating Harry when she broke up with him and married Alec. But that was many years ago and had been long forgotten because Harry had married another young lady. But Alec had been put out when Harry had shown up at his door around midnight.

"What in the world do you need, Harry? I was about to go to bed," Alec had said grumpily.

"Hey, Alec, don't get mad. I need your help," Harry had said with a long face.

"Are you drunk, Harry? What can I possibly do for you this time of night?"

Harry was holding a small black square package, which Alec eyed.

"I am borrowing a plane, but I need to have you drive my truck to where I need to land the plane. I'll have passengers meet me there later because they can't meet me in Roosevelt," was Harry's strange request. "I'll drive you home after I get the plane to where I need to meet my passengers."

"I'm not available in the morning," Alec had said. "I need to be at the airport to work on a plane at eight. So, I can't do that."

"No, not in the morning, right now!" Harry had demanded.

"I can't do that either," Alec had protested. "I've had a little too much to drink tonight."

"Let me come in, and we'll talk about it. I'll make it worth your while." Uninvited, Harry had slipped past Alec and entered the house. He'd placed the black package on the living room sofa. "That's yours," Harry had said.

"I don't need whatever that is," Alec had protested mildly.

"It's on me. It's something to show my appreciation. It has a big surprise inside, but I don't have time for you to look now. Let's go." Harry started back for the door.

"Take your package, Harry. I don't want whatever's in it."

Harry had stopped and turned to Alec as he removed a tiny device with a red button on it. He had looked angry. "See this?" he'd said and waved it around before putting it back in his pocket.

"What is it?" Alec had demanded, starting to get a bad feeling.

"It's a remote. If I push the button, that black box goes boom! And your house disappears." He'd laughed. "I was hoping you would cooperate and I wouldn't have to threaten you, but you give me no choice."

"W-why?" Alec had stammered.

"Because I need your help, cousin. Let's go now. You'll drive my truck. And if you try anything stupid, I'll push the button," Harry had said darkly.

At Harry's direction, Alec had driven to the airport in Roosevelt, fuming the whole time. Harry had parked beside the plane he'd planned to fly.

"Hey, you can't use that plane," Alec had protested. "That's the one I was going to work on today. One of the owners is flying to Seattle in the afternoon. He needs it worked on and ready to go in a few hours."

"It'll be back here, and he knows that, so don't worry," Harry had lied. "I'm renting it is all I'm doing."

"I'm telling you it could be dangerous to fly that plane until I complete some work on it," Alec had said angrily. "I'll need my tools, and it will take me a few hours."

"Don't lie to me. The owner says it's fine. Here's where you are to drive my truck." Harry had reached out with an object in his hand. "This is a GPS device. It will direct you to where you need to go.

I'll fly the plane, and I'll be waiting for you there. And remember," Harry had said ominously, if you don't show up there, your house goes boom."

"I'll just throw the bomb out," Alec had said angrily. "I am not going to do what you think you can make me do."

"Oh no, you don't want to touch the bomb. You see, after I put it on your sofa, I set it with this remote to explode if it is moved so much as a half inch," Harry had warned him.

"You are a no-good stupid man—" Alec had begun.

Harry had hushed him before he could finish what he had to say. "Don't be calling me names. Oh, one more thing, Alec. If you don't do what I ask you to do, there is an important thing you need to know. You see, cousin, I know what happened to your wife. We both know it was not suicide."

Alec had felt his gut begin to churn. He had no idea how Harry knew what had really happened to her.

"I'll give the sheriff an anonymous tip if you do anything foolish. Now, here are my keys. Get going and don't waste any time. The truck is full of gas, so you won't need to stop anywhere."

Several hours had passed after that. Alec had done what he'd been told to do with two dangerous threats hanging over his head. His wife's death had been ruled a suicide, but Alec knew it wasn't. Prison for life was what would await Alec if he didn't do exactly as his nasty cousin had told him to do.

After Alec had arrived at the backroad Harry had directed him to, he saw that the plane had safely landed there. Harry was a good pilot, and it was no surprise that he could land on a dirt road. Alec had stopped beside the plane, on a wide spot on the road.

Harry had climbed in the truck with Alec, saying, "You're still driving, cousin. So don't get out."

"I'm guessing you're taking me home. And you will take the bomb with you, if it really is a bomb."

At that point, Harry had pulled out a small handgun and pointed it directly at Alec's head. "No, we have another place we need to go first. Now get driving. I'll give you directions."

At that point, they drove into the nearby mountains. At one point, Harry said, "Stop here. You'll need to walk back."

"What?! I don't even know where we are," Alec protested.

"Get out, you fool. You'll figure it out. I ain't got time to argue with you."

With a churning gut, Alec did as his cousin told him to do.

"Walk into the trees, Alec," Harry ordered, keeping the small handgun directed at his chest. "Turn around now. I'll shoot if you try anything foolish."

Alec did as he was told, with Harry following. Once they were out of sight of the road, Harry stepped up beside him and brought the gun down violently on his head. That was the last thing Alec remembered before waking up sometime later, only to find that he'd been bound tightly with rope. And he'd been left there on the ground.

Alec figured he would lie here until he died. He had no food, no water, and no way to move. His hands were behind his back and his legs pulled up and tied to the rope around his wrists. He struggled for an hour but was unable to loosen the knots. In fact, he was afraid all he did was make them tighter with all his struggling. He realized that Harry intended for him to die there. There was nothing he could do about it.

But then he had a thought. He could still feel his phone in the front pocket of his jeans. Maybe when he was reported missing, the sheriff or his people could track him by his phone. With that small ray of hope on his mind, Alec let himself slip into blackness again.

***

At Alec's house, Detective Sergeant Parker said to Jim Rogers, "I don't like the looks of that box, Jim. I think we should have our bomb dog come in. I'll call the sheriff and tell him why we need it. The dog's handler lives in Roosevelt, so it shouldn't take long."

Jim was anxious to get to the airport, not that there was anything he could do there. So instead, he called the partner who was waiting there and explained the situation. The two men discussed the plane for a minute. Both were worried that whoever had taken it could have engine trouble. They didn't know how serious the problem was, but they figured it had needed to be worked on before it was flown again. Alec had planned to do it, and when the issues with the plane had been explained to him, he'd agreed that it shouldn't be flown until it was repaired.

Jim's partner explained that he was making arrangements to rent a plane so he could still go to Seattle in a few hours. The Roosevelt Police had already broadcast the description and wing number of the missing airplane. All airports in the state and beyond had been alerted to watch for the stolen plane. At that point, nothing more could be done. Jim decided he should wait with Hank for the deputy with the bomb dog to come and check out the black box.

In the meantime, the men waited outside just in case there was a timer on the bomb, *if it was a bomb.* So, they waited.

***

Harry Jones decided, just for the fun of it, to detonate the bomb. He didn't expect Alec to survive anyway, nor did he think he would be found, so there was no way for anyone to connect the bomb to him. Not that he cared, because he didn't plan to return to Ballard. He and his son would resume their theft business from the location they were en route to in a few minutes. First though, they decided it was time to demand the ransom. He would do it using a burner phone. But after Harry and Elliot discussed it further, they decided to do that a little later. The longer they waited to call, the more they would demand, assuming that Jim Rogers and his wife would grow more and more desperate and would pay anything to get the two hostages back.

So, as he drove, he reached in his pocket and pushed the red button, chuckling to himself. He'd waited all these years to get his revenge on Alec for stealing his girl from him and then for causing her death a few years ago. He knew that was what happened. It was not suicide. Harry and Sharon had been secretly seeing each other again. She had health problems, but she had planned to leave Alec and get back with Harry. Alec had somehow figured it out, and shortly after that, Sharon had died. She'd told Harry that she was afraid of Alec, and he had believed her. Now Alec was going to die as well, and he had earned it. He would have plenty of time to think about what he'd done before death overcame him.

***

Jim and Hank were leaning against Jim's truck when the deputy with the dog pulled up. He and the dog got out, and Hank explained the situation. "It may be nothing, but we decided that we shouldn't touch the black box until your dog checked it out."

The dog wasn't needed. As the three men were talking, a sudden loud explosion tore Alec's house apart. Burning debris rained down on the men as they scrambled to get out of the way.

"I guess it was a bomb," Hank told the other men, shaking his head. "That would have killed us if we'd been in there."

It took hours after that for the fire department to douse the flames of what was left of the house. The state fire marshal arrived to investigate, even though there was little doubt that it had been a bomb detonating, but they needed to know for certain that it wasn't some problem with the natural gas in the house.

Jim was finally able to go to the airport. No sign of the stolen plane had been reported. An effort had been made to trace it by the GPS feature it contained. But it appeared that the GPS had been disabled by the thief. Whoever stole the plane apparently knew enough about planes to take precautions. Harry Jones was considered a prime suspect, but at this point, there was no way to prove that he had taken it. All Jim and his partners knew for sure was that their valuable plane was gone. And so was their mechanic, Alec Harmon. Who knew where he may have gone to?

The sheriff decided that they should try to trace Alec's phone by its GPS feature, if it had one, or by the *find a phone* feature, which Jim was sure it contained. Jim and his partners all knew that the phone Alec carried was an iPhone. A fairly new one. And all four of them had his number stored in their phones.

Hank, who had gone back to the sheriff's office in Duchesne, called Jim, who had finally gone home. "We know where the phone is," Hank told Jim. "At least, we think we do. I'm heading that way. Do you want to come?"

"No, but I've been talking to our two private detectives. I think they'd probably like to go with you. I know it's a slim connection, but since we suspect Harry Jones of kidnapping Gina and Sammy, and now of stealing the plane, and for that matter, of blowing up Harmon's house, I want to keep those investigators in the loop."

Chapter 13

WITHIN A FEW MINUTES, HANK HAD BEEN JOINED BY BOTH PIs—Detective Carter Keefe and Detective Bentley Radford. They headed east in Hank's sheriff pickup. Alec Harmon's phone was located somewhere in Daggett County, north of Vernal.

"Let's hope that Alec is with his phone and that he's okay," Hank said to the PIs. "We need to also consider the fact that it might be a spot where there's a cabin or some kind of building that Harry and Elliot are holding Gina and Sammy in. Alec may be a hostage for some reason, though I have no idea what that might be."

"I did a lot of searching in several counties, including Daggett, but I didn't find any other property listed to Harry or Elliot Jones," Carter said, "except for that one place we checked out that was empty."

"It could be within the national forest," Hank said. "Or if not, then it may be on private property near the forest. I just hope we get lucky and find Alec and Gina and Sammy when we reach Alec's phone."

"We need to be very cautious when we get close, because they may try to resist arrest and attempt to engage us in a gun battle," Hank said. "If Harry really did steal the plane and kidnap Gina, Sammy, and Alec, then he and Elliot are very dangerous. That bomb in Alec's house may well have been intended to kill someone. We're lucky it wasn't any of us. It was a close call, to say the least."

It was a long drive, but eventually they could tell that they were getting close to where Alec's phone was located. At least, they hoped so. They were on a very rough and seldom-used road, if it could even be called a road.

"This may be a false lead," Hank said. "I can't imagine a cabin being on such a horrible road. I'll bet hunters are all who ever travel this road."

Bentley was using his phone to track Alec's phone. "I think maybe we should park your truck here and approach on foot," he said. "And I think we should circle around in the forest a bit so we don't approach it from this road, just in case Harry and Elliot have plans to ambush us. I know it's unlikely that they have any idea we're coming, but I think it would be best if we are very cautious."

Hank and Carter agreed, so they pulled the truck into some trees, barely off the road, locked it, and hiked deeper into the forest. They were spread a few feet apart and were looking all around them. It was Carter who spotted what looked like a large lump of some kind a short distance ahead. It was hard to see through the tree limbs and brush. He wondered if it was a bag of garbage. He signaled the other men, and they approached him.

"It's impossible to tell from here," Hank whispered, "but let's consider it to possibly be a man there on the ground. I think we're safe to approach whatever that is. But let's circle around first out of an abundance of caution."

"Guys, my phone tells me that Alec's phone is right about where that is," Bentley said in a soft voice.

The other detectives nodded, and they moved quietly around whatever it was. They didn't see anyone lurking in the trees nearby, nor was there any sign of a cabin or any other structure. Hank signaled. "Okay, let's move in."

With pistols drawn and on the constant lookout around them, the three investigators approached. "It's a person," Carter said as a knot formed in his stomach, nearly making him sick. "I hope it's not Gina."

The men put their pistols away. "It's not Gina," Bentley said. "I'm thinking it must be Alec Harmon. This is where his phone is at. It's a man, not a woman."

Bentley was right. Alec was bound tightly with ropes and was very still, making no movements of any kind, but when Hank felt his carotid artery, he said, "He's alive. You two cut the ropes off while I take some pictures with my phone. He's really bound tight. He'd never get out on his own." He began snapping pictures before Bentley and Carter had their knives out.

Alec groaned when they tried to straighten him out after the ropes were off. "Help me," he said weakly, clearly in anguish. "I've been here for several hours."

"That's what we're doing," Bentley said as Hank got on his satellite cell phone to make a call.

"I'm calling the Daggett County Sheriff's Department," Hank said and then stepped back a few steps.

He reported the fact that he'd found a man who was kidnapped from his home in Myton. He was asked if he needed an ambulance.

"We don't know yet," Hank responded. "He was bound tightly, but he's alive and breathing. This is a tough location. An ambulance might have a hard time getting in here." He went on to explain how they found him.

By the time Hank was off the phone, Alec was conscious and sitting up on the ground. Bentley and Carter were helping him drink water. After a moment, he was able to speak.

"I'm Alec Harmon," he said in a shaky and strained voice. "My cousin, Harry Jones, made me drive his truck out here while he flew a plane he borrowed."

"He stole the plane," Hank said with disgust.

"I'm not surprised," Alec said.

"The plane has a problem that I was supposed to fix. I told him that, but he flew it anyway," Alec said. "And then, instead of driving me home, he took me out here at gun point and knocked me out. When I came to, I was all tied up like you found me. How did you find me? I'm sure Harry meant for me to die."

Hank chuckled. "He forgot to take your phone away. That's how we found you."

"I got lucky, didn't I?"

"Alec, how did he get you to drive his truck for him?" Hank asked.

"He put a bomb in my house and said he could detonate it remotely. If I didn't do what he told me to, he said he'd blow my house up."

"And you believed him?" Hank asked.

"Why wouldn't I?" Alec asked. "I saw the box he said was a bomb, and he showed me the remote control he had." Alec coughed, and it was a minute or two before he could speak again. "I know he meant what he said," Alec finally finished.

Hank noticed something in Alec's eyes. He had a feeling there was more to it than what Alec was telling him, although the bomb was real. He asked, "Is there something else he held over your head?"

Alec diverted his eyes. Hank stared at him. "Alec, look at me!"

Alec finally did, but he quickly shifted his eyes away again. Hank was a brilliant detective. He had a feeling that he knew what Harry was holding over Alec's head. He said again, "Look at me!"

It took Alec a moment, but he finally looked up at Hank, who was glaring at him. Then Hank said what he had guessed. "Your wife didn't kill herself, did she? You killed her, didn't you? And your cousin Harry knew it."

Again, Alec dropped his eyes. But the look in them told Hank that he was right. "No, she killed herself," Alec said in a very small, anguished voice. "I need to go home now. Are you guys going to take me?"

Hank decided to be anything but gentle at this point. He'd never believed that Mrs. Harmon had killed herself, but he and the sheriff couldn't prove otherwise. "Mr. Harmon, you don't have a home anymore. The bomb was real. It exploded while I was there with Jim Rogers and a bomb dog and its handler. We were lucky it didn't blow us up. But we stayed outside while we were waiting for the bomb dog to come. It went off before the dog could help us," Hank said. "We're lucky to be alive. So, tell me the truth."

"He blew my house up?" Alec asked in obvious dismay. For a moment, the airplane mechanic said nothing more, his head hanging between his knees. Hank and the PIs waited. Finally, Alec said, "My wife was Harry's girlfriend, but I stole her from him. I thought he'd gotten over all that years ago."

"Mr. Harmon, look at me." Alec finally looked up again. Then Hank asked, "Why did you kill your wife and try to make it look like suicide? The sheriff and I never were quite comfortable with calling it suicide."

Alec looked down again. "I don't have a home no more. So take me to jail. At least I'll have a place to live."

"You're admitting that you killed her?" Hank pressed.

"Okay, you got me. Yes, I did, but she was awful sick. She'd have died soon anyway." The guilt in his voice was evident.

Hank looked at Bentley who had his phone in his hand. "Did you record that?"

"I did," Bentley said.

"Mr. Alec Harmon, you are under arrest for the murder of your wife." Hank then gave Alec the Miranda warning. The detectives helped him to his feet as soon as Hank was finished.

"Was Harry taking a young woman and a little boy somewhere?" Carter asked.

"You mean the girl and little boy that were kidnapped? I saw that on the news."

"Yes. Where was he going to fly her to?"

The defeated man simply shook his head. "I don't know. And that's the truth."

"Surely he said something to you that might have indicated where he was taking her," Carter insisted.

"He didn't say anything about his passengers. He didn't tell me why he had the plane. When I warned him about flying it before I could repair it, he called me a liar—said he didn't believe me," Alec said as they started to walk him toward the rough forest road. He was stumbling and having a hard time walking. Carter and Bentley were helping him, one on his right side and one on his left. "Can you trace the plane's GPS?" Alec asked. "I want him in jail with me. I want to kill him!"

"The GPS in the plane has apparently been disabled. Keep going," Hank said coldly. He was angry with Alec for killing his own wife. He had thought about the death of Mrs. Harmon many times, and it had never felt right to him. And now, he finally knew the truth.

"We've got to find Gina," Carter said, his voice breaking just as Alec stumbled and had to have Carter and Bentley keep him from falling.

They moved slowly toward the road. Hank could tell Alec was in pretty bad shape. He wondered how long he'd been tied up. Despite himself, he began to feel sorry for him.

Carter was clearly still thinking about Gina and Sammy. "How are we ever going to find them now? Harry and Elliot could be taking them anywhere," he said.

"Someone will see the plane," Hank said. "It must be fueled up if they go far. Every airport in the state and all our neighboring states are on the lookout for it. We'll find them."

"I sure hope so," Carter said, close to tears.

"It had a full fuel tank," Alec informed them.

"Are you talking about the stolen plane?" Hank asked.

"Yes. I know that because Jim and his partners always filled it when they returned to the airport in Roosevelt after a flight."

"That's good to know," Hank said. "It will help us figure out how far he can fly without having to fill up."

They walked for a few more minutes. Carter and Bentley practically had to carry Alec now. He was extremely weak. But they finally reached the truck, and Alec leaned against it, his legs shaking.

"Now get in the truck," Hank said. "We'll help you."

"Aren't you going to handcuff me?" Alec asked as he looked bleakly at Hank.

"Don't need to. There are three of us, only one of you, and you are in bad shape. Get in. Carter, will you sit next to him?" Hank asked.

Carter nodded, and after their prisoner was in the truck, he climbed in beside him. As Hank started the truck a moment later, Alec said, "I wish you would have let me die out there. I deserve it."

Hank made no comment. He was angry at Alec, but it wasn't his problem to make things worse for the guy. His job had been to arrest Alec once he had confessed to murdering his wife. He'd done that, and in all honesty, he hated having to do it. But the late Mrs. Harmon deserved justice.

Now the pressure was rising to find Gina Rogers and her cousin Sammy Anders before it was too late.

Chapter 14

GINA AND SAMMY SAT TOGETHER IN THE BACK SEAT OF THE TWO-SEATER plane. The Joneses, father and son, sat in the front. The supplies, food, and other things were stored behind the seat the two prisoners sat in. Gina was disoriented. She wasn't sure what direction they were flying in, even though she'd flown a lot with her father. Not that it mattered. She feared they were going somewhere far away, or else they wouldn't be in an airplane. She was very discouraged, but she promised herself and Sammy that she would never give up.

Gina knew the plane they were in. She had taken several flying lessons in it in addition to flying many times with her dad. This plane belonged to her father and his three partners. Harry Jones, who was flying it now, had stolen it. That only added to the terrible things her parents were going through.

If she could see past the two men in the front, she might be able to catch a glimpse of the control panel. If she could, she would be able to figure out which direction they were flying, what their altitude was, and how fast they were going. The instrument panels were very familiar to her. But the men blocked her view. She would keep trying, no matter how unlikely it was to help.

Harry and Elliot were speaking to each other through their headphones. She could only catch a word or two here and there. At one point, she thought Harry had mentioned the name Alec Harmon. She couldn't tell what he was saying about him, but she did know who

Mr. Harmon was. He was an aircraft mechanic who took care of this plane. He was also a pilot. She even knew that he lived in Myton.

She couldn't imagine why they were talking about Mr. Harmon. Surely he didn't have anything to do with Harry taking her father's plane. He seemed like an okay guy to her, although there was something about him that made her a little uncomfortable the few times she'd been around him. He was kind of rough around the edges and didn't use very good language. Her dad had told her he was an excellent aircraft mechanic, that he'd learned his trade working on planes while he was in the air force.

There was something else she recalled. Alec's wife had died of a suicide. Her dad had been very upset about that. He couldn't imagine why she would do something like that. He'd told her Mrs. Harmon had been ill for a while, but he didn't believe that was something that would make her take her own life. At any rate, it was terribly sad, and her dad had told her and her mother that Mr. Harmon had never been as happy and carefree as before her death. Gina could not imagine how hard that would be.

She kept looking out the window. For the past hour, they had been flying over mountainous country. Below, there were trees as far as she could see on either side. It made her sort of nervous. Her dad had always told her that it was safer to fly over or near highways so that in the unlikely event the plane lost power, they would have a better chance of landing safely.

There were no roads that she could see on either side of them. She hadn't seen roads below them for many miles. Sammy seemed quite fascinated by the sight outside the windows of the plane. She was glad about that, at least. He'd been terrified when their captors had first forced them into the plane, and she'd had a difficult time settling him down. His voice was definitely gone, or else he would have screamed when he was put in the plane. He'd been frantically fighting Elliot, but it had done no good.

Gina had finally helped him become calm. Now, to her relief, he was totally mesmerized by the scene below them. Occasionally, they would pass over a stream or a lake. The lakes were all relatively small, as was the case in the mountains she was familiar with, the High

Uintas. She knew they were not over the Uintas. The country below them was extremely rugged.

She looked at Sammy and touched his arm. When he looked back at her, she said, "It's pretty down there, isn't it?" He nodded in agreement, a small smile on his face. "We'll be okay." He looked at her with hope in his eyes. Then he turned back to the window on his side and watched as the wild but beautiful country passed beneath them.

A stray thought crossed Gina's mind. What if they were lost in that vast forest? That would be horrible. That thought had barely crossed her mind when she felt the plane begin to shudder. Without warning, it began to lose altitude. When Elliot shouted at his dad, she knew that it was not something Harry had planned or was doing intentionally.

The plane shook harder. Then, to Gina's sheer terror, she realized that she could no longer hear the engine; they were flying without power. Harry, even from her vantage point, looked frantic. Elliot continued to shout. She could tell what he was saying now that the engine had stopped. "Start the engine! What do you think you're doing?"

"I'm doing the best I can!" Harry shouted back. "Shut up and let me think! I don't know what's wrong." He said nothing for a moment and then added, "We have plenty of fuel. I've got to find a place to set it down." More frantic shouting from Elliot was followed by Harry once again shouting, "Look for a road of some kind or even a large meadow."

Sammy's face was very pale. Gina was scared too. They were going to die. She prayed frantically as she grasped one of Sammy's little hands. She tried to speak to the little guy, but the continuous shouting of the men in the front made it impossible.

She saw a meadow to the right. Harry must not have seen it. She leaned forward and reached around the seat back and punched Harry to get his attention. Then she shouted for all she was worth. "There's a meadow to the right coming up. It's large."

She didn't know if Harry had heard her, but apparently Elliot did, for he started shouting again at his father and pointed at the approaching meadow. The plane was losing altitude rapidly. Harry, however, had seen the meadow. It was not very far ahead of them now. Harry dropped lower rapidly. The ground came up to meet them. Gina's stomach was in her throat. Gina put an arm around the terrified boy beside her and helped him to lean forward as she did the same.

As the plane approached the grassy meadow at much too great a speed, she simply prayed. Her prayer was desperate and ended when the airplane hit the ground and then slid forward. If it would stop now, they would survive, she thought as the plane lost speed even while it bumped and bucked terribly. To her surprise, she heard little Sammy scream. It took unbelievable terror to restore his voice again.

The plane continued to rush through the meadow. "Stop the plane!" Elliot shouted at the top of his voice. There was no reply from his father. "No! No!" Elliot screamed only seconds before the plane struck the trees at the edge of the forest. Gina didn't have time to scream before she struck the seat in front of her, and then there was nothing.

***

Carter Keefe was terribly discouraged. There was very little conversation as they rode back to Duchesne. Hank would occasionally make a call on his phone and ask whoever he called if there were any reports on the stolen plane. There were none, so he would wait for a while to check again.

Alec, in the back seat with Carter, mostly slept, occasionally mumbling something. Whatever he said was unintelligible. Carter couldn't be sure if he was talking in his sleep or if he was trying to say something to him. Either way, his mumbling made no sense.

Carter tried to tune him out. All he could think about was Gina. The longer she was gone, the more he realized how very important she had become to him. He closed his eyes but did not doze. No, what he did was silently talk to his Father in Heaven about Gina and Sammy. He prayed that they were safe right then and that they would continue to be safe and that they would be rescued and returned to her family—*and Gina returned to him.* But as he prayed, his heart was heavy. He had no idea why. But his concern ratcheted up a notch or two. He prayed some more. He didn't know if it was okay to beg Heavenly Father, but that is what he did. He begged that Gina's and Sammy's lives would be spared.

Hank pulled into the sally port at the jail where he turned Alec over to the jail staff. Carter listened as he said, "I'll be back to talk with you later, Alec. If you can think of anything that might help us find where Harry and Elliot have taken Gina and Sammy, I . . . we would appreciate it."

Carter didn't doubt that Gina and Sammy had been taken in the stolen plane. Alec claimed he hadn't seen the two of them when he'd met up with Harry where he'd landed the plane on a straight stretch of dirt road. But there was no other reason Harry would have taken the plane. Harry and Elliot apparently intended to take the two missing ones far from their home. That didn't make sense if it was their intention to demand a ransom at some point.

Alec stopped walking as he was being escorted by two corrections officers. He looked back at the three detectives, who were getting back into their pickup. "I don't know if this will help or not, but there's an old cabin that belonged to my grandparents, which means Harry's grandparents, since we are cousins. I have been there before, but it's been several years. It's in Daggett County."

Carter was very interested. Clearly Hank was too, for he asked, "Can you tell us where it is?"

"I think it's near where you found me. It might be within a mile or two," Alec answered.

"What are your grandparents' names?" Carter asked. "If the property is still in their names, I might be able to find a record of it."

Alec gave him the names of the grandparents.

"Thanks, Alec," Hank said. "We will find it, and maybe there will be a clue there as to where Harry was going to fly to. I'll talk to you later, probably tomorrow sometime."

Alec choked up, but before he let the officers take him into the jail from the sally port, he said, "I loved my wife. She was in pain. I know I shouldn't have killed her. But I didn't like how she was suffering. I did it out of love, but Harry would never understand that."

The two corrections officers looked at him with some surprise on their faces. One of them asked Hank if Mr. Harmon was being charged with murder.

"Yes," Hank said. "I'm afraid so."

Chapter 15

When Gina came to, she had no idea how long she'd been unconscious. It took her a minute to remember what had happened. When it came back to her, she looked over to where Sammy was sitting. She feared that he was dead. His head rested against the back of Elliot's seat, which had been shoved back a little in the crash, just like Harry's seat had been shoved back against her, but when she reached an arm out and touched his shoulder, he moved his head a little.

Then he looked at her. "Are we dead?"

She remembered him screaming just before the crash. Terror had taken his voice. Had it been even greater terror that restored it? That was the only thing she could think of, and it sort of made sense to her.

"No, sweetie, we are alive," she responded to his innocent question. "Do you hurt anywhere?"

"A little, but I think I'm okay. How come we aren't dead? The airplane crashed. Airplane crashes kill people."

"They don't always. We're alive because Heavenly Father saved us, Sammy. I was praying when we crashed. I think I'm sort of pinned, though. I need to see if I can get my legs free, and then I'll get you unstuck too."

"Are those bad men still alive too? Did you pray for them or just for us?"

Sammy's innocent question made her smile. "Just for us," she said. "I don't know if they are alive. We'll figure that out when we are able to free ourselves from the wreckage."

"Why didn't the plane explode?" Sammy asked. "On TV, they explode when they crash." His bruised eyes looked earnestly at her.

Gina grinned. "This is real life, but I think we should try to get out as quick as we can, because I suppose it still could catch on fire."

"If it does, will it burn those guys?"

"I will try to save them if they are alive," Gina responded. "I'm sure glad you have your voice back."

A gruff voice from the front of the crumpled airplane said, "You little rat, you. You were faking not being able to speak."

"No, he lost it because you scared him so bad, Harry," Gina said angrily. "It was your fault. You are a horrible man."

"Whatever," Harry said, his voice weak and filled with pain. He said nothing for a couple minutes or so while Gina worked at getting her legs out from between her seat and the back of Harry's.

"You got to help me, girl," Harry said in a weak voice. It sounded like he was trying to say something else, but he started to gurgle and he didn't continue.

The very thought of helping him made her cringe. But Gina was a righteous girl, and she knew that she would help him even if she didn't want to. She needed to free herself and then Sammy before she would try to do anything for the kidnappers. Once they were both out of the plane, she would check on Harry and Elliot. She had a feeling that they were probably hopelessly pinned in the wreckage, but she would make sure and help them if it was humanly possible.

Gina continued to struggle to free herself. The first thing she did was undo her seat belt. She'd been thrown so forcefully against the seat belt that the parts of her it had cut into ached terribly. Her legs hurt badly too, as did her head. But she had no choice but to endure the pain as she'd endured the pain Harry had inflicted on her. She gritted her teeth as she tried to move her legs. After a painful few minutes, she finally managed to pull one leg out. To her relief, it didn't appear to be broken. The second one took a little longer, but she eventually got it loose. Once again, it seemed that it was not broken either, just badly bruised. She sent a short prayer of gratitude to Heavenly Father.

Once she was no longer pinned, she helped Sammy. She soon discovered that he wasn't pinned. All she had to do was get the seat belt off him. She heard occasional groans from the front seat area. But she paid them no mind. Her first responsibility was to herself and Sammy.

Sammy's seat belt proved to be quite a problem, since there was nowhere for her to put her legs while she worked on getting it unlatched. Reaching over to Sammy's seat belt was a strain. She finally managed. The entire time, Sammy stayed silent. She was amazed at how incredibly brave he was, but maybe he was in shock. That concerned her too.

The next problem Gina faced was getting a door open and getting out to the ground. The doors were both in the front. Elliot was slumped over, near the door on Sammy's side of the airplane. To get to it, she realized she would have to squeeze past the back of Elliot's seat. She couldn't do that without hurting Sammy. "Sammy, we must trade places in order for me to reach the door. I've got to get my feet out from under me. Can you help me?"

"I can stand on the seat if I bend over. Then I can try to get past you," Sammy said bravely.

He didn't seem to be in a lot of pain, and he was able to first kneel up and then get to his feet, his head and shoulders hunched over. He began to step slowly past her as she leaned forward the best she could. He had to climb on her back for a minute, but then he was past her. Finally, she was able to move toward his seat. He was soon seated on her seat, and she was on his, her legs still curled beneath her.

"Sammy, if you can slide to the edge of the seat, I think I can get my legs straightened out," she said. They were getting cramped, and the pain grew worse with every passing minute.

Sammy did as she suggested, and soon, she had her legs across the seats, touching him. At that point, she was able to turn her body over and face the front. Gina was careful not to kick the little guy. Now she faced the problem of getting to the door and forcing it open. She was not able to get into a position where she could push on it. She examined it closely. It was jammed very tightly from the collision with the trees.

She could tell that there was no way it could be pushed open. The one on the other side was in much the same shape. She had succeeded in getting her head and shoulders past the back of Elliot's seat. She looked around up front, trying to see if there was any way to get out of the plane. She spotted a solution immediately: the entire windshield was gone. There was broken glass all around, but she could see that she would probably be able to get out that way and onto the tree limbs outside. One limb was very large, and it came right against the front of the smashed plane. She was soon convinced that she could do that.

She looked closer at the two men. Harry in the pilot's seat was still moaning some. Elliot was not moving at all. She felt for a pulse at his carotid artery, but there was none. Elliot Jones was dead. It was nobody's fault but his own for thinking he could kidnap her and Sammy to collect a ransom from her parents. She shoved that thought aside. What she needed to deal with now was getting both Sammy and herself out of the wrecked airplane.

She continued to study the broken windshield and the large, broken limb that was touching the plane. They would need to crawl over Elliot. She searched her feelings, but she was unable to feel sorry for him. She didn't hate him or his father, but she also felt very little pity for them. He wouldn't feel anything as she and Sammy crawled over his body in order to get out of the airplane, but the thought of it made her gag. She pulled her head and shoulders back and looked at little Sammy. She smiled through her pain. The little guy smiled back. Gina felt a strong surge of love for him.

"Sammy, I've found a way to get out of the airplane," she began. "It won't be pleasant, but we're going to have to crawl over Elliot to get to the open windshield."

"He'll be mad," he said. "He might try to hurt us."

She shook her head sadly. "Sammy, he won't know. He can't feel anything now."

Sammy showed once again how intelligent he was. "Is he dead?" he asked after thinking for a moment.

"Yes, he's dead. Let's bring some of the supplies behind our seats up here by us, and then we'll get out. I'll have to come back in several times to get everything we need. But first, let's get out and to the ground."

Sammy trembled. "A bear might get us," he said with a catch in his voice.

"No, Sammy, we'll be okay. Heavenly Father helped us survive the plane crash. He won't let a bear get us. And when I start getting stuff out, I'll bring one of the kidnapper's rifles."

"You can shoot it if it sees us," he said.

"Yes, I can if I need to, but I don't think we will. Should we see what we can reach behind us?"

"I can help do that," he said.

"The most important thing is the food," Gina told him.

"Yeah, we've got to eat," Sammy said, sounding almost close to cheerful. "And we need the gun and bullets."

Gina once again realized what an amazing and wonderful little boy Sammy was to think of such a thing.

"Yes, we do," Gina agreed. What she needed most right now was some Tylenol or something else that would help numb the terrible pain she was experiencing. She was really hurting quite badly, even though she knew she didn't have any broken bones. But she could only ignore the pain for so long. Surely there was medicine in the plane. Then she remembered. Of course there was. Her dad and the other owners kept a well-stocked first aid kit in the aircraft, and she knew right where it was.

Sammy and Gina pulled out the sacks of food and one of the rifles. Then she got the first aid kit from where it was kept in the back on the inside of the plane's wall. "That will do for now," Gina said. "Let's see if we can get out of here."

She made her way past the seat Elliot was in. He looked terrible and smelled worse than ever. She tried to control her stomach as she crawled over the dead man's body. She helped little Sammy join her.

"Help me," Harry said in a voice so filled with pain it was hard to hear him.

Apparently, he could still speak, but she ignored him. She honestly didn't know how she could help him. He was pinned tightly. She was sure he had a lot of broken bones, even badly crushed bones.

"Get me and Elliot out," he demanded weakly again. "I mean it."

"I've got to get me and Sammy out first. You might try to help yourself. That's what I did," she said coldly. Then she worked her way out of the windshield and onto the large tree branch. She was able to help Sammy onto the branch as well, and then they carefully worked their way to the ground. It really wasn't far, because the front end of the plane had collapsed quite a bit.

They rested in the shade of the trees for a few minutes. Gina was sore all over, but Sammy claimed he felt okay despite his bruised face.

"I need to get back in the plane and get our supplies," Gina said.

"Get the gun and bullets first," Sammy said as he looked nervously into the trees. And please hurry, Gina. I'm kind of scared out here."

She smiled at him and then gave him a hug. "We will be okay," she said. "I'll hurry."

"Don't get Harry out, please," Sammy added.

"I couldn't if I tried. He's pinned badly," she said. "And his bones are probably crushed beyond help."

"But I guess you can give him some water and food." Sammy said, much to Gina's amazement. He was a good boy, a special boy. Oh, how she loved Sammy Anders. His parents had taught him well, she thought to herself.

Gina went to work trying to get all the supplies she felt they could use while they were in the forest attempting to make their way back to a highway or a town. As Sammy had asked, she handed down a rifle and some ammunition to him first, even though he couldn't shoot the rifle. He kept it right beside him when she headed back up the large limb to the plane. She wasn't very concerned about wild animals, but he was scared, and he certainly had good cause to be worried after their encounter with a bear in the cabin.

She carried the first aid kit and a bottle of water on the next trip she made into the plane. She knew the first aid kit would be full, for her father was the kind of man who would make sure of that. As soon as she was back on the ground, she opened the kit and found a full bottle of Extra-Strength Tylenol. She put three in her mouth and swallowed them with water from the bottle. She also gave Sammy a drink.

"Thank you, Gina. I love you," he said.

"I love you too, Sammy," she said and kissed his forehead.

She rested for about half an hour, giving the pills time to kick in. When she began to feel some relief, she returned to the task at hand. Each time she crawled over Elliot's dead body with more food and water, Harry would curse weakly at her and tell her to get him out of the plane. At one point, she said, "Here, you may have a bottle of water and a piece of jerky." Only one of Harry's hands was usable. The other one was pinned, and she suspected it was broken very badly, probably smashed. She couldn't imagine the pain he was in, and despite herself, she felt bad for him. She helped him take a drink of water and gave him three of the Tylenol pills, even though she knew she might need them before she and Sammy were rescued. She placed the water bottle on his lap and handed him a large piece of jerky. On the next trip with supplies from the back, she carried another first aid kit that she'd found in a box of canned food. It was small, but she was not about to leave it.

"There," she said to Harry. "You'll feel better in a few minutes."

She swallowed another one of the pills herself. All the climbing in and out of the plane was increasing her pain. But she didn't wait any longer for the Tylenol to ease more of the pain. She was anxious to get all the supplies she could out of the plane and on the ground.

When she once more crawled from the backseat and over Elliot's body with a handful of clothes, Harry said, "I can't chew this," and he dropped the jerky onto his lap. "I need you to get me something soft."

On the next trip, she carried some Twinkies. She unwrapped one and handed it to Harry. Not once did he so much as offer a thank-you to her. He was truly an evil and ungrateful man. She ignored him after that. She knew that there was no way she could free him from the wreckage. It actually made her feel bad to know that he would die there. If she could have helped him, she would have, even though he didn't deserve it.

Finally, Gina had retrieved all she could and spent a few minutes sitting beside Sammy on the pine needles inventorying what she had. She'd brought out some bags and boxes that she hadn't looked in. She was surprised to find a small .38-caliber pistol in a holster wrapped in some of the men's clothes in one of the duffle bags. There were boxes of bullets in the bag as well. She knew how to shoot rifles and pistols. She'd hunted with her dad many times. She hoped she wouldn't need the firearms, but they gave her a feeling of security.

She wanted a large knife. She'd only found a couple of small pocketknives that were, at least, in better shape than the ones they had found in the cabin. She had Sammy put one of them in his pocket.

She put the other one in one of her pockets. "I wish we had a long and sharp knife," she muttered.

"I know where one is," Sammy said.

"You do?" she asked.

"Yes, Elliot has one on his belt," he said. "You should go get it."

"I didn't think about his knife," she said even as the thought of going back in and somehow taking the knife off Elliot's body made her gag. But Sammy was right, and she would do it no matter how repulsed she was by the idea. It took her several minutes, but she finally managed to get the knife and the scabbard from his belt. His smell was so bad that she threw up on him as she retreated with the knife.

"Get me out of here," Harry demanded once more. His voice was getting much weaker. Once she got back to the ground, she returned to where Harry was trapped with a bunch of men's clothing in her hands. She covered him with the clothes as best she could, knowing it would get cold. That was all she could do to help him, but then she had a thought.

Harry and Elliot both had wallets that might have money in them. She might need the money once she and Sammy were out of the forest. So she pried Elliot's from his pocket. It made her gag again, but she eventually got it. She kept the wallet and the large wad of cash in it but emptied everything else it contained on his dead body. With a lot of effort and a little resistance from Harry, she was able to get Harry's wallet as well.

She took the money out of it and dropped the wallet on his lap. "That's my money," he said in a weak, slurred voice. "You can't just steal it. That's mine."

She couldn't resist saying, "So says a thief. You don't need it. Anyway, this is my dad's plane, so everything in it belongs to me."

"Get . . . me . . . out . . ." he begged once more.

"I can't," she said. "Or else I would." She truly meant that. She didn't hate him. She disliked him and knew he was a thoroughly evil man. But she wasn't someone who hated people, no matter what they did.

He tried to say something else, but he couldn't do it.

"If I could find your phone or your son's, maybe I could call for help," she said.

"Do that," he said so weakly that she could barely hear him. Then his voice faded away.

Gina searched for their phones but couldn't find them. They were probably someplace unreachable in the wreckage. She finally gave up, but as distasteful as it was, she took the time to remove the watch from Elliot's wrist and put it on her own. It was too large, but she'd see if she could make the band smaller later. It was an expensive watch, but more importantly, it did what she needed it to; it told the time and the date. That would be helpful, she thought.

Gina left the plane for the last time, tears pouring down her face. She was crying for Harry. She knew that was strange, but it was true. He was suffering. She didn't like to see anyone or anything suffer. She prayed that he would not have to suffer long. He was going to die, and there was nothing she could do about that. But she asked her Heavenly Father to let him die soon.

Back on the ground beside Sammy, she told him again that she loved him. He told her that he loved her too, and they both shed tears for each other. They hugged and then they prayed together. This time Gina gave thanks to God for sparing her life and Sammy's. She also prayed that they would be able to somehow find their way out of the mountains they had crashed in. She prayed that her family and Sammy's would be comforted. She also prayed for her friends. Toward the end of her prayer, she said, "Please bless Carter. Help him find Sammy and me."

Sammy also prayed, and he thanked God for protecting them and for freeing them from the bad men. Then he said, "Please help me and Gina that bears and lions and wolves won't hurt us."

After they'd prayed, she counted the money. Between the two men, they'd been carrying over a thousand dollars in bills of various denominations, mostly hundreds and fifties. Sammy was watching as she shoved the bundle of money in a pocket of the jeans she was wearing and tossed Harry's wallet back into the plane.

Chapter 16

It was getting close to sundown. Gina and Sammy had inventoried everything she had taken from the wreckage. There was enough food and water to sustain them for several days if they rationed it. Since they had no idea how long it would be before they found their way out of the forest, they thought rationing would be wise. They also had several books of matches, so if they were careful, they could have a fire at night.

"The fires will keep us warm," Gina said.

"And it will keep the animals from getting too close to us," Sammy added.

"That's right, Sammy."

There were a couple of notebooks and some pens and pencils in one of the boxes, which made Sammy smile. "I can still draw," he said. "My notebook and pencil are still in the cabin. I put them in that big cupboard and forgot to grab them when they made us leave."

"Then you can draw when we take breaks," Gina said with a smile.

Gina wrapped the food and other supplies in one of the blankets and slung it over her shoulder. They had jackets, ones much too big for them, but they were at least fairly warm. Sammy had only the clothes he was wearing, but Gina had saved a few extra shirts, jeans, and socks that they could wear. Sammy was small, but she told him, "I can roll up the sleeves and pant legs for you, and it will be better than nothing."

"Thanks, Gina. You're wonderful."

When they finally started walking away from the wreckage, Gina was carrying the blanket with supplies over her shoulder. It was quite heavy, but she was determined to carry all they could with them. The long knife and small pistol were strapped to her waist. Sammy carried the rifle and the extra blanket. It was hard for him, but he did not complain. Gina had made the decision to travel in the same direction she thought the plane had been flying. That may not have been the best choice, but it was the best she could think of.

"How far will we go tonight?" Sammy asked. "It's getting dark."

"We will go until we can't see well, and then we'll make a fire and eat some food. We probably won't get far tonight, but we'll go as far as we can. If we get too tired, we'll stop and take breaks. We don't want to wear ourselves out. Are you feeling all right, Sammy?"

"I don't hurt much, but I think you do," he said.

"It's not too bad. I can stand it," she responded. "We're both lucky that we don't have any bad cuts or broken bones."

"We were blessed," he said, and she marveled at his faith and maturity. "Gina, I have the gift of the Holy Ghost. I've been baptized."

"So do I," she said. "The Holy Ghost will help us make good decisions."

It was very difficult walking once it was nearly dark, so they picked a spot beneath the trees. They cleared a place for a fire pit with their hands. Then they gathered firewood, making sure they stayed together. Gina picked some dry grass, which she placed beneath some small twigs, and then she put larger sticks over that. She lit a match. To her relief, it only took one match to get a fire going. Then they hunkered down next to the fire and, using a pocketknife, opened a can of stew. They used sticks they whittled to use as spoons and ate the stew.

They both wanted more, but Sammy agreed with Gina when she said, "That's all we'd better eat." They each drank a bottle of water as the evening progressed and burned the plastic bottles in the fire. Gina stomped on the empty stew can until it was flat and put it with the other supplies. "We don't want to litter the forest," she said. "If we had a shovel, we'd bury it, but we don't, so I'll carry it out with us."

"Maybe God will protect us if we keep the forest clean."

Gina had to smile at what he'd said. She hoped he was right.

They huddled together with the two blankets wrapped around them and then lay on the ground and tried to sleep. Sammy fell asleep quite easily. Gina only dozed off and on. It was going to be a long night, but she was determined to endure it.

***

The plane had not landed in any airports as far as the cops could tell. Nor did it stop for fuel. Carter, Hank, and Bentley had searched for the cabin that day, but by the time they found it, it was dark. They had made the decision to sleep and then search the cabin and surrounding area as soon as it was light.

They had food and water. They also had blankets in Hank's truck. It wouldn't be comfortable, but searching with flashlights wasn't effective enough.

Once they located the cabin, they were able to tell that something had broken the door. Inside, things were relatively clean and neat, although there wasn't much in there.

"I'll bet they made Gina keep this place clean," Hank said with disgust.

"I know her well," Carter said. "I'll bet she did it without being forced. Even though she was a captive, I can imagine her cleaning and keeping things straight. That's just the kind of girl she is."

There was a stove and some firewood in the cabin as well as matches. Hank started a fire in the stove. With the broken door propped up in the door opening, the fire soon had them feeling reasonably warm. "It'll get colder during the night, but if we keep a fire going, and with the blankets, we'll be okay."

There were two beds in a small second room and a cot in the main room.

"I'm the youngest," Carter said. "You guys each take a bed, and I'll sleep on the cot." The beds were not comfortable, but it was better than sleeping on the floor. The cot was the most uncomfortable of all, but Carter was okay with it.

Carter tried to rest that night, but sleep mostly eluded him. The men were not cold, because they did what Hank had suggested and kept a fire burning in the stove. It wasn't the cold or the uncomfortable cot that kept Carter awake. It was thinking about Gina and wondering where she was and if she was okay. The longer she was missing, the fonder he became of her. He prayed for her a lot during that long night. He knew that the longer the search for her and Sammy went on, the more difficult it would be to ever find them. He couldn't bear to think of that, though. He simply kept repeating in his head that Gina and Sammy were alive. He prayed that they would find them soon.

Early the next morning, Hank got on his satellite phone and checked in with the sheriff. The plane had not landed in any airports within the range of where that plane could fly on a tank of gas. When he ended the call, he reported to the others what he'd learned. "Our biggest worry is that the plane might have broken down in the air. The engine problem that Alec had planned to fix could cause the engine to fail." That was of great concern to all of them.

Also of concern were the large bear tracks all around the cabin and the deep scratches on the damaged door. "It looks like a bear got in the cabin at some point. I wonder if anyone was hurt. I don't see any blood around," Hank said from where he was searching inside.

"There's some on the porch," Bentley informed the others. He'd been searching outside. The others joined him, and they looked at the blood and worried. All three continued to search into the trees.

Carter shouted at the others. "Hey, guys, I found the source of the blood. There's a dead deer here that's had some meat cut out of it."

"That's a relief," Hank said. "It's a wonder the bear hasn't been back and found this carcass. But I'm glad it didn't."

"They clearly have rifles. Maybe they killed the bear. If so, its remains will be in the forest somewhere," Bentley said. "But that's not our biggest worry right now. I keep hoping we'll find something to give us a clue as to where Harry and Elliot planned to take Gina and Sammy from here."

They took a break and ate some MREs (Meals, Ready-to-Eat) that were packaged for long-term storage. Then the three detectives began to search again. Carter was the one who opened the large cupboard. It was empty except for a short pencil and a large notebook. He picked the notebook up and opened it. His heart nearly stopped when he saw a pencil drawing of Gina and one of Sammy. "Hey, guys!" he shouted. "You've got to see this."

The others came running. "I don't think Gina is an artist. She's more into sports and music, but someone is," Hank said.

"Sammy is an artist, and he's a very good one," Carter said.

The three men went to the small table and started at the front of the notebook, looking at what had been drawn on each page. There was an excellent drawing of a bear standing on its hind legs, its front paws reaching upward.

Carter looked up and spotted a shelf up high. "Could Sammy and Gina have been on the shelf, out of reach of the bear?" he asked as he pointed out the shelf to the others.

"They had to have been, but where were the Jones men?" Hank asked. "Were Gina and Sammy afraid to leave, so they stayed here without being tied up?"

"That must be the case. We need to search that spot," Carter said. "But how did they get up there?"

The men looked around the room.

"The only way would be if they climbed up on the big cupboard and shimmied over there on the rafters," Hank said.

They left the notebook for a moment and pulled the table beneath the shelf. Hank climbed on it. He was barely able to see onto the shelf. "There are wrappers up here and empty water bottles," he reported and then jumped down from the table."Now we know that they were up there, and that saved them from the bear. Let's look in the notebook some more. Maybe we'll find clues in there."

They moved the table back and studied the drawings once more. They came to the page that Carter had opened to when he first found the notebook. "Gina and Sammy," Hank said, rubbing his chin thoughtfully. "At least we know that they were still together while they were here in the cabin." There were also drawings of Harry and Elliot Jones. "These pictures are solid proof that these men kidnapped Sammy and Gina," Hank concluded.

They looked at the rest of the pictures Sammy had drawn.

"These people are his parents. This little guy is an amazing artist. The detail in these pictures is so good, they could almost be photos. I'm going to take pictures of every page," Hank said. As he began to take pictures with his iPhone, he added, "This notebook is dynamite, but you two keep searching. We still have no idea where they might have taken Gina and Sammy from here."

"At least we know that Gina and Sammy were both okay when they left the cabin," Carter said. "I hope they still are. I believe that they took Gina so they could make her family pay to get her back. They must have taken Sammy only because he was with Gina when they'd left Maya's house."

Hank stopped taking pictures for a moment. "I wonder why they haven't made a ransom call yet."

"This makes me so angry," Bentley said, and indeed, the anger in his voice was strong.

They went back to searching but found nothing more of value except for boot tracks and tire tracks, which Hank photographed. He also took pictures of both the inside of the cabin and the outside. "Wildlife resources will be interested in the poached deer," Hank said as they were finishing up. "Of course, if we can nail them for kidnapping, the poached deer won't be worth bothering about."

A few minutes later, they started the long drive back to Duchesne. There was still no word of the aircraft having landed or even being fueled up anywhere. Their biggest fear now was that the plane may have crashed. That was not something Carter even wanted to think about, but he knew it was possible. That very thought made him sick.

Chapter 17

Gina was terribly sore. They had eaten a small breakfast, put the campfire out, and started hiking again. The weight of the blanket filled with supplies on her back was making it harder than ever to keep walking. Little Sammy was also struggling. The rifle was heavy, even though it was a small one, a .30-30, so Gina took turns carrying it. They stopped frequently to rest. Gina wanted to push harder, but neither of them had the energy to do so. They trudged slowly on, rested, and trudged on some more. Gina had never imagined anything could be so hard. But she was a girl with a strong will and great faith. She vowed that she would never give up.

They each ate a candy bar for lunch. At one point, Gina looked around, confused. "I think we must be going in circles," she told Sammy. "Didn't we pass this crooked tree a few hours ago? It looks familiar to me."

Sammy studied it for a moment, and then he, too, looked around. "Yes, Gina, I think we've been here before. How could that have happened?" he wondered, a look of discouragement on his face.

"I wish we had a cell phone. Even without service, we could use the compass on it to make sure we keep going straight. We need to start looking at landmarks and find a way to go straight," she said.

They rested by the crooked tree. Suddenly, they heard something crashing through the timber behind them. Gina's heart felt like it was about to burst from her chest. Sammy handed her the .30-30 rifle and then snuggled up tight to her, whimpering. They stood against the crooked tree. Gina made sure there was a round in the chamber and the safety off in case she needed to shoot.

The crashing sound became louder. "There's more than one," she whispered to Sammy.

"It isn't bears," she assured him with some relief. "Bears don't run in packs."

"Wolves do," the little boy said.

"It's too loud for wolves," she assured him as the rapid beating of her heart decreased.

A moment later, a half dozen elk pounded past them. There was nothing chasing them, so she had no idea what had spooked them or why they were running. After they disappeared, Sammy said, "They're pretty. I'm glad it wasn't wolves."

Gina chuckled. "I'm glad too."

They started to walk again. They tried to stay straight, but that was impossible because of the valleys and ridges and the many fallen trees. After walking for another hour, according to the watch she'd taken from Elliot, she saw the wrecked airplane. Her heart sank.

"What are we doing back here?" Sammy asked in confusion.

"I don't know," Gina said as exhaustion and discouragement overcame her. She sank to the ground, and despite her best effort, she started sobbing. She felt a little hand on her shoulder.

"It's okay, Gina. Maybe we were going the wrong way in the first place. Heavenly Father will help us."

Ashamed of her weakness, Gina took the little guy in her arms and held him for a couple minutes. She finally controlled her emotions. "Okay, Sammy. I'm okay now. We'll go that way," she said, pointing in the exact opposite direction from the one they'd gone before.

They each took a small drink of water, and then she said, "I want to look in the plane before we start walking again."

"Do you think Harry is dead now?" he asked with a touch of fear in his voice.

"I think he is, but I just want to be sure." With that, she climbed up the limb and peered into the plane. The odor was the worst she'd ever experienced. She held her breath while she looked closely at Harry. There was no question that he was dead. She then proceeded down the limb and took a deep breath of fresh air.

Sammy looked up at her with a question in his eyes.

"Yes, Sammy, Harry is dead. Let's start walking."

"I'll carry the gun for a while," Sammy said.

She handed it to him, and then she put the blanket with their supplies in it over her shoulder, and took the other blanket in her hands so Sammy wouldn't have to carry it for a while. They set off.

Gina concentrated hard on where they were going, and using the sun as a guide, she tried to keep going in one general direction. She could only hope that by hiking in the current direction, they would find a road that they could then follow.

***

Sheriff Terry Goldman got a call at his office from a Sheriff Lawson Connor in Colorado, who said, "Sheriff Goldman, I received a report of a downed plane from a pilot who had flown over the mountains in my county. The pilot told me that his passenger saw something below them reflecting the sun at the edge of a meadow. She thought it had to be something metal. He said he circled and came in lower to investigate what she saw. He told me it is most definitely a plane. He thought it looked like the pilot was trying to land, because there was a disturbed area in the meadow right up to where the tree line began. The plane struck the trees pretty hard. It is in a very remote area a long ways from any roads. It's a large and dense forest. I know you've been looking for a missing plane."

"That's right. It was stolen from the airport in Roosevelt," Sheriff Goldman said. "We know that a nasty character by the name of Harry Jones stole it. We also believe that there were four people on board. Jones and his son kidnapped a teenage girl and a young boy from Duchesne. They were probably on board and being taken to parts unknown."

"We can't be sure of anything about the plane because the pilot that spotted the crash couldn't be sure of the description," Sheriff Connor said. "It was a single-engine plane. White with blue stripes. But neither the pilot nor his passenger could read the wing number. He gave me the approximate coordinates, and I'm sending some officers to the location in a helicopter. They'll be leaving in a few minutes."

"I appreciate the heads-up," Sheriff Goldman said. "Our missing plane is white with blue stripes and is single engine. It sounds like it could be the one we're looking for."

"I'll let you know as soon as my officers locate the crash site. It did not catch fire as far as the pilot could see. If it had, we'd probably have had a serious forest fire."

"Let me give you the descriptions and names of the four people we believe were on board the stolen plane," Sheriff Goldman said. Then he relayed that information to Sheriff Connor.

The two sheriffs talked a little more, and it was agreed that a detective from Duchesne County would drive over and be there to identify the people in the plane if needed. "I will send Detective Sergeant Hank Parker, and there may be someone else with him. I will determine that after I meet with my detective."

"I'll be expecting him then, Sheriff," Sheriff Connor said. "And if need be, we'll take him to the crash site."

Sheriff Goldman summoned Detective Sergeant Parker to his office. "Hank, I'm afraid I just got what could be very bad news. A crashed plane has been spotted in the mountains in Colorado. It may not be the plane Elliot Jones stole, but I'd say the odds are high that it is. That's the only plane reported missing in the last few weeks, and it is the right color." He explained what the Colorado officers were going to do.

"Do I need to go to Colorado?" Hank asked.

"Yes, I told Sheriff Connor that I would send you. I would like you to meet the officers when they return with the helicopter or possibly just get a report from them. If it is our missing plane, then you will need to have them give you a lift by helicopter out there. Sheriff Connor has already told me that he will get you to the scene if it is our missing plane."

"It's going to take me a while to drive there," Hank said. "I'll pack a bag and get on the road."

"I can't spare another officer to go with you, but if either of the PIs would like to go, if they are available, that would be fine. In fact, take them both if you want to," the sheriff instructed Hank.

***

About forty-five minutes later, Hank Parker and Carter Keefe were on the road. Bentley Radford was in Salt Lake working on another case, so he couldn't go, even though he'd made it clear that he wished he could when Hank called him.

"I hope it's not Jim Rogers's plane, but we need to be prepared for the worst," Hank said to Carter as they started their journey. "I'm sorry about this. I can see you are very worried. I am as well. The sheriff and I made the decision not to notify Gina's family yet. We don't want to either cause more worry or give any false hope to them."

"I have a feeling that it is them," Carter said sadly. "I'm just praying that they survived."

***

Gina and Sammy had spent another night in the forest after leaving the plane wreck for the second time. It had been tough going. Gina's pain had gotten worse, but she didn't mention it to Sammy. He was a brave boy, but even though he was eight years old, he was small for his age. He was getting very tired, and they had to stop often and for longer periods of time on each stop.

They continued to eat their food very sparingly. Gina wasn't too worried yet about running out. But she knew they could be in this forest for a long time. She knew it was large, because she'd watched the forest as they'd flown over it, and it seemed like it went on forever.

They refilled their water bottles each time they came to a stream, which was quite often. Thirst was not a problem, but they had wet feet much of the time. Sleep, on the other hand, was a problem. Neither of them slept very well on the hard ground, and Sammy worried constantly about wild animals. Gina kept a good fire going all night long, which was of some comfort to Sammy—and to her, too, for that matter.

They had hiked for several hours that day. Gina felt like they were no longer walking in circles. She used the position of the sun to stay oriented, and she felt like she'd done quite well. They had seen a couple of small planes fly over, but Gina didn't think it likely that anyone would spot the wreckage in such a large forest. And the planes were quite high.

"Gina," Sammy said as he sat next to her in front of a log around noon that day, "do you think it'll be much longer before we come to a road?"

"That's a good question, Sammy. I have no idea. All we can do is hope for the best. God is watching over us," she responded.

"I know that He is," Sammy said

Gina was thoughtful for a moment. "Sammy, if Carter and the other detectives have found the cabin where we were at, they'll at least know we're still together."

"Yeah, because I forgot to bring my notebook, and if they find it, they'll see both of our pictures in it. Do you think they found the cabin?"

Gina put an arm around his shoulders and pulled him close to her. "They are very smart detectives. I think they will find the cabin. In fact, they probably already have."

"I hope they have," Sammy said. As they rested, he used a pen with blue ink to draw in one of the two notebooks they'd found in the plane. Gina's face was appearing on the page. It made her smile.

"Do you think we should get going again?" Gina asked.

"Yes, let's go. It's hard, but I'll try not to get too tired."

"You are doing very well," Gina told him, once more tugging him close to her.

They got on their way again. Gina kept watching the sun, and she felt like she was doing okay as far as being consistent on the direction they were traveling. She constantly prayed that she was. She also prayed that they would not encounter any dangerous animals. So far, they'd seen quite a few elk and deer, as well as lots of squirrels and a variety of birds.

Chapter 18

Sheriff Lawson Connor welcomed the two detectives from Utah to his office that afternoon. "My chopper is on its way back to take you men out to the crash site. We've got the wing number, and it matches that of your missing plane."

"Are there any survivors?" Hank asked as Carter stood wringing his hands.

"There are two men dead in the plane's cabin. There's no sign of the girl or the boy who you believe were on the plane with them," Sheriff Connor explained.

"That could be good news," Hank said. "Gina and Sammy might have gotten out and are trying to walk out of the forest."

"Let's hope so, but I've got to tell you that will be a very difficult hike. That plane crashed many miles from any roads. The forest is large and rugged."

"It will be harder if either of them is injured. How did they get out of the plane if they were in it?" Hank asked.

"That I don't know. You will probably be able to tell a lot more when you get there. We do know that the two dead men are pinned badly. It's not going to be easy to recover their bodies," Sheriff Connor explained. "My pilot will be here for you men shortly."

Thirty minutes later, Hank and Carter were onboard the helicopter and on their way to the crash site. When they arrived at the meadow, the pilot set the helicopter down a short distance from the wrecked plane. The two men got out and walked over to the plane where they were greeted by Sheriff Connor's deputies.

The lead officer there was a man named Alfred Stringam. He was a sergeant, about six feet tall with a slender build. He and the other deputy had masks on their faces and were working without success to free the bodies of Harry and Elliot Jones.

"I assume that's who they are," Sergeant Stringam said. "I suppose you men will be able to identify them for us."

"If their faces aren't too messed up, we will," Hank said.

The helicopter pilot joined them and handed masks to Hank and Carter. Hank climbed up onto a large branch that reached up to the missing windshield. He held his breath as he peered inside. There was no doubt who the two men were. He climbed back down and reported his confirmation to Sergeant Stringam.

Carter was studying the ground in front of the plane. When Hank got back to the ground again, he said, "The grass is flattened right here." He pointed to a spot in the grass where a large branch reached almost to the ground.

"We noticed that too," Sergeant Stringam said. "And we noticed more flattened spots just inside the tree line. It has clearly been tromped down a lot. I think your two kidnap victims must have either sat or reclined here. And we found tracks back in the trees—a very small shoe track and a larger one. There's no sign of blood, which could mean they weren't injured too badly. Of course, that doesn't mean there aren't any broken bones."

Hank and Carter followed the tracks for a short distance while the Colorado deputies resumed the horrible task of freeing the mangled bodies from the wreckage. Hank, who had quite a bit of experience tracking people, noticed something and pointed it out to Carter. "The same tracks come back toward the plane." He was silent for a moment. "It's possible they got disoriented at some point and returned to the plane. The tracks coming back are fresher than the ones going out."

Carter looked closely at the ground. He wandered farther away from Hank. After a few minutes, he returned and said, "I don't see any other tracks leading away again. Do you think they may have gone a different direction?"

"Let's walk around the edge of the meadow and see if we can find any tracks leaving it in another direction," Hank suggested.

It didn't take long to see where Gina and Sammy had crossed the meadow and entered the forest on the far side. They followed the tracks for a short distance before turning back. "I wish we had tracking dogs," Hank said. "Maybe we could find them that way. I can't imagine that they're going very fast. I'd be surprised if they aren't both injured to some degree. Sammy, as we both know, is a small kid. Even though he's eight, he's more the size of an average six-year-old."

"I've been around him a lot. He is very fit and strong for his size."

"Let's talk to Sergeant Stringam and see if they have any dogs that might be available," Carter suggested.

They did that and were told that they had one in the department and that they would fly it out with its handler early in the morning.

"Right now, let's fly you two back to town. We'll be here a while longer. These bodies are not coming out easily. We'll have the pilot bring some equipment that will help us get the bodies out. And we'll need body bags. We'll work until the chopper gets back from delivering you two to town, and then we'll have to call it off until morning. We can't do anything after dark."

The helicopter flew in the direction the tracks had been heading away from the meadow, which was also the general direction back to the sheriff's office. Carter and Hank watched out of the windows of the helicopter just in case they might spot Gina and Sammy. Unfortunately, they had no luck, and after a while, they had returned to Sheriff Connor's office.

They spoke briefly with the sheriff, who said, "You men be here about an hour after sunup, and we'll take you back out to the crash site. We think we can send a tracking dog and its handler. We'll have our people out there again before daylight. One of my deputies will stay there overnight to protect the scene from scavenging animals."

"Thanks for what you're doing, Sheriff," Hank said. "We'll be here in the morning."

"It's our job, as you both know, since the crash happened in my jurisdiction," Sheriff Connor said. "The Feds are also sending a team to investigate the crash. The lost young people are also our responsibility. In addition to a dog, we'll send some search-and-rescue people out to search for them. The only thing that could complicate things is the weather. I am concerned about a storm that has been forecasted to hit. Hopefully, it won't be a significant one."

Afterward, the two detectives found a motel where they got a room and took their bags in. Then they found a café to get some dinner. Both men were very tired and went to bed early.

***

The weather was changing. Dark, heavy clouds formed early in the morning. Shortly after sunup, it began to rain. Gina and Sammy huddled around their fire. They were hunkered down at the base of a tall ledge, which had a large overhang that gave them some shelter from the rain. They gathered a big pile of wood before it got too wet, and then they stayed under the overhang with their blankets around their shoulders.

"I know we need to get going, Sammy, but if we get wet, it might make us sick," Gina said. "Are you okay with us waiting to walk again until the storm is over?"

"Yes," he said. "I don't want to be wet. It's bad enough getting our feet wet crossing streams."

"We can dry our shoes and socks by the fire since we can't go anywhere yet," Gina responded.

As they spoke, lightning struck a tall tree a short way down the hill from them in a burst of light and loud thunder. It was followed by a hard downpour, which kept the fire of the burning tree from spreading and even put the fire out after a few minutes.

Gina didn't ever remember seeing such a hard rainstorm. Water was soon pouring from the ledge above them and splashed to the slope about ten feet in front of them before rushing down the hill like a river. But Gina and Sammy stayed dry and reasonably warm. The heavy rain lasted for well over three hours before finally slowing to a more normal rainstorm. At least what was normal from Gina's experience.

Gina's sore body was healing, but she still felt a lot of pain. It felt good to be leaning against the wall of rock beneath the overhang as she watched the rain pour beyond her. Even though the intensity of the storm had decreased, water still cascaded down the mountain above them and over the ledge they were sheltered beneath.

They had conserved their food and were doing okay. Thirst was not a problem because all of their bottles were full. The pistol was still strapped to Gina's side, and the rifle lay on the ground next to her. Sammy was still worried about bears and cougars and wolves even though they had seen no wild animal tracks besides those belonging to deer and elk. But she understood his fear after how close they had come to being killed by the bear in the cabin.

"I miss my mom and dad," Sammy said. "I hope they get well soon. But at least I have you and your family for now."

"I'm glad you could be with our family while your folks are healing," Gina said.

"I love your family," Sammy said as tears slipped down his face.

"I know that my family is praying for both of, us," Gina said. Gina had been thinking about Carter. She was sure he was doing something to help find her. She just wondered what. She also knew her father would be doing something to help find her, but it was Carter she found herself longing for.

I'm glad I have you, Gina," Sammy said as he turned his head toward hers. "I love you. I wouldn't know what to do without you. Heavenly Father blessed me by sending you to take care of me." As he spoke, he leaned into her, and she put an arm around his shoulders and tugged him tightly to her side.

She felt an outpour of love for Sammy. "God sent you to take care of me," she said, smiling at him.

"You're funny," he said with a small smile. "I can't take care of you."

"Sammy, just having you with me is a great comfort and keeps me from being lonely. That is how you are taking care of me. You are being a companion and friend to me."

"I guess we are taking care of each other, then," he said, wiping a tear from his cheek.

After about an hour, the intensity of the storm increased again. The mountains echoed with the sound of thunder, and lightning lit the sky almost constantly. Gina watched the lightning and falling torrents of rain and the huge cascading stream going right over the top of them. The water was eroding the ground in front of them, but she didn't feel like it was any danger to them. Not yet, anyway. The biggest problem was the thick mud they'd have to walk through when they finally left their shelter to continue their search for a road. And that was a very worrisome thought.

Chapter 19

The storm was so bad that the helicopter was unable to fly. Hank and Carter were assured that they would be taken out to the crash site as soon as the storm passed. The recovery party had been taken before daylight, before the worst of the storm had blown in.

"The really bad news," Sheriff Connor began, "is what this storm does for the dog's ability to track. I hate to say this, but the dog's handler says it would be a total waste of time now. The same is true of the search crews I've assembled. Any tracks will be totally washed away. A little storm wouldn't have been a problem, but this one is not a little storm. I've been in touch with my deputies at the crash site. It seems the storm is much worse there than it is here. Sergeant Stringam said there are streams of water all around them. They're under a tarp they set up, so they are sort of out of the weather. But the bodies in the airplane are getting soaked as the rain pours in through the missing windshield.

"I was afraid of that," Hank said. "Besides washing out Gina's and Sammy's tracks, the heavy rain will also make it a hundred times harder for them to walk through the mountains. I just hope they've found some shelter."

That concerned Carter more than anything. They could be washed away with flooding torrents of water. His heart ached for Gina. He wished he could do more. But other than praying for her and Sammy, there was absolutely nothing he could do right now except wait for the storm to pass.

"I'll still have the chopper take you back out to the plane wreck when it clears up enough to fly, if that's what you men want to do," Sheriff Connor said.

"We'd like to go back out there. Gina and Sammy returned to the plane once; maybe they will again," Hank said hopefully.

"A couple of planes will begin to search from the air when the conditions permit it," Sheriff Connor said. "We will do all we can to find those two young people."

While they waited, both detectives made some phone calls to report what was happening. Hank explained the unfortunate circumstances to Sheriff Goldman while Carter listened in.

"I'm arranging for some planes from here to fly there and do some searching from the air when the weather over there permits it," Sheriff Goldman said. "We have good weather here. Bentley and Gina's father are renting a plane. They'll be heading that way as soon as the weather clears. Others are preparing to fly and assist in the search from the air as well."

"The storm here is very bad," Hank said. "And it's apparently much worse in the mountains. Sheriff Connor says it is one of the worst he's ever seen."

"I've been looking at the forecast for that area. It should be clearing up in the next few hours. Our planes here will head that way as soon as it is conducive to searching from the air."

"That's good news," Hank said.

"With planes coming from Duchesne County and some to help from here as well, we will have the best chance at finding Gina and Sammy," Carter said as soon as Hank's call was over.

***

Gina looked at Elliot's watch every so often. She'd managed to take some links out of the band so that it fit her. The only thing about checking the time was that it continually reminded her of the horrible men who had forced her and Sammy into this situation.

The day was dragging on. The storm continued. Finally, at about one in the afternoon, it stopped raining, and the sun peeked out of the clouds. She had already decided that they would need to wait longer before setting out again, because it would be so terribly muddy. And she could imagine that the water would gather into new streams as it drained to lower country.

To pass the time, Gina and Sammy told each other stories. Sammy had a very fertile imagination. The energetic way he got into his stories made Gina smile. And he listened intently to her when she told him stories, hanging on to every word she spoke. Sometimes she made the stories up, like Sammy did. Other times, she told stories of experiences from her life. He mostly liked her to tell him about the softball games she'd pitched. Even though the story of one game wasn't often different from others, he listened intently, cheering when she told him about striking a batter out or of making a good hit when she was batting. They became engrossed in their storytelling as the water continued to flow over the overhang where they were sitting. They both had to talk very loudly to be heard over the rush of water.

Gina paused in a story she was telling Sammy about a softball game she'd pitched a no hitter in. What caused her to pause was a roaring that was louder than the water falling past them. The ground seemed to shake as the roaring came closer. "It's from somewhere up there," Sammy said, pointing upward. "Or is it an earthquake?"

"I think it's a huge mudslide," she shouted to him as the noise became almost overpowering.

Soon it was absolutely thunderous. The ground they sat on shook so hard that Sammy whimpered. Gina could feel his little body trembling and knew he was terribly frightened. A few small rocks were dislodged from the ledge above them and dropped harmlessly in front of them. They huddled together in fear as whatever was happening turned the water gushing over them into thick mud. That confirmed what she'd suspected. Then the noise became deafening and the ground shook harder and more tiny rocks fell around them. They put the blankets double over their heads in case any rocks hit them, but none did.

Soon the water was replaced with rocks, trees, and tons of mud. It all hit the ground ten feet in front of them and piled up. Mud splashed onto them as the volume of the slide increased by the second. It kept coming and coming. It was a literal landslide. She wondered what the mountain above them looked like. She had a feeling it was bare of trees now considering how many were coming over the cliff and sliding down the ever-growing pile of mud and rock and the steep slope beyond.

Gina knew they were in trouble when the slide became much wider. Within about ten minutes, it had closed off both sides of the overhang with more building up in front of them.

Sammy cried frantically. "It's going to bury us!" he screamed.

Gina had barely been able to hear him. She had to suppress her own screams for fear of making Sammy even more terrified.

She feared that Sammy might be right, that it might bury them. She prayed hard as she and Sammy were forced to crowd tighter against the rock wall behind them. Gina used sticks to pull the fire closer to them. Soon there were only about five feet between them and the wall of mud and rock. She didn't know what to do besides plead with God to save them once more.

The flow of mud stopped suddenly. It appeared that it had run its course. The wall in front of them towered a good ten feet into the air, but it did not reach the edge of the overhang. Over the next long hour, it slowly settled, but it was moving away from them and down the slope in front of them, not closing them in tighter. Finally, the earth seemed to settle, and all became still and quiet.

"Gina, we're trapped," Sammy said fearfully.

"Not entirely," she consoled him. "I think that, by morning, we might be able to climb over the mud. It will dry some and become more stable."

Gina hoped that would happen, but there was no way to know for sure. All they could do was wait and see what the next day brought. For now, there was nothing they could do but try to stay warm. They huddled together with both blankets pulled close around them. Their supplies and the firewood she'd collected were piled on either side of them and their small fire was tight against the newly formed wall of muddy dirt and rock. They had to shift to one side a little bit and move their supplies and firewood to where the fire wouldn't burn them.

Gina kept the fire small. She didn't have a lot of wood left, but it no longer took a large fire to keep the area around them warm. They waited and prayed, and finally, after the fear had receded from their minds, they told a few more stories. There was no use in even thinking about trying to get out of there until the next day. They huddled and talked and prayed and slept from time to time as the day wore on.

***

The deputies at the crash site had strung a large tarp from the wreckage of the plane to the trees near it. They had a fire burning just beyond the edge of the tarp and had succeeded in keeping it burning during the storm by piling large chunks of pine wood on it. It was a place for them to dry out whenever they climbed from the plane. The water had soaked the interior of the plane, which made their work harder as they tried prying the badly mangled metal from around the dead men's legs.

By the time Carter and Hank finally arrived, they had succeeded in removing Harry's body. The deputies were still working to free Elliot's body. Carter and Hank pitched in and took turns working inside the plane. After a few minutes, the helicopter pilot suggested that Carter and Hank come with him and search for Gina and Sammy from the air. They could fly lower than the fixed-wing planes that would also search.

Hank spoke with Bentley using his satellite phone. He and Jim Rogers were in one of five planes that had begun flying once the storm had moved out. Hank explained what he and Carter were going to do. When they were in the air, the pilots of the different aircraft communicated with each other on a radio frequency that they could all use. That way, the search was fairly coordinated.

They were all flying east of the wreckage but attempting to stay within a radius of about five miles. No one believed the two young people could have gone farther than that. In fact, four miles seemed like a stretch considering how rough the terrain was and how thick the forest was with large trees, downfall, and streams of water.

Carter was especially discouraged after they'd flown for an hour. It was very difficult to see through the trees, even though they were flying low. He couldn't imagine how Gina's father and Bentley or any of the other personnel in planes could see anything from higher up. One of the things that they watched for was smoke rising above the trees, thinking that Gina may have managed to make a fire to keep them warm.

"I doubt they've done much walking today, if any," Hank mentioned to Carter above the noise of the helicopter. "I think they probably settled down someplace and stayed there, despite the storm or, rather, because of the storm."

"I wonder if they found anyplace close to cliffs or even if they might have found a cave," Carter suggested.

"I don't think that they would want to use a cave for fear of bears," Hank countered. "I would imagine that Sammy and Gina were scared enough of bears after their close call that they wouldn't be likely to dare step foot in a cave."

They spotted a tall cliff with a substantial overhang that had lots of mud and rock in front of it. Above and beyond the cliff, a large area of the mountain had slid down and over the cliff. Most of the trees had been brought down, along with mud and rock. If Gina and Sammy happened to have taken shelter beneath that overhang, the slide could have and probably would have spelled disaster.

Steam was rising from the mud as the sun shined directly onto it. "If they were there and had a small fire against the cliff, and if it was still burning, it would be impossible to see the smoke with all the steam," Hank said.

"Let's hope they're not there," Carter said. "They'd be buried."

"We need to move on," Hank said as the pilot did exactly that.

They searched longer, but then they headed to the airport for fuel before returning to the crash site. When they got back there, the deputies had finally succeeded in getting the badly broken body of Elliot Jones from the plane. He was now in a body bag beside his father beneath the tarp.

After landing, another helicopter approached and landed near the one Hank and Carter had ridden in.

"Hank," Sergeant Stringam said, "they are the federal investigators. They're from the National Transportation Safety Board. I've been expecting them. They'll take over from here. Their job is going to be very difficult in a different way than ours was. When they're through, we'll need to have a very large helicopter lift the wreckage out of here."

"I don't suppose there's much more that Carter and I can do here," Hank said.

"These federal boys are going to want to examine the bodies," Sergeant Stringam said. "But that shouldn't take long. If you men can wait for a little while, you could take the bodies back with you in the storage bin beneath your seats. The sheriff has arranged for them to be taken to the state medical examiner right from the airport."

About an hour later, the bodies had been loaded in the storage compartment of the chopper, and Carter and Hank were in the air and on the way back to the airport. When they arrived there, the bodies were loaded into a couple of hearses, and then the pilot refueled his helicopter and headed back for the crash site.

Bentley and Jim landed in the rented plane, and they joined Hank and Carter. After discussing what they had all seen during the search, which wasn't anything helpful, they all went to dinner together. Then Jim announced that since there were still a couple of hours of daylight left, he was going to search for his daughter again. Bentley insisted that he would go with him. They parted company, and Hank and Carter began the long drive back to Duchesne.

Chapter 20

Gina and Sammy had heard what Gina believed was a helicopter late that afternoon. There was nothing they could do to attract the attention of whoever was on board, even though she had a strong feeling that they were looking for her and Sammy. Gina had known that it would be virtually impossible for the people in the helicopter to see them behind the huge wall of mud. She was discouraged to think that there were rescuers so close and yet had to fly past them.

From time to time, Gina thought she heard airplanes overhead too. Were they looking for her or were they looking for the plane that she'd been in? It seemed likely that they would be searching for her dad's plane. Or was it nothing but coincidence that planes and a helicopter were flying over this huge forest? No matter which scenario was right, it wasn't helpful to her and Sammy. No one was going to be able to see them whether they were looking or not.

She checked Elliot's watch. It was getting very late. It would soon be dark. Another long and miserable night loomed ahead. She worried more about her young companion than she did herself. There wasn't much food left. Their water was also running short despite all the rain that had fallen earlier. They were conserving it the best they could. Gina was getting very discouraged and depressed, but she told herself to snap out of it. She had to be positive for Sammy's sake. He would sense her mood, and she didn't want him to be as depressed as she was.

She became aware of movement to their right. She looked closely at where the wall of muddy earth was piled against the cliff over there. She froze in shock when she realized the movement was that of a snake slithering down the wall of mud. It wasn't just any snake; it was a rattlesnake, a very large one. She watched it, nearly paralyzed with fear. Gina had always had a fear of snakes, which was usually unfounded, but in this case, it was a valid concern because of how deadly rattlesnakes were.

She hoped Sammy didn't see it. At the moment, he appeared to be asleep. She prayed that he would stay asleep. She instinctively knew that the safest thing to do was for her to be totally still and quiet. She didn't think the rattler would harm them if it didn't perceive them to be a threat.

The snake slithered in their direction along the base of the cliff. When it reached her, it paused momentarily and then passed right over the top of her legs, across Sammy's, and then went beyond them. She thought maybe it would once again ascend the wall of muddy earth, but instead, it turned toward the cliff, and to her surprise, it disappeared. There had to have been a hole in the rock, for it had gone right into the rock face.

Was that its nest, and had it simply been finding its way home? Possibly. But that also meant that it would be here for who knew how long. Would she even dare sleep for fear it came out again? Perhaps she should crawl over to where it had entered the rock and stuff dirt or small rocks into the hole to block the snake from getting out again.

Sammy stirred, then said, "I'm hungry, Gina."

"So am I," she whispered. "In a minute I'll see what we have left that we can eat. But first, there's something I need to do over there," she said and pointed the few feet to where the snake had vanished.

"I need to use the bathroom," he said.

He wasn't the only one. And that was a problem. She needed to figure something out. But first, she needed to plug the snake's hole into the ledge. She passed Sammy and located a hole that was not more than an inch wide. With her heart pounding like a hammer in her chest, she began to gather handfuls of small rocks and dirt. She pressed what she'd gathered into the hole. She added more, pushing it back into the ledge. She had no idea how far in the ledge the snake was, but she pushed several small handfuls in before hoping she had filled the hole enough to trap the snake.

Sammy had crawled over and joined her. "Why did you do that?" he asked.

"A snake crawled in there. I don't want it to get out," she said, knowing she had to be honest with him. "It's not a danger to us now. Let's see what we can do about creating a bathroom."

"Okay," he said.

Privacy was the issue. She had an idea. "I know what we'll do, Sammy. Let's use the rifle to prop up one corner of the blanket and then put another corner against the wall of muddy dirt. Then we can each take a turn behind it."

That worked fine. After that, they shared a few bites of crackers that were part of their dwindling food supply. Then they waited for darkness to descend while Sammy busied himself with pen and paper. He drew a coiled rattlesnake.

***

Carter and Hank drove late into the night as they reluctantly headed home. Bentley stayed with Jim, for Jim was determined to search for his daughter as soon as it was light enough to see. Hank and Carter traveled through the night and arrived home a couple hours after midnight. Carter was so tired that he fell asleep quickly despite thoughts of Gina filling his mind. He awoke about the time the sun was coming up. He showered, ate some breakfast, and then wondered what to do that day. He was restless, discouraged, and filled with sadness.

There was nothing more he could do to aid the search for Gina and Sammy. But he needed something to do. He thought about Gina's best friend, Maya Warwick, and realized that she must be sad and hurting as much as he was. Perhaps he should visit her and see if he could do anything to lift her spirits. He waited until around nine o'clock and then drove to the Warwick home and parked on the street in front. She must have heard him drive up, because before he was halfway up the sidewalk to her house, she came out and rushed toward him. She threw her arms around him and began to sob.

Carter felt awkward, but he held her until she pulled back and looked up and into his eyes, rubbing the tears from her own. "I'm sorry, Carter," Maya said. "I don't know what to do with myself. I'm all torn up inside. You probably are too."

He nodded, fighting back tears of his own. Then, doing his best to control his emotions, he said, "She will be found, Maya. I've got to believe that."

"I must believe too. I feel like I need to do something. But there's nothing I can do," she said, choking back a sob. "Gina's mom came over to see me. She is such a wonderful woman. Here she is thinking of me when her heart must be broken."

"She is a good woman," Carter agreed.

"She told me that Gina and Sammy were not in the wrecked plane. Is that true?" Maya asked.

"That's true. I've also been wondering what to do with myself today, but I just had an idea," he said. "I think I'll drive to St. George and visit Sammy's parents and see how they are feeling. Maybe we can comfort them with an assurance that we believe Sammy will be found. I don't know what good that will do, but at least it will fill the hours for me since there's nothing I can do here to help find Gina and Sammy."

"Would you like some company?" she asked. "I'd like to go with you if it's okay."

"That would be great," he said. "I guess you don't have a game today?"

"That's right. Even though it's Friday, I don't have any classes I need to go to, so I stayed home. Not that I'm doing any good in school. I can't concentrate on school or softball," Maya said. "The whole team is messed up. Gina is the only good pitcher on the team. We can't win a game. It's awful. Are you sure you don't mind me going with you?"

"If it's okay with your parents, I would love to have you accompany me," he said.

"I'll go ask right now. I'll be right back," she said and ran to the house. When she came back out a couple minutes later, she had her purse. "Mom said it would be good for me. I'm ready, or do you need a few minutes first?"

"Nope, we can go right now," he said. "Wait, maybe you should get an overnight bag. I have one in the truck all the time. We probably won't need them, but it's always good to be prepared."

"It will only take me a minute," Maya said, and she ran to the house again. She was back in a very short time. "Okay, now I'm ready."

In a few moments, they were on the road for the five-hour drive to St. George. Carter didn't know how much comfort he could give to Sammy's parents, but he felt impressed to go to Saint George.

***

Gina was anxious to attempt the climb over the pile of mud and rock. Sammy was ready too. But before they left, Gina, who had a soft heart, decided she couldn't leave the snake to die in the hole she'd filled. Using a leftover stick from the fire, she carefully dug out what she'd pushed into the hole. She and Sammy didn't wait for the snake to come out.

It took ten minutes to get themselves and their rifle, blankets, and what was left of their dwindling supply of food and water over the mud pile. By the time they got down the far side and out of the path of the slide, they were both muddy and exhausted. They walked until they found a stream, where they washed in the cool water, letting the sun dry the clothes they had bathed in. They also washed the muddy blankets and hung them up in the sun to dry. When they finished, they were on the far side of the stream, because that was the direction Gina wanted to walk.

By then it was almost noon, so they decided to stay put until they were dry, and their blankets had also had time to dry somewhat. With the sun shining brightly, it wasn't long before they were ready to start out again. From time to time, they heard an airplane, but even though they tried to get out of the trees and in sight, they were never spotted. So, weak, sore, and hungry, Gina and Sammy trudged slowly onward, unsure of what lay ahead.

Chapter 21

Maya and Carter stopped for lunch in Cedar City. They had been on the road for four hours and needed a break before driving the final hour to St. George. Carter had learned more about Gina from Maya, lots more. She told him all about their childhood growing up as best friends. The more he learned about Gina, the more he admired her and the more anxious he was that she'd be found. He wanted to spend more time getting to know her on a personal level.

One thing Carter learned from Maya that buoyed him up was that Gina cared for him a great deal and talked a lot about him to Maya. He desperately wanted Gina in his life, and from what Maya had told him, Gina felt the same as he did.

They ate a quick lunch and headed south on the interstate again. Carter had the address where Sammy lived with his mother and father. It was technically in Hurricane, which was just north of St. George. He had set his GPS to the address before leaving Duchesne, and he drove directly there after they finished their lunch. The house was a small older white frame home in an older part of town. He pulled up across the street from the address.

A small white Ford that showed its age was parked in the driveway and a newer black Nissan was parked in front of the house.

To Maya, Carter said, "The Nissan is Sammy's dad's car." He'd familiarized Maya with what he knew about the injuries and illness of Sammy's parents.

"I wonder if he's not healed enough to go back to work yet," Maya said.

"That was what I was thinking," Carter said. "I guess there's only one way to find out. Let's go knock on the door."

"I hope they're both a lot better," Maya said.

Then, they got out of the pickup, crossed the street, and went up the sidewalk to a small porch on the front of the house.

Carter looked at Maya. "Should I ring the bell or knock?"

She shrugged her shoulders and said, "I don't know. The bell I guess."

Carter pressed the doorbell and they waited. A moment later an attractive, short, slender woman of around thirty opened the door. Her short light brown hair was mussed, as if she'd been running her fingers through it, and her green eyes were red and filled with tears. She was pale and looked very weak.

"I'm kind of busy here," Ophelia said. "This isn't a good time. You'll have to go."

"I'm Detective Carter Keefe, a private detective from Duchesne," he said as he produced his credentials. "This is my friend Maya Warwick. We are both friends of your niece, Gina Rogers."

Ophelia ran her fingers through her hair, mussing it worse. Just then, a man who was probably about five six with dark hair limped behind her, supporting himself with a cane.

"This is Samuel, Sammy's father. We are very upset about a phone call we got a couple hours ago. We were just talking about it." She sobbed and Samuel put a hand on her shoulder.

"Why don't you two come in? Since you are a detective, maybe you can give us some advice," Samuel said.

His wife said, "Yes, please do." She turned and her husband slipped an arm around her shoulders. "Come sit down."

They entered a very clean and attractive but quite small living room. Ophelia pointed to a sofa and said, "You may sit there." She then sat down on a chair across the room from them and Samuel sat next to her on a matching chair. He reached over and took her hand in his.

Carter and Maya exchanged a quick glance. Then Carter said, "What do you need advice on?"

"As I said a moment ago, we were made to understand that Gina and Sammy were kidnapped by the same person. But now we don't think that's right. We don't know much about what has happened the past few days, but contrary to what we were told in a disturbing call we got this morning, that can't possibly be right."

Carter pulled his phone from his pocket. "It is exactly right," he said. "Let me show you some pictures taken by a sheriff's deputy and forwarded to me. I was a witness to him taking the pictures. I want you to look at these and then tell me about the phone call."

He scrolled for a moment, found the pictures he was after, and then stood and crossed the room and dropped to one knee while he held his phone toward the parents of Sammy Anders. "These pictures are from a notebook that we found in a cabin where both Gina and Sammy had been held for a while. Your son is an excellent artist, is he not?"

"He is," the parents said in almost perfect unison as Maya stepped over and looked over Carter's shoulder.

"Does this look like something he would draw?" he said as she showed them the page where, on one side Sammy had drawn a picture of Ophelia and Samuel and on the opposite page had sketched a picture of himself. "These were drawn in pencil. We have the pencil."

Both Ophelia and Samuel gasped, and their faces lost color. It was Ophelia that spoke first. She said, "Sammy drew those. No one else could have done that."

Samuel said, "I agree with Ophelia. That is Sammy's work. What else is in that notebook?"

"I'll show you all of it in a moment, and I'll tell you what my fellow detectives and I have pieced together from what we found in this notebook and other evidence in the old cabin." He flipped to another page, several pages later in the notebook. "You will recognize your niece, Gina," he said. Maya grabbed onto his shoulder and began to weep.

"Sammy drew that too, didn't he?" his distraught mother said.

"You tell me," Carter said as Maya's hand gripped his shoulder tighter.

"It's his work all right. What a pretty girl our niece is. You must both be worried to death about her. May we see the rest of what Sammy drew?" Ophelia asked.

"Yes, but do you want to talk about the phone call first?" Carter asked them, looking first at one and then at the other.

"No, let's look first while you tell us what you know so far."

"Are you sure? I would like to hear about the phone call," Carter said.

"It was very disturbing, but it can wait. I want to see what Sammy drew first. Please," Ophelia said.

"I agree with Ophelia," Samuel said.

One by one, Carter thumbed through the pictures on his phone. As he did so he explained about the evidence that a bear had been there and that Sammy and Gina had climbed up to a small shelf out of reach of the bear.

"That bear, was it trying to get to them?" Samuel asked as he pointed to the current picture on Carter's phone.

"We think so. It got in the cabin by breaking the door down."

"They had food and water up there, so they must have climbed up before the bear got in."

"Wait, are you telling us that they were alone when this happened?" Samuel asked. "Where was the man who kidnapped them?"

"We have no idea, but he must not have been there, so yes, they were alone. We think they didn't dare leave the cabin out of fear that the kidnapper instilled in them. Okay, here we go." Carter then continued to show them the pictures.

"Okay, now let me go forward in time. Harry Jones stole an airplane which belonged to Gina's father and three other men. He and his son, Elliot, and Gina and Sammy were on that plane."

"How do you know that?" Ophelia asked skeptically. "I don't think Sammy could have been."

"Because of the phone call you received?" Carter asked perceptively. "I really need to know about that call."

"I will tell you in a minute. But first, what makes you think that Sammy was in the plane?"

"I'll show you some pictures we took at the crash site," Carter said. He explained step by step what the investigators had figured out and why. He didn't give small details, as he knew them, but he did tell them about the tracks they'd found and showed pictures of the tracks. "These are small tracks, like your son would make, and larger ones like Gina would have made."

Ophelia leaned forward and looked closely at one of the small tracks that had been taken in a spot of soil without grass. "That's Sammy's shoe!" she said as her face went pale. "I mean it was made by Sammy's shoe. I just bought him two pair of new shoes a couple weeks ago. They were identical."

"Do you have the other pair?" Carter asked.

"Yes, I'll go get them," she said and got up and left the room. Samuel stayed with Maya and Carter.

"Carter, show me pictures again of Gina's," Maya said softly.

He did as she asked. The picture he showed her had been taken in the same patch of dirt where the one of Sammy's shoes had been taken. Maya looked closely at it, nodding her head, and then she said, "Look at the shoes I have on. Gina and I bought matching shoes a couple months ago." She slipped around beside Carter and lifted one of her feet.

Carter looked at the tread on her shoe and then at the one taken from the crash site. They appeared to be alike to him. He snapped a picture of the bottom of Maya's shoe just as Ophelia came back. She sat down and Maya stayed where she was. Ophelia handed one of the shoes to Carter. He compared it to the photo and said, "They match."

Ophelia and Samuel looked closely at the photo and the shoe in her hand. They looked up and Ophelia said, "You're right. They match."

Carter then took a picture of the tread on that shoe as well. Then he put his phone away and said, "A massive search for the two of them is underway, but so far they have not been found. It is a very large area and is heavily forested. It is difficult to search. We were going to use a tracking dog and several search and rescue personnel, but there was such a heavy storm that the dog handler said it would never work. And there was no way the tracks that Gina and Sammy made could have survived the rain."

"Oh, Samuel," Ophelia moaned. "They will starve."

"We were able to tell that supplies from the wrecked plane were taken. We are quite certain that they have blankets and some food and water with them. Oh, and we believe they also have a first aid kit, one that had been in the plane. But we will need to find them in the next day or two or they may run out of food. There is water in the forest there, so they won't go without water."

"That's good to hear," Samuel said.

"Gina is very bright and I can assure you she will take good care of your son," Maya said.

Then Carter spoke quite sternly. "Now about the phone call," he said as he and Maya crossed the small living room back to the sofa.

"Well, it's like this. Some guy called us this morning and said that he has Sammy and that we will only get him back if we give him a hundred thousand dollars," Samuel said.

"That's why we told you we didn't think that Sammy was with Gina. I was told that I was not to tell the police or he would kill my son," Ophelia said. "That's why I didn't want to tell you about it at first, because you are kind of like the police and we were afraid to." Samuel nodded in agreement.

"I work very closely with the cops and assist on some of their cases," Carter said. "So I understand but I can tell you that unless the police are involved, very few kidnapped people are returned alive even when a ransom has been paid. But that doesn't apply here. Some criminal out there is trying to collect money even though he's not the actual kidnapper because we know that Sammy was in that airplane that crashed and is now in the forest with Gina. And in this case, as I explained, both of the men who kidnapped Gina and Sammy are dead. I saw the bodies for myself, so I know it's true."

"What do we do now?" Ophelia asked, wringing her hands.

"Tell me this," Carter began. "If you had to pay a ransom, would you be able to pay a hundred thousand dollars?"

Samuel and Ophelia both shook their heads. "There's no way," Samuel said. "But I'm sure the man, whoever he is, will be calling back. He told us he will probably call either tonight or in the morning. What should we do now that we know he doesn't have our son?"

"I'll make a call, or maybe more than one call. I'll find out what you need to do," Carter said as he pulled his phone from his pocket.

Chapter 22

Bentley and Jim had not had any success searching from the air. None of the volunteer pilots had either. The two men had returned for fuel, and both of them were hungry. Jim Rogers was very worried about his daughter. Just when they had a new lead, she was still out of reach. He'd prayed silently all day.

"I don't know if we should go up again today, Bentley," Jim told him as they were waiting for their late lunch to be served at the nearby café. "I'm totally exhausted, and if I fly more today, we could crash, and I can't take that risk. Is it okay with you if we start again at daylight in the morning?"

"Absolutely," Bentley replied as his phone began to ring. He pulled it from his pocket and looked at the screen. "It's Carter. I'll see what he has on his mind."

Bentley accepted the call and almost immediately Carter spoke. "Bentley, I need some advice. There's a strange situation taking place."

"Has someone contacted you about needing PI help?"

"Not exactly, Bentley. I'm in St. George," Carter revealed.

"What are you doing there?" Bentley asked in surprise.

"I was going crazy with worry about Gina and decided I needed to do something. I thought about Sammy's parents and decided to drive down and visit them and see if they're healing okay. I didn't know if I could do them any good but I wanted to try. I was visiting Maya, bringing her up to date on the search for Gina when I thought about going. She's with me."

"Okay, so what's happened down there?" Bentley asked as Jim watched curiously from across the booth.

"First, have you guys had any success looking for Gina and Sammy today? I am so worried about them."

"No, I'm afraid not," Bentley replied. Then he quickly explained that he and Jim were on the ground and would not go back up until early in the morning. He told Carter why, and then he said, "So what's going on with Mr. and Mrs. Anders?"

"Some guy called them and told them he had Sammy and that unless they gave him a hundred thousand dollars that he would kill him," Carter said. That made Bentley angry. He said nothing at that point but his mind was working. Carter continued to explain. Carter told him more about the call the Anders had received, and then he got to the point of his call to Bentley. "I need to tell the Anders what to do. They now know all about what's happening with Sammy. I showed them the pictures of the notebook Sammy had been drawing in. They confirmed it was Sammy's work. I also told them about the plane crash and showed them pictures of tracks of what we believed were Sammy's and Gina's. Get this, Ophelia recently bought Sammy two identical pair of shoes. The prints on the soles of the shoes she has here in the house match the ones in the photos we took. And that's not all. Maya is wearing a pair just like the ones Gina is wearing. The girls bought matching shoes a couple of months ago."

Bentley couldn't help but smile to himself. Carter was working out to be an excellent detective, and his enthusiasm was great. To Carter he said, "You are doing some great work, Carter. Did you take pictures of the ones Maya is wearing and the ones like Sammy's?"

"I did."

"Excellent. Hank will need copies of them," Bentley said.

"I'll text them to him. Now what I need is advice for Samuel and Ophelia about what to do about the call."

"This is an interesting situation," Bentley said. "The caller is obviously someone who knows Sammy was kidnapped. But why would he think he could collect a ransom if someone else might have already called for a ransom? This is strange indeed."

"My thoughts exactly," Carter said.

"The local police need to be notified. But why don't you call Hank first. I'm thinking that he might have Sheriff Goldman call the cops down there. Let's see, the Anders actually live in Hurricane. The sheriff might even know the police chief there. You are doing great work, Carter. Keep me informed."

"I will, and Maya and I are going to get hotel rooms for tonight but will stay here with the Anders until the local officers do what they feel they need to. I'll call Hank now."

After the call ended, Bentley said, "Jim, this is strange." Then he told him what he'd learned from Carter.

"He's a mighty fine young man. I wouldn't feel bad at all if he were to one day become my son-in-law," Jim said. Then his eyes clouded over. "If we find Gina." His voice filled with emotion.

"We'll find her somehow," Bentley assured him, hoping he was right.

***

Hank was in his office when his phone rang. When he saw that it was Carter, he answered.

"I need advice," Carter said. "I just talked to Bentley. He said to call you and said you will want to talk to the sheriff."

"He's in his office. Let me walk in there and put my phone on speaker. Then you can tell both of us what you need advice about."

Hank tapped on the frame of the sheriff's open door.

"Come in, Hank," Sheriff Goldman said.

"Carter Keefe is on the phone. He needs our advice."

"About what?" the sheriff asked.

"I don't know yet. Carter, I'm with the sheriff now. I'll put my phone on speaker."

"I'm in Hurricane at the home of Samuel and Ophelia Anders," Carter told them.

The sheriff and Hank looked at each other, both puzzled. "What are you doing there? Do you have a case that's taken you that far away?" Hank asked.

"No, it's about Sammy Anders." Carter then spent the next few minutes telling them what he'd already told Bentley. The two veteran officers listened intently to what Carter had to say. "So I guess what I need to know is how to advise Samuel and Ophelia."

"We know that whoever called the Anders can't hurt Sammy," Sheriff Goldman said. "They need to call the police there in Hurricane and let them deal with it. The caller has committed a serious crime and needs to be found and arrested."

"That's what I thought, but I wanted to make sure I wasn't giving them bad advice," Carter said. "I'll tell them now and help if I can. Thanks, guys."

"It would be really interesting to know who this scammer is and how he knew about Sammy's kidnapping," Hank said. "Let us know what happens, Carter."

After the call ended, Sheriff Goldman said, "That young man is becoming an excellent investigator. I'll call the police chief down there right now."

***

Two detectives showed up at the Anders's modest home within fifteen minutes of getting a call from Samuel, and they explained that their chief had received a call from Sheriff Goldman just moments ago. They made a plan to catch the scammer. Carter and Maya stayed around another hour, and when there hadn't been another call by then, they went in search of motel rooms. Samuel and Ophelia assured Carter that he would be kept up-to-date on any developments.

They had checked into hotel rooms next to each other and then gone to find something to eat when Carter's phone rang.

"Detective Keefe, this is Samuel Anders. We got another call from the man who wants a hundred thousand dollars. He told us that Sammy would die if we involved the police. The call was recorded."

"Did they give you a location and time to deliver the money?" Carter asked.

"Yes, and on advice of the detectives, I told him that I would not be able to get the cash together until Monday since the banks won't be open on the weekend."

"So did you set a time for Monday?" Carter asked.

"The man wouldn't accept that," he told Carter. "He said he needed the money tonight, that I could borrow the money or go to a bank that stays open late. He told me that if I didn't get it to him that I could start planning Sammy's funeral."

"So what are you going to do?" Carter asked.

"I pretended that I would find a way to get the money, no matter what I had to do. I told him that I would not let him destroy my innocent son."

"Is a place to leave the money set up for tonight then?"

"Yes, and it's the same location he gave me earlier. The cops are going to be in plain clothes around the area. They promised that they would be placed where he could not see them but where they could capture him before he could get away. I hope they catch him," Samuel said. "I'd really like to know who he is and why he is after our money—money that Ophelia and I don't have."

"What time did he tell you that you had to have it there?" Carter asked.

"Ten o'clock. He wanted it after dark."

"Maya and I are going to eat, but we will be back in an hour or so if that's okay with you," Carter said.

"Of course it is. We'll see you then," Samuel said, and the call ended.

Maya, who had only heard half of the conversation, was watching Carter with an expectant look on her face. "So it's set up, right? You know, to get what the scammer thinks will be a bunch of money," Maya said.

"Yes, Samuel has to have the money, or what he hopes the scammer will *think* is the money, at the location the guy told them to use at ten o'clock," Carter responded.

"You're going back to their house?" Maya asked.

"I am. Probably around nine o'clock."

"That's over an hour from now," she said. "May I come with you?"

"Of course you may," he said. "We'll eat slowly and then head over to their house."

"Thanks, Carter. You're a nice guy. Gina is a lucky girl," she said, and then all of a sudden, she began to sob. "She's really unlucky right now. I am so scared for her. I can't even imagine what she and Sammy are going through."

"Apparently they haven't been found yet or I would have been informed," Carter said. "I'm afraid for her too. I've been praying so hard for her. I have to believe that they will be found."

"I've never prayed so much in my whole life," Maya said after she was able to control her crying. "I'm trying to have faith, but it seems like the longer she is gone, the worse it is for her and Sammy. But I'm trying to believe that Heavenly Father will save her. He's got to."

They'd been waiting for a server to take their orders. The place was busy, which wasn't too surprising as it was Friday night. They had already been given glasses of water. They finally ordered, but Maya said, "This will be on separate checks, please."

Carter quickly countered. "No, it will be one check," he said to the waitress. Then to Maya, he added, "I am paying. And please don't argue."

"Thank you, Carter," she said softly.

"You're welcome. I'm so glad to have your company. This trip would have been hard for me if I was alone."

They ate slowly, and then an hour later, they decided to drive back to the Anders' house.

***

Sammy and Gina were both growing very weak and very discouraged. She was rationing their supply of food, and both of them were hungry all the time. Water wasn't a problem because there were pools of rain water and occasional streams.

They had been lucky enough to find another cliff, and that's where they were spending the night. There was no overhang, but it still felt better than being in the trees. The ground wasn't too muddy as the sun had shone brightly all day and it had been quite warm. It had cooled off dramatically as the evening progressed, though. They built another fire and then settled down between it and the cliff. The sun had gone down, and it was almost dark now.

"I miss my parents," Sammy said, his little voice breaking.

"I'm sorry, Sammy. I miss mine too."

The two of them then sat silently. Gina worried about her little companion. He was getting very weak. He hadn't been able to carry the .30-30 rifle most of the afternoon. And he was still worried about wild animals. Since they'd had an encounter with a snake, he now worried about snakes too.

As if that wasn't enough, as darkness descended, they heard some kind of animal approaching their little camp. Sammy huddled close to Gina, shivering with fright. He let out a little moan when the eyes of a critter reflected their fire. The eyes looked red, and they were about two feet from the ground, as near as Gina could tell.

"It's a bear," Sammy said as Gina lifted the rifle from beside her, took the safety off, and pointed it in the direction of the animal.

The animal moved closer. The fire made it light enough to see that the animal was large, but she couldn't tell much more. She waited with her eyes constantly on the dark figure in front of them. The rifle rested on her knees, but she was ready to lift it to her cheek and fire if she needed to.

The creature moved closer. Then, to her immense relief, the light of the fire shone on a large set of antlers. It moved a couple steps closer, and she could tell that it was a large buck deer. She heaved a sigh of relief.

Sammy said softly, "Look, Gina. It's a big buck. I think he likes us."

As if to prove Sammy right, the buck stepped closer, lowered its mighty head, and gazed at the two wanderers. Then after about a minute, he quietly turned and walked gallantly down the slope.

Gina looked at this visit by the mighty king of the forest as a good omen. She turned and smiled down at Sammy, who returned her smile. She put the safety to the rifle back on and laid it beside her. Sammy spoke again. "That was special, wasn't it?"

"Yes, it was, Sammy. I think Heavenly Father sent the big buck to remind us that He loves us," she said reverently.

Chapter 23

AS THE HOUR APPROACHED FOR SAMUEL ANDERS TO TAKE THE NEWSpaper-stuffed bag to the drop site, Carter watched the couple closely. They knew their son was not with this man behind the ransom, but concern still etched across their faces. He hoped the plan that the police had in place would result in his capture. Because of the location, other police agencies had become involved. If the scammer actually showed up at the drop site, he would most likely be captured.

Finally, after kissing his wife, Samuel left. He returned in less than a half hour. "The bag is in place, and I didn't see any cops around, but I know they're there. I hope this crook comes so he can be arrested. I'm really anxious to know what he has to say for himself," Samuel said.

Only about fifteen minutes later the Hurricane police chief called and asked for Samuel. The chief's name was Ron Childers. They had met him earlier, and he seemed to be both competent and truly concerned. Carter was glad to see that.

"We caught him," Chief Childers said. "He tried to knife one of my officers, but he failed and after a short scuffle, he was subdued."

"Do you have any idea who he is?" Carter asked.

"I sure do. He had his driver's license in his wallet," the chief said. "His name is Larry Jones."

"Are you serious?" Carter asked. "The dead kidnapper is Harry Jones. Could they be related?"

"Let me text you a picture I took of him before my officers put him in a patrol car. Take a look at this." Chief Childers forwarded the picture to Samuel, who showed it to Carter.

"Oh my word," Carter said. "He looks exactly like Harry. He's even as rough looking. He has the same sort of beard and hair and facial features."

"We think he might be a twin brother," the chief revealed. "It's possible the two were in communication. So far, he has refused to talk."

"Has anyone searched the Internet for information on him?" Carter asked.

"Not yet."

"I have my laptop here. Would you like me to see what I can learn about him?"

"Yes, Detective Keefe, that would be great."

With Maya sitting next to Carter, he booted up his computer. It did not take long to learn that Larry Jones was, indeed, a twin to Harry Jones and that they had a younger brother whose name was Barry. To Maya he said, "This is weird. Why would parents give a younger brother a name that rhymes with his older twin brothers?"

"That is weird. I wonder what that third brother is like and where he's at," Maya said.

"Give me a minute, and I'll see if I can find out. I wonder if Larry was working with Harry in an attempt to get a ransom, even though he knows he could never have returned Sammy since he doesn't have him," Carter said.

"We have Larry's cell phone," Chief Childers said. He was still talking to Samuel who had his phone on speaker. "Once we get him in an interview room we are going to try to get him to open his phone. If he opens it, then we'll look at whatever communications he and Harry may have had. I have an officer working on obtaining a search warrant for Larry's phone and his house and pickup."

"Wow," Maya said. "I wonder if he's also a kidnapper."

"Could be," Chief Childers said. "And when you learn more about the brother called Barry, maybe we will need to see if he is also involved in major crimes."

"I'll see what I can find out," Carter promised.

"I appreciate it," the chief said. "I'll be at the Anders' home in a few minutes. As soon as I have a chance to speak with Ophelia and Samuel, I'll be going down to the county jail to see what we can learn from Larry."

The chief arrived and visited with them for a few minutes while Carter was looking for information on the younger brother, Barry, and then he said, "I guess I'll be going. Detective Keefe, since you have been such a big help, would you like to meet me at the jail in St. George?"

"I'd love to," he said. "But first let me tell you what I just learned about the younger brother."

The chief looked at him with interest. "That was fast. Where is he at?"

"He's in prison in Colorado," Carter revealed.

"So we know he's a bad character. What's he in prison for?"

"Attempted murder," Carter said. "But I don't like this. He's due to be released on parole in a few days. I'll bet he's been in touch with Harry or Larry or both of them."

"We need to make sure we know when he's paroled. He could cause us more trouble," Chief Childers said. "I'm glad you discovered that. So, would you like to follow me to the jail down in St. George?"

"I would," Carter said as he closed his laptop. Then he looked at Maya. He could tell that she was drained. "Maya, I'll take you to your room before I meet with the police at the jail."

Ophelia spoke up before Maya had a chance to respond. "Why don't you stay here with Samuel and me? You can rest if you want to. I can tell you are very tired."

"It's okay. I can go back to my room," Maya said.

"Despite the lateness of the hour," Chief Childers said, "I will be coming back here to report to Ophelia and Samuel, and I bet your PI friend will too."

"Will you, Carter?" she asked.

"Of course," he said.

"Then I'll stay here. Thank you, Ophelia," she said.

Carter followed the chief of police out of the door and once he was in his truck, he followed him to the interstate. He called Hank on the way to the county jail. "Hank, they caught the guy who was after the ransom. You aren't going to believe this, but he is Harry Jones's twin brother. His name is Larry. They have a younger brother named Barry who is in prison in Colorado, but he is due to be paroled in a few days."

"That's a whole new twist," Hank said. "We'll want to figure out when the brother is paroled. I wonder if the twin brothers had planned to demand a ransom this way even though Harry knew Larry wouldn't ever see the boy. At least, I would think he wasn't going to let him. But who knows."

"I wonder if Larry even knows that Harry is dead. For that matter, I wonder if the other brother knows. I hope to find that out in a little while. Chief Childers of the Hurricane Police Department is going to let me watch the interview with Larry at the county jail. He is also going to search Larry's phone, his truck, and his house after his officers get a search warrant," Carter said. "I hope I get to help with that or at least watch."

"I wish I was down there," Hank said. "This is really interesting. Have you called your boss yet?"

"No, but I will when I get to the station," he said. Then he paused for a moment as he realized what time it was. "I got you out of bed, didn't I? I'm sorry. I should have waited until morning."

"It's okay, Carter. You're doing great work."

"I hate to call Bentley this late. He and Jim Rogers are probably trying to get some rest before they search again in the morning," Carter said.

"Carter, I have some advice for you. Call Bentley. He's used to being jarred awake at strange hours, and I can assure you that he will want to know what you've just told me. And furthermore, if you learn anything of significance from the interrogation of Harry's brother or the search of his property, don't hesitate to call me."

Carter agreed and continued the drive to the jail. While he drove, he followed Hank's advice and called Bentley.

Bentley sounded groggy when he answered the phone after three rings. "Hey, Carter, what's up? Something must be or you wouldn't be waking me."

"I was going to wait to call you in the morning after I realized I'd called Hank so late. But when I told him what was going on down here, he said that I should call you, even though it's so late," Carter said.

"He's right. Okay, so tell me," Bentley said. "It must be important."

Carter explained the situation to Bentley, who grew more interested by the second.

"Carter, I'm glad you went to St. George. That was a great idea. I will be interested to hear what you learn. I wish I was with you right now."

"That's what Hank said," Carter told him. "I'll call you back. I'm just pulling into the jail parking area. Chief Childers and a detective are waiting for me to go in with them."

"Call me back about anything significant that you learn. As long as Gina's dad is getting some rest so he can fly us again tomorrow, it'll be okay if I'm tired," Bentley said. "I'm really curious as to why this brother of Harry's demanded a ransom."

"I'll let you know if I find anything out," Carter said. "I'm going to watch."

A few minutes later, Chief Childers and a detective entered the interrogation room while Carter watched from the observation room through one-way glass. Larry was advised of his rights, and then Chief Childers said, "I want you to tell us why you demanded a ransom for someone you didn't even have in your control, but first, we have learned that you are the twin brother of the man who kidnapped Sammy Anders."

"That's right," Larry said. "Not that it makes any difference. I got nothing to say to you. I want an attorney."

Chief Childers said, "You are going to be locked up now. We'll see about getting you an attorney on Monday."

"You got no right to jail me. I didn't do nothing wrong."

"You mean *anything* wrong?" the chief asked.

"Yep, didn't do nothing wrong," Larry repeated.

"But you did *something* wrong, something illegal," Chief Childers said. Carter had to smile at the way the chief corrected Larry's bad English and how Larry didn't even realize it.

"I want an attorney tonight," Larry said, the little English lesson having flown right over his head.

"If you can get one, go ahead," the chief said.

"I can't afford a lawyer, so you gotta appoint one."

"Monday," the chief repeated. "I won't ask you any more questions until you have an attorney. Oh, and one more thing: we have a search warrant for your phone, your truck, and your house."

"Ha, ha," Larry said. "My house is locked, my truck is locked, and my phone won't open without it seeing my face. So good luck with that."

"We won't need luck because we have the keys to your truck and your house. If we need to, a lab can open your phone for us," Chief Childers told him.

"My keys are in my pants pockets, and my pants are in the jail," Larry said with a smirk.

"Not anymore, they aren't," the chief said, and he walked out of the room. A moment later he joined Carter and an officer who had been with Carter in the observation room. "That went about as well as I thought it would. Let's go do some searches."

The truck had been towed to a location in Hurricane. "Let's do Larry's house first since he lives in St. George. I'll have some officers from St. George assist us," the chief suggested. "We can do the truck last."

"Where is his phone?" Carter asked as they walked out of the jail.

"It's in my truck in an evidence bag," Chief Childers said.

"Where is the search warrant?" was Carter's next question.

"An officer is on the way down with it. Why? Did you have something in mind, Detective?"

"Well, I was just wondering what it would take to get it open. Do you think we could have them bring Jones out to us again and then maybe we could wave the phone right in front of his face and ask him if that's his phone?"

The chief looked puzzled for a moment, and then he said, "I got it. That will open it."

"It should," Carter said modestly. "I think it would be worth a try."

"That's right smart thinking, Detective. I'll have my officer meet us here before we leave, and we'll go in and have them bring Jones back to the interrogation room. I should have thought of that myself."

"I got to thinking about it when he said his phone would only open with his face. He doesn't have to be holding it," Carter said.

Chapter 24

When Larry Jones was brought back into the interrogation room, he was angry. "I don't see no lawyer here," he said. "So I still got nothing to say."

"This will only take a minute," Chief Childers said.

Carter was in the observation room with two other officers. A third officer was in with the chief and the prisoner.

"I just wanted to give you a copy of the search warrant," Chief Carter said, and he handed it to Larry. "This covers your house, your truck, and this phone." He pulled the phone from his pocket and held it right in front of Larry's face.

"This is your phone," the chief said. It wasn't a question, just a statement of fact.

"'Course it is. Give it here. You got no business with it."

Chief Childers handed the phone to his officer. "You know what to do," he said.

The officer grinned and nodded an acknowledgment. He came right into the observation room with Carter and the officers from Hurricane. He began to work the phone, which had opened nicely with Larry's unsuspecting face. One of the officers had a laptop, which he opened and then the officers proceeded to download the entire contents of Larry's cell phone to the laptop.

Carter glanced into the interrogation room where the chief was talking to the prisoner. Carter heard him say, "Mr. Jones, we'll bring you a receipt on Monday for everything we seize from your home and truck."

"What about the phone? I want a receipt for it. It ain't going to do you no good anyway cause you can't open it," Larry Jones said with a snicker.

"We already did," the chief said and walked out as Larry watched him with a puzzled look on his face. He wasn't a very smart guy.

A moment later, the chief joined the others in the observation room. As soon as the contents of the phone were downloaded to the laptop, the chief had the officer begin to look through the phone while it was open. "Anything you find that is even remotely related to Sammy and Gina's kidnapping and Larry's attempt to collect a ransom I want texted to my phone. Be thorough. Even though we have everything on the laptop, I would like access to what you find while we're conducting the other searches."

Carter met the chief and his officers and a couple of St. George officers at Larry Jones's home.

"We'd like you to help us, Detective Keefe," Chief Childers said. "It's thanks to you that we have accomplished so much."

Carter was glad to do it. He thought that there might be something in the house that referred to Gina's abduction and possible other ransom demands. He found a letter in plain sight on Larry's kitchen counter with other mail. It was sent through the United States Postal Service. It was postmarked from Myton and was from Harry Jones to Larry Jones. It was time stamped several days previous. So Larry hadn't had it very long. A second letter was written in pencil and mailed from the prison in Colorado. It was clearly from the little brother, Barry.

He called out to Chief Childers. "I've got something here I think you'll want to see."

With latex gloves on, Carter pulled the single sheet of paper out of the envelope that had Harry's Ballard address on it as the chief entered the room. "I've got a couple letters here that could be interesting," Carter said as he showed him both of them. "We'll read this one first, and then we'll see what the one from Barry, the inmate, says."

Carter and Chief Childers scanned it together. It was short but to the point, and it made Carter's stomach churn. He went back over it a second time. It read:

Hey, my brother, as soon as you collect the ransom on the boy from down in your area, I have another ransom I need to have you collect. This one applies to a young lady by the name of Gina Rogers. We need to make some money from her parents for our efforts. She is from Duchesne, and her parents are Jim and Sue Rogers. I'll text you their phone numbers when I figure them out. Don't contact them until you've had the ransom on the Anders kid for a couple of days. Ask a hundred thousand from them just like you are going to ask for the boy. I was going to make the demand, but I think I'd rather have you do it. Go to Duchesne and get familiar with the town and figure out a good place for the ransom drop. You'll get a generous split for each one of the two you collect.

It was signed by Harry Jones.

"So they were going to attempt to collect a ransom on the Rogers girl as well," the chief said.

"It looks that way," Carter said. "I'll bet there's a text from Harry on Larry's phone with the numbers for Gina's parents."

"Where did you find these?" the chief asked.

"Right here with these other pieces of mail." He pointed to the stack of mail. "It was on the top."

"Let's read the one from Barry now," Chief Childers suggested.

Carter opened that envelope and extracted the letter from inside. The letter, like the address on the envelope, was written in pencil, as was typically the case with inmates. They were not allowed pens. Carter supposed it may have been because they could possibly be used as weapons.

With the chief once again looking with him he read: *Hey, big brother. You guys have been having too much fun while I've been locked up on bogus charges. But I will be out in a few days and I'll join in the fun. I'll do some burglaries, and we'll make us some big money selling what I get. I've been in here too long. I'll text you when I get released and we'll get together with Harry. Your brother, Barry.*

"It looks like they were planning more crime," the chief said.

"This is a bad family," Carter added.

"I think we need to go through the rest of this mail. By the way, there are some texts between Harry and Larry about the ransom on Sammy Anders. But my officer going through the phone hasn't seen anything about this. I'm surprised they used both the texting feature and regular mail as well," Chief Anders said. "I'll need to take that and add it to the inventory. Actually, it's the only thing of interest we've found so far from Larry's house."

"Let me take a picture of both of these first," Carter said.

He photographed both envelopes and letters and then handed them to the chief. The two men then went through the rest of the mail. They found one other letter that Harry had written to Larry giving him instructions on how to collect ransom for the Anders boy. That was all they found of value in the pile of mail. It was some very important evidence, though.

Carter took pictures of the third letter and envelop and then he texted all six pictures to Hank. As soon as he'd sent them, he called Hank on the phone. "Sorry to wake you up again," Carter said.

"I told you to if anything of significance showed up in your searches and interrogation down there. I take it you have something," Hank said, sounding very tired.

"I just sent you a text with six pictures you will be interested in," Carter said.

"Hold on while I look at the text," Hank said.

A couple of minutes later, Hank came back on the line. "This is something I never expected, but with criminals, you really never know what to expect. Did you learn anything from Jones in the interrogation?" Hank asked.

"He demanded a lawyer," Carter explained. "But we did get his phone open and an officer downloaded it to a laptop and is going through it while we search here."

"How did they get the phone opened?" Hank asked.

"I suggested that Chief Childers hold it to his face and tell him that we had his phone. That was all it took to open it," Carter explained.

"Carter, that's good work. If there's anything else of significance, let me know," Hank said, and the call ended.

The search continued, and what they found in a drawer in the main bedroom was interesting. It appeared that Larry had done a lot of burglaries. The room was full of what appeared to be stolen items. There were no other references to ransom demands, but Carter said, "I'll bet some of these suspected stolen items will be mentioned in texts between the Jones brothers."

Several items of interest were collected, but none of them were of interest to Carter. It was obvious that Larry Jones was a very busy burglar. The officers collected the suspected stolen items.

"I think we will be able to close a number of burglaries from around the county with what we've found here," Chief Childers said.

Later, they searched Larry's truck at the lot it had been towed to in Hurricane. There was nothing in it that tied it to the Sammy Anders case or the Gina Rogers case. But several burglary tools were collected. Larry Jones had been a busy crook.

Back at the hotel, Carter decided that there was nothing he needed to call Hank about that couldn't wait until morning. So he said his evening prayers. It took him a while for he had a lot to talk to Heavenly Father about. Of course, the most important part of his prayer was about Gina Rogers.

He set the alarm on his phone for eight a.m. It was almost five right then. Three hours would have to do. But then he had a thought. He needed to call Bentley before he went to sleep.

He thought that Bentley would probably be up and getting ready to fly with Jim Rogers again. So he made the call. Bentley answered right away.

"I hope I didn't wake you," Carter said, "but I wanted to tell you what I've learned before you were up in the plane where I probably couldn't reach you."

I was just about to take a shower before I meet Jim for breakfast. He wants to be in the air by shortly after sunup," Bentley said. "So, what have you learned?"

Carter went through everything as quickly as he could. When he'd finished, Bentley said, "Harry and Elliot Jones were really bad men. I shouldn't say this, but I'm glad they're dead. Something needs to be done about that other brother. You've done great work. You probably need some sleep now."

"I sure do. But if you guys spot Gina and Sammy, please call me right away."

"I'll do that, Carter. Talk to you later."

Carter also considered calling Hank Parker, but he decided that call could wait until after he'd had some sleep. And he didn't want to wake Hank up, because he knew he wouldn't have had a lot of sleep.

Carter was asleep within minutes of his head hitting the pillow. His ringing phone woke him up rather than his phone's alarm. He looked at the time. His alarm would be going off in a few minutes anyway. So, he answered the phone. "Good morning, Maya," he said.

"You sound really tired," she said.

"I am, but we need to head home soon."

"I'm dressed and ready to go whenever you are," she said.

"Give me twenty minutes, then we'll go find some breakfast," he said.

"Any news on Gina?" she asked.

"She still hasn't been found, but I have learned some important things that I'll tell you about over breakfast. I'll knock on your door when I'm packed and ready," Carter said.

Chapter 25

Maya was interested in the things that Carter and the officers had learned during the night. "I know I shouldn't say this, but I don't feel bad that those awful men are dead and that Harry's brother is in jail. I wish the younger brother wasn't going to be getting out of prison soon."

"All four of them are very bad men," Carter said as they both finished their breakfast. "Well, I guess I should say that Harry and Elliot *were* very bad men and that the other two still are. "I'll pay for breakfast, and then we'll head north. I'll drive first, but I'm afraid you're going to have to take over for me after a while. I don't want to fall asleep while driving."

"I'll drive as much as you need me to," Maya said. "I rested better than I thought I would."

As soon as they were in the truck, Carter called Hank Parker and filled him in.

"I wonder if any of our unsolved burglaries may have been done by Larry, or even by Harry and Elliot," Hank wondered. "And I think a deeper search of Harry's house is in order. I wish we had his phone, but at least we have Larry's. But right now, searching for Gina and Sammy is most important."

"I'll talk to you after we get home," Carter said. "I'm hoping that Bentley and Gina's dad will finally spot them today."

After the call ended, Carter said to Maya, "I'll drive for a few more minutes, but I think I'll have you drive after we get to Cedar City."

"Whatever you say," Maya said agreeably.

***

Gina and Sammy were having a tough time. They'd come to a stream that they didn't dare wade through. It was too deep and wide. It was really more of a small river. "I guess we should follow it downstream, Sammy. Maybe it will lead us out of the mountains. We'll be going downhill if we do that."

"Okay," the tired boy said. "Do we still have some food left?"

"Not much," Gina responded.

"Hey, Gina, look," Sammy said excitedly as he pointed at the stream. "There are fish here. If we catch one, we could build a fire and cook it."

"That's a good idea, but how can we catch one? We don't have a fishing pole."

"You have that pistol. Could you shoot a big one and then we could grab it and get it out of the water?" he suggested.

Sammy had quite an imagination, but Gina decided it wouldn't hurt to try. So, they stopped alongside the stream and watched the fish flashing about in the water. "It's shallow on this side of the stream. Maybe we can do that," Gina said.

"Or we could make a net out of one of the shirts we had our food wrapped in," Sammy suggested.

"Now that is a great idea," Gina responded. So, they got a shirt out, shaped it as best they could into a net of sorts. Then using some tape from the first aid kit, they taped a stick to the shirt. "There, that should work. Should we try it?"

"Okay, where is the best place to try?" she asked Sammy, intent on keeping him thinking about fishing rather than how weak and hungry he was.

He studied the stream. She followed him up and down the bank while he was thinking. Finally, he said, "Right here. Look at all those fish, and they're close to the edge."

"I'll try, Sammy," Gina said and dipped the net—the shirt on a stick—into the water. She dragged it toward the fish, which began to swim frantically. She felt a tug on the makeshift net and jerked it from the water and away from the bank.

"You got one!" Sammy said, laughing and looking delighted. "Let's see how big it is."

She made sure she walked away far enough that the fish couldn't make it back to the stream before she tipped it out. She couldn't believe how hard it was flipping around. To her amazement, three fish fell from the net.

"Wow!" her little companion shouted gleefully. "You got three of them. And they're big ones. You are a great fisherman." He was dancing around about as much as the fish were flipping. It was like all the strain and tiredness had disappeared when he saw the fish.

As soon as the fish quit flipping around, Gina said, "You gather some small sticks for a fire while I gut these fish."

"Do you know how?" he asked skeptically.

"Do you?" she asked him.

"I don't," he said.

"Well, I do. I've done it lots. My dad and little brother love to fish. And Dad made sure we both could gut a fish and get it ready for frying. This will surprise you, but I know how to fillet them," Gina said.

"What does that mean?" he asked, looking at her with a little frown on his face.

"It's what has to be done to get the bones separated from the flesh. Here, before you look for sticks and wood, watch me do the first one."

Gina took the pocketknife from her pocket. It wasn't as sharp as she would have liked, so she spent a couple of minutes whetting it on a rock. When she was satisfied, she gutted all three fish and then filleted the first one. She laid the finished one on the wet shirt that had made such a good net. Then when she began filleting the next one, Sammy gathered small sticks and then larger ones. By the time she had finished with the fish, he had more than enough wood to cook the fish.

She found some small green trees along the bank of the stream and cut three of them down. "We don't want to use dry sticks because they would catch on fire while we are roasting the fish. These green ones won't burn easily," she explained for Sammy's benefit. Then she sharpened one end of each of the small trunks. While she was doing that, to her amazement, Sammy, using only one match, got a fire started. She put a stick into each of the fish. Then while she held two of them over the fire, Sammy held the other one.

Gina was surprised at how they were able to cook the fish to perfection. She offered a blessing on the food, and then she ate two of the very tasty fish while Sammy ate the third one. They ate with their hands, and that worked just fine. When they had finished eating, Sammy said, "Gina, I am full for the first time since we left the plane. Thanks for being such a special friend to me. I love you, Gina."

"I love you too, Sammy." That was true. She loved that boy like he was her very own little brother.

They rested with their stomachs filled with fish. Then they put the fire out, packed their diminished supply of food, the first aid kit, their extra clothes, and the net they had so miraculously caught fish with. They were soon ready to start hiking.

"I'll carry the rifle for a while," Sammy offered. "I feel stronger now."

The fish had truly been a miracle.

"We'll try to catch more for our dinner tonight. Can you eat fish twice in a row?"

"I can eat them every meal, Gina. I guess it's good we're following the stream because then we can have fish whenever we get hungry."

She hoped that she would be able to catch more. Sammy didn't seem to think it was even a question. His faith amazed her. If he believed, then so did she.

The hiking was difficult, but not any worse than what they'd already done. They occasionally had to hike out of the way to get past fallen trees, but they made steady progress. She believed they might really get out of this forest.

***

Carter and Maya stopped for lunch in Fairview. Then they continued their trip. They arrived in Duchesne at about six o'clock that night. Hank was expecting them and met them at Maya's home. "Thanks for keeping Carter company, Maya," Hank said. "You guys had a very successful trip."

"We did, didn't we? But Gina is still missing. I believe she will be found, though," Maya said with a small smile.

Her dad and mother met them as she was grabbing her bag from the back seat. Dale, her father, asked, "Did you kids have a successful trip?"

Hank answered for them. "It was more successful than I would have ever guessed. Now, we detectives have got a lot of work to do because of what Carter learned in St. George."

"Thanks, Maya," Carter said. "I know more about Gina now than I would have learned in a long time. She is lucky to have such a good friend. "Brother and Sister Warwick, thanks for letting her come with me. She drove over half the way home while I slept. I was up most of the night."

"I'll tell you all about it, Mom and Dad. Thanks for taking me, Carter. You're an amazing detective," she said.

"I'm just learning, but working with Hank and Bentley has been very educational," he said. "Good night, Maya. I'll see you at church tomorrow."

When they parted ways, Hank said, "I know you're exhausted, but before you go home, I'd like you to come up to the sheriff's office. We'll meet in my office there so I can make sure I know everything you learned on this trip of yours."

"I will be glad to," Carter said. "I just wish Bentley and Jim and the other flyers would have found Gina and Sammy today. I think they're going to try again tomorrow, even though it's Sunday. Maybe the Lord will make the Sabbath a successful day for them."

"The sheriff is going to sit in on our meeting, Carter. He's impressed with what you learned and wants to be very familiar with everything," Hank said. Then the two men got in their trucks and drove to the sheriff's office.

Chapter 26

After Carter made his report to the sheriff and Hank, Sheriff Goldman said, "I think another search of Harry's house is in order. Hank, will you set it up? I think we can shoot for Monday. There's no need to do it tomorrow."

Hank agreed, and he and Carter walked out to Carter's truck. "You need to get some rest," Hank said. "Take all of tomorrow to rest too, since it's Sunday and there's nothing you can do until Monday. Then, if you'd like, you can give us a hand searching Harry's place again."

Carter was torn. "I'll help on Monday, but I'll go to church in the morning. I can't just sit at home all day and not do anything. Gina and Sammy are out there somewhere in the wilderness in Colorado."

"There is nothing you can do about that," Hank said sadly.

With that, the detectives bid each other good night. Carter went to his apartment and went to bed early. He looked forward to attending church the next day and partaking of the sacred emblems of the sacrament.

***

Gina and Sammy had spent another long, cold night in the forest, but at least they had something to eat, as Gina had succeeded in netting three more fish for their dinner. It had taken longer than the ones they'd caught earlier, and she'd only caught one at a time, but it still had taken her only about a half hour.

The sky had been clear, so they'd built their fire in a small clearing surrounded by a thick stand of pines. Gina had filleted the fish, and they'd roasted the fillets over the fire. They hadn't had to touch the tiny amount of food they still had left. Gina said, "We'll try for more fish tomorrow if I can catch them."

"You can catch them, Gina. I'm glad we're hiking near this big stream because we won't run out of food or water," Sammy said. They had a small fire going and were warming themselves beside it when Sammy asked, "What day is it?"

Gina looked at the watch she wore, the very expensive one she had taken from Elliot's wrist. It had the date and the day of the week displayed on it. "Oh my goodness, Sammy, it's Sunday."

"Then we should not walk today," he said very seriously. "We're missing church. I miss my primary class."

"I miss Relief Society," she said as she considered what he'd said about not walking today. "Sammy, Heavenly Father has provided us with food, so I think it would be a good idea to rest today."

"Yes, we should do that. Sunday is a day of rest," he said with a grin.

"We will need to catch and roast some more fish, but I'll bet we could get by with two big meals today. Does that sound good to you?"

"Yes," he agreed.

The faint sound of thunder carried in the distance. Gina didn't like the sound of that. Another hard storm would be very difficult for them.

Sammy had heard it too. "I hope it doesn't rain."

Gina recalled that though there were some steep slopes above the stream, she hadn't noticed any cliffs they could shelter near. She glanced at the trees surrounding their little clearing and an idea came to her. "There are some small pine trees just beyond these big ones. Maybe we should build us a lean-to and cover it with branches. We might be able to stay mostly dry if it storms. But we would need to hurry."

"You better catch some fish first," Sammy said.

"I'll tell you what. Let's get some long sticks if we can find them and make a framework up against this big tree near the fire. Then

I'll catch the fish while you cut branches with lots of pine needles on them. Can you do that?"

"Yes," he said with his lips trembling. "I don't dare go very far from you."

"You won't have to. I'll show you where the small trees are. I think you can cut them with this big knife of Elliot's. Well, I guess it's my knife now."

She hurried, and they were able to find some dry sticks about two to three inches in diameter. She leaned them against the big tree and helped Sammy cut the first few small branches and place them on the sticks. He was enthusiastic about the work, so he said, "I can get more while you catch the fish."

She could hear thunder getting closer, and the sky above their clearing was filling with dark clouds. She went to the stream with the net they'd made. She walked up and down the bank for a minute, listening every few seconds for Sammy. She found a pool near the bank that had several large fish in it.

She slowly and noiselessly lowered her net to just above the water and watched as the fish swam back and forth. Two very large ones approached, and she swiftly lowered the net into the water and caught both of them. She lifted them from the water and hurried back into the clearing before she let them out of the net. She knew they were two or three times larger than the others she'd caught so far.

She and her dad and brother had done enough fishing that she could accurately estimate the weight of fish. These two had to have been at least five pounds each. Each fish would make a good meal for the two of them.

Sammy came into the clearing lugging some small tree branches. When he saw the fish, he whooped. "Those are giants!" he exclaimed.

"They are big," she agreed. "If I could catch one or two more, we'd have enough fish to eat today and tomorrow. Are you okay getting more branches while I try to get more?"

"I'll be okay," he said. "I'm trying not to be afraid."

"You are very brave, Sammy. And look at how many branches you've cut already." She looked up at the sky. The storm hadn't reached them yet. She thought she'd have time to try for two or three more fish, and then she'd help Sammy finish getting the branches.

Gina succeeded in catching three more large fish from that same pool within just a few minutes. She let them squirm on the grass while she helped gather more limbs for the lean-to. "I'll clean and fillet the fish from inside our lean-to if I have to. First, I think we should also get more firewood and stack it beside the lean-to. We'll rebuild the fire near one of the openings at the side and stack the firewood on the other side."

Gina kept looking up at the darkening sky. They were nearly out of time. As soon as she had what she felt like was a sufficient supply of dry wood, she built another little fire pit where they could hold the fish over the fire while they were under the lean-to. Lightning and thunder grew closer. She started another fire while Sammy put their blankets, the rifle, and the remaining supplies, including the first aid kits, under the low end of the lean-to.

When the rain came, it started out quite light, and she had two of the five large fish cleaned and filleted before she had to join Sammy inside their lean-to. They hung one of their blankets to close the opening where the firewood was stored. They were soon warm and comfortable. They talked about Jesus Christ and the prophet and other church topics. Gina told Sammy that that would have to do for a Sabbath-day meeting.

The rain, even when it came down harder, didn't last long, and the young lost kids stayed dry. The lean-to didn't look like much, but it did what they had hoped it would do.

Gina cooked, and they ate another of the large fish for dinner that Sunday night. They once again told each other stories. Some they made up, some were from the scriptures, and others were from their lives. When the storm had passed, they ventured outside the lean-to. The grass in the clearing was very wet, and the trees around it dripped water for quite some time after the storm.

After a few minutes of walking around, Gina and Sammy roasted the rest of the fish fillets so that the fish would not spoil. "We'll eat one cold in the morning, and another one later in the day," Gina told Sammy. "That way we won't have to use any more of the food we brought from the plane."

"We can probably keep catching fish as we go," Sammy said hopefully.

"I'll keep trying," Gina promised. "Heavenly Father has blessed us a lot."

***

Jim Rogers and his passenger, Detective Bentley Radford, flew again on Sunday after they'd both attended sacrament meeting at a local ward. But they gave up when a storm moved in a little before noon. It wasn't as strong as the one before, but it created a lot of lightning, which caused Jim to return back to the airport because of the danger of lightning striking the plane.

He was terribly discouraged by their lack of success. "Bentley, my heart tells me to stay and keep flying. But my brain tells me it is a waste of time. We're the only ones who flew at all today. All I can do at this point is pray that God is watching over my daughter and that He is keeping them safe, wherever she and Sammy are in the large, rugged forest."

"I'm sorry," Bentley said. "But I understand."

"We'll refuel and leave once the storm has passed out of the area," Jim explained.

***

Carter had spent a couple hours after lunch studying Come Follow Me and reading scriptures. Then he spent another two hours on his computer doing genealogical research.

Carter was restless and decided to go for a five-mile run. He dressed in his running clothes and headed out. The course he was running took him past both the Rogers home and the Warwick home. As he passed Maya's home, he heard her call out to him. He stopped and looked back. She was sitting with her mother in some wicker chairs on their front porch.

Carter jogged back.

Maya met him on the sidewalk halfway to her porch. "Have you learned anything more today?" she asked.

He had to tell her that there was still no sign of Gina and Sammy. "Bentley and Jim both got home a short while ago. Apparently the search is doing no good at all. All of the planes have quit looking for them. No one seems to know what to do now. I sure don't have any ideas."

"I was hoping for good news," Maya said. "Hey, I wanted to go for a run, but I didn't dare after what happened to Gina. Would you mind if I joined you?"

"That would be nice," he said.

"Let me run in and change. I'll be right back."

She joined him again in just three or four minutes. As soon as she was with him, they headed out. They mostly ran in silence, each of them absorbed in their own sad thoughts.

***

Barry Jones was anxious to help his brothers again. He'd spent too many years in prison. In his mind, his imprisonment had been totally unjust. He had always hated cops, but now he hated them worse than ever. He would take any chance he got to harm cops without being caught.

He was a free man now. He had been paroled the day before. He was supposed to stay in Colorado until his parole terminated in three years. But since when had he ever done what he was supposed to do? He planned to check in with both of his older brothers in Utah. He hadn't heard from either one of them for a few days, but they would be glad to hear from him. They were a close family.

Barry had thought a lot about his nephew, Elliot. Barry was getting to the age that he was constantly thinking about getting a serious girlfriend. Elliot had sent him pictures of two high school girls from Duchesne. One, of course, was the one that had been kidnapped by him and his dad. The other one was very cute. Maya Warwick was her name. *She would be perfect for him.* Yes, he would find a way to get her for himself.

He no longer had a home, but he had his phone again. It had been returned to him by the prison. But of course, it was dead. He would need to find a charger so he could use it. It was terribly outdated because he'd spent the last eight years in prison. But he had money in the bank, which the cops hadn't known about. And he had the money he'd been given by the jail upon his release.

He'd asked them to call him a taxi so he could go to a motel. He had found a charger that would fit his phone at a store next to the motel. Once his phone was charged, he'd tried to call Harry, who didn't answer. So then he'd called Larry, who also didn't answer.

Barry had been puzzled. Using his phone, he looked up the news. He hadn't seen the news in prison because it was never on the television he'd been allowed to watch in a commons area. He knew that Harry and Elliot had kidnapped a girl and a young boy that they were going to collect a ransom on. Larry was actually going to collect a ransom for the boy, even though he didn't have him. He'd been asked to do that by Harry.

He'd worked backward through the news on a local channel. A lead story from several days ago was about a plane crash in the forest. The pilot was Harry Jones. His brother. Barry sat back in shock. His brother was gone. To add to the grief, Harry's son, Elliot, had also died in the crash. A teenage girl and a little boy survived, and they were lost in the forest and had not been found.

The death of his family members upset Barry terribly. They shouldn't have died. Someone would pay for their deaths.

Angry, he continued to look at stories related to the kidnapping of the young woman and the boy. A detective by the name of Hank Parker with the Duchesne County Sheriff's Department and two private investigators were working the case. He found the names of the PIs and swore to get vengeance against the three detectives who, in his mind, were to blame for the death of his brother and nephew. He swore he would make them pay for targeting his fine family.

Additional searching on news from Washington County, Utah, shocked him again. Larry was in jail in St. George. One of the PIs from Duchesne was credited with giving the local police the information that led to his arrest. Carter Keefe. He swore in his wrath that he would make him pay. He needed to head to Utah. He would enact revenge against the detectives. No one should have messed with his family. He would soon take care of the people who had caused him so much sorrow.

Chapter 27

After eating cold fish for breakfast, the two lost souls cleaned up the campfire and tore down the lean-to.

"Sammy, we'll never be back this way again, and even though it's not likely that anyone will ever pass through here, I want to keep the area looking as good as we can."

"I think that will make Heavenly Father happy," Sammy said.

"Yes, it will," she agreed. "We need all the help we can get from Him."

In a few minutes, they were on their way again. They both felt stronger after having had their stomachs full for a few meals. Sammy was able to take turns carrying the rifle. The blanket with supplies was a lot lighter, so Gina used both blankets together to haul the supplies over her shoulder. She was determined to make things as easy for Sammy as she could.

They took several small breaks, and at about one in the afternoon, they took time to eat another fillet. They were able to share just one. The big fish she'd caught had made it so they could go a fairly long time without having to eat the small amount of food they had left from the wrecked airplane.

"We'll try to catch more tomorrow if we haven't found a road yet," Gina said as they started hiking once again. She was concerned though as the terrain became much more rugged. It forced them to move away from the stream, but not so far that they couldn't hear it.

***

“Harry must have been more careful about what he keeps and what he throws away than his brother is,” Carter said to Hank, Bentley, and a Uintah County deputy. They had been carefully searching Harry’s house. They hadn’t been able to start until about one in the afternoon because the judge on call hadn’t been able to sign the search warrant until well after noon. It was frustrating but not terribly surprising. By three in the afternoon, they still hadn’t found a single new piece of evidence.

They were looking specifically for any records Harry might have hidden somewhere that might shed additional light on the burglaries that they knew Larry had committed and ones they had probably committed, as well. Carter added, “Harry was definitely more careful than his brother about leaving incriminating evidence in his house.” They’d looked in every nook and cranny they could find but found no stolen property.

Now they turned their attention to Harry’s garage. The garage was a mess. There wasn’t room to park a bike in it, let alone a truck. It was filled mostly with items that appeared useless to Carter. Maybe someone like Harry would have found use for some of the junk, but Carter couldn’t see anything that looked of any use.

The junk was making the search more tedious. They kept at it though until they had searched through everything. But despite their efforts, they found nothing important.

“I guess Harry wasn’t as careful about what he left in his garage,” Carter said. “Who knows, something in here may have been stolen, but I don’t know how we’d know if it was.”

They finally gave up around five that evening.

Sheriff Connor in Colorado notified them that the wrecked airplane had finally been removed from the crash site. The federal investigators had determined that the crash was caused by the very same engine problem that Alec Harmon had been planning to fix but that Harry Jones had scoffed at. Harry had died, along with his son, because he’d refused to listen to Alec.

The federal investigators still wanted to do a more thorough examination of the wreckage before it was hauled back to Roosevelt, and Jim and his partners wanted that too. "So we'll need to keep it here for another three or four days," Sheriff Connor explained to Sheriff Goldman. "When they're through here, then someone from over there can haul it back to Roosevelt."

***

Gina and Sammy struggled up a very steep mountainside that went right to the edge of the large mountain stream. It was tiring and discouraging. But they didn't see any alternative. The farther they climbed, the more distant the stream with their supply of fish was. Gina kept hoping that they would be able to get past this rugged ridge and be able to descend next to the stream again. They needed more fish. It was the only thing she could think of to keep their stomachs full and their energy up.

When six o'clock rolled around, they were both extremely fatigued, especially Sammy. His short legs had a hard time climbing over rocks and fallen timber that littered the mountainside. But then the land once again descended closer to the stream. However, the water was running much faster, and Gina was afraid it would be hard to find fish with the stream flowing so rapidly. She needed pools near the bank in order to use the net she'd built.

"Can we stop now?" Sammy asked. "I'm tired."

"Yes, I think we'd better. I'm tired too. That mountain was rough. But you know what Sammy? We are getting stronger."

"Do you think so?"

"Yes, Sammy, I think so. But we need more fish to keep us strong. Should we eat the rest of the fish we have left?" Gina asked.

Sammy looked seriously at her. "Maybe we should only eat half of it and save the rest of it for tomorrow."

Gina was impressed with Sammy's wisdom. She'd thought that, but when he suggested it, she knew that it was okay to save some of it. "Let's find some wood and make a fire beside these rocks." The rocks she was speaking of were huge boulders, many of them five or six feet high and just as big around. They were near the side of the rapidly running stream at the base of the mountain they had descended. Gina had found that it was nearly as difficult coming down as it had been going up. That may have been partly because they had been very tired already from the climb before beginning the descent.

With the rocks as shelter, a small fire kept them quite warm. They nibbled slowly on the small pieces of fish that made up their dinner. It eventually became dark, but Sammy had fallen asleep shortly after he'd finished his fish. Gina watched him fondly in the light of the fire as he slept on one side, one arm beneath his head and the other stretched out in front of him. He was truly a wonderful boy. She prayed that God would help her get the little guy out of the mountains to safety.

They had not encountered any wild animals for many hours. But as they worked their way through and around the boulders the next morning, they saw what Gina guessed were mountain sheep. They were high above them on the steep mountainside, bounding gracefully from one small ledge to another as they picked at the sparse grass that grew there. "How do they do that?" Sammy asked as he gazed in wonder at the beautiful creatures. "It doesn't look like there's anything to put their feet on."

"I don't know how they do it. It looks impossible. It would be nice if we could do that," Gina said wistfully.

They sat down, leaned against a large rock, and watched the wild sheep until they had all worked their way around a steep ridge and out of sight. Then the two wanderers set out again. Gina didn't say what she was thinking to Sammy, but she wondered if they were going to be able to keep going this way or if they would have to turn back. It would be terrible if they were forced to do that.

However, the mountainside was soon not as close to their stream, and the bank of the stream was smoother, making for much easier walking. Eventually, the stream slowed, and pools of water once again appeared near the bank with fish swimming lazily in them.

"Gina, we can get more fish here," Sammy said as he pointed to one smooth pool. The backs of fish glistened as they effortlessly moved about in it. "There are lots of them."

He was right, and Gina spent the next half hour catching fish with her crude but trusty net. She finally stopped when she had eight nice-sized fish squirming on the bank. It was well into the afternoon by then, so she decided, with Sammy's agreement, to clean and fillet the fish. When that was done, they built a small fire, and over the next hour and a half, they roasted all of the fillets. They filled their bellies and then saved the rest to take with them.

There were still a few hours of daylight left, so they put out the fire and moved along beside the stream. They moved slowly but steadily. Gina became concerned again as the mountainside crowded closer to the stream. It wasn't as steep as it had been back where they had watched the mountain sheep, but if they had to climb it, it would be very difficult. She tried not to worry about it and simply kept moving forward.

An hour later, Gina noticed a distant roaring coming from somewhere ahead of them.

Sammy noticed it too. "What is that noise?" Sammy asked. "It sounds scary."

Gina had an idea what it was, and it worried her. She didn't want to further worry Sammy, who was already concerned about the sound, so she said, trying to sound cheerful, "I don't know, but I guess we'll find out. At least it's not a bear."

Sammy grinned when she said that. "A bear doesn't sound like that. I know because one roared at us when we were in that cabin."

Gina looked at her watch. There was only another hour of daylight left. They would need to find a place to camp for the night and eat more of the fish. Frankly, she was becoming very tired of eating nothing but fish. But she was grateful for what she'd caught and roasted. Without it, they would have already run out of the very small amount of food they had left. Had that happened, they would have been in serious trouble by now.

She didn't complain about the fish to Sammy, and he didn't complain to her, even though she knew he must also have been getting very bored of it. But she was grateful to her Father in Heaven for providing food for them. It reminded her of the story of the Israelites in Moses's time being supplied with manna from heaven. In a way, she considered the fish to be their manna from heaven.

The loud roar became deafening. She felt chills down her spine as she anticipated what it might be. The stream grew wider and was moving slowly. She couldn't see beyond it. They had to circle around some rocks and trees beside the stream. When they got to the far side, she gasped. There to the left of them, the stream reached a drop-off, becoming a raging waterfall. The water plunged two hundred feet or more straight down and created a large pond at the bottom. The sound of the falling water was almost deafening, and yet it was somehow beautiful.

She grasped Sammy's shoulder as they stared at the beautiful sight. She didn't want either of them to get any closer to the edge. After watching for five minutes, totally in awe, Sammy looked up at her and shouted so he could be heard above the loud sound of falling water. "How do we get past here, Gina?"

She knew the answer, and it wasn't a good one. In fact, it was a terrible one. The only way to go, as far as she could tell, was to climb the mountain. But that would have to wait until morning. Right now, they would eat some fish and camp for the night. It was going to take a lot of energy to climb that daunting mountain in the morning. And it was going to be hard to sleep with the loud noise, but she saw no alternative.

Chapter 28

CARTER KEEFE KNEW THAT HE HAD TO SNAP OUT OF HIS FUNK. HE had to get busy and do something that would help keep his mind off Gina. Some people in town and even in the ward were saying they feared that Gina and Sammy would never come home, that something terrible had happened to them in the Colorado forest. He knew it was possible, but he would not allow himself to believe it.

He needed something to keep his mind occupied. He needed a case to work on. When Bentley called him that Tuesday morning at seven o'clock, he was given something to do. Bentley had just been retained by a defense attorney in Vernal to attempt to find evidence that would prove a client he represented had not done what she was accused of doing. "This is an embezzlement case, and the attorney is convinced that his client has been set up to take the blame for something she hasn't done. The attorney emailed me everything he has on the case."

"I'll be glad for something to do to keep me from worrying so much about Gina," Carter said.

"This should help," Bentley said. "I'll pick you up at nine, and we'll drive to Vernal. The first thing we need to do is meet with the defendant, a young lady about twenty-two years old by the name of Susan Bingham."

***

CHAPTER 28

Barry Jones had found where the PI Carter Keefe lived. He was watching the apartment from a short distance away in an old pickup he'd stolen before leaving Colorado. A late model dusty blue Ford F150 pulled up. The driver got out and stretched his arms. Barry wondered if that was Bentley Radford, the other PI. A moment later, Keefe came out of his apartment and joined Radford at his truck. They talked for a moment and then climbed into Radford's truck and headed in the direction of Main Street.

Barry followed them, staying far enough behind them that he figured they wouldn't spot him. He'd follow them to wherever they were going. He would avenge the deaths of his brother and nephew and the arrest of his other brother. Barry laughed as an idea came to him. He wanted the detectives to know they were in extreme danger and that there was nothing they could do about it. He had a phone call to make. But he'd do it in a little while, he decided. Once he had them worrying for a while, he'd take his revenge.

***

Carter was glad to have something to do that would keep him from worrying about Gina every minute. As they rode to Vernal in Bentley's pickup, Carter thumbed through the file that Bentley had put together. It included the material sent to him by the attorney on the case and the notes Bentley had taken while he'd been speaking to the attorney on the phone.

When they were about fifteen miles from Vernal, Carter closed the file and looked at his boss. "Bentley, it doesn't look good for this lady."

"That is precisely why we are being hired to look into it," Bentley said. "Her attorney says he is positive that she has been framed. It's our job to confirm that if he's right. And he is convinced that he is."

"Well, all I can say right now is that we have a steep hill to climb if we are going to be able to find evidence to refute this," Carter said.

***

If Carter had been able to see what Gina was looking at right at that moment, he would have been absolutely dismayed. She wasn't looking at a steep *hill*, she was looking at a steep *mountain*, and she and Sammy had no choice but to climb it and hope that it would be easier for them to hike after they reached the top.

There were a few trees on the mountainside and clumps of grass and brush along with lots and lots of rocks of varying sizes, all of which they would have to either go over or around. It was indeed a daunting task. They prayed together and began to climb.

Gina was grateful that it wasn't as steep as the one where the mountain sheep had been grazing. The first hundred feet were not too bad, but after that, it got steeper, lots steeper. She was carrying the blankets filled with what few supplies they had left, which now included the roasted fish. The pistol was strapped to her belt on one side, and the large knife was strapped to the other. She was carrying the rifle because there was no way Sammy could do that and still climb.

At times, they had to crawl and use clumps of grass and brush to keep from sliding back down the steep slope. Gina would have to put the rifle and the blankets with their supplies above her as far as she could reach and then do the same thing again when she reached them, as she needed her hands free to climb. She also kept Sammy ahead of her and boosted him when he needed help. At one point, she said, "Whatever you do, don't look behind us; only look ahead." She was trying to do what she instructed him to do.

That proved to be impossible, for they had to rest frequently. When they rested they had to sit on the mountainside. And when they did that, they had to face back down.

"I can't help but look down there," Sammy said. "I can't believe how steep that is."

"I can't either, but when we're climbing, we shouldn't look back, because it could make us dizzy and cause us to lose our balance."

Sammy looked down and then turned and looked up. "We have farther to go than we've already climbed." The discouragement in his voice echoed what she was feeling.

"That's true, Sammy, but look at the bright side. All that we have already climbed is that much we don't still have to climb. I think we are doing pretty well."

He nodded at her and offered a weak smile.

The hours passed slowly, but they continued to make progress. They did not attempt to hurry. It was essential that they took their time so they didn't slip and fall. They eventually sat behind some boulders perched on the mountainside while they ate fish and drank water. They had enough water if they didn't waste any, and they certainly needed it since the sun was shining brightly on their backs as they climbed, making them sweat profusely.

They finally reached the top, but beyond that, there was still more climbing following a few hundred feet of relatively flat terrain. But it was not steep climbs like the one they'd just completed. "We can do this, Sammy. I'm so proud of you."

He beamed a tired smile at her and said, "I couldn't do it without you."

***

Carter had thought that by working on the embezzlement case for Susan Bingham it would take his mind off Gina, but to his dismay, Susan looked very much like Gina. She had long blonde hair and eyes the same shade of blue as Gina's. And she was built like her. She could have been Gina's sister. So instead of working with her getting his mind off Gina, it only made him long for her more. Susan's voice even resembled Gina's. The resemblance made him think that this poor lady had been framed as her lawyer believed. She seemed so much like Gina, so wholesome and good.

Carter made up his mind that since he couldn't do anything for Gina, he would work hard to help her lookalike. As he and Bentley went over the case against Susan, they both began to see serious holes in it.

"Tell us who you think may have set you up," Bentley said.

She looked down at the table that separated her from the two detectives. "I hate to point fingers. What if I did point fingers and I was mistaken about who was behind it? If I did that, I'd be no better than whoever is blaming me," she said.

"Don't worry about that. You give us a name or names, and we will take it from there. We won't accuse anyone without hard evidence—like what has been done to you," Bentley promised her.

She nodded. "Okay, it's either another secretary or the company's accountant." She looked at the detectives before giving names. She surprised Carter when she said, "You're looking at me like you think you've met me before, Detective Keefe. Is it because I look so much like my cousin Gina Rogers? My dad and mom both say I look like her."

"Yes, you do," Carter mumbled in shock.

"Wait, are you the guy she told me about at my birthday party a month ago?"

"I don't know," he said.

"You are. I just know it. She said you were a PI. And she said you were the most handsome guy she'd ever seen." Carter felt himself going red. She continued. "You've got to find her. She's a good girl. Please, find her. Our whole family is worried."

"We are trying, but we're stumped," Bentley said.

"Keep trying, please," she said as tears filled her pretty blue eyes. "Is it true that she's lost in some huge forest in Colorado?"

"Yes, I'm afraid so," Bentley said.

"I know that my attorney picked the right men to help me. If Gina cares for you as deeply as she told me she does, then I trust you, Detective Keefe. And I trust you as well, Detective Radford. She mentioned that you two work together and you're both good at what you do."

"Thanks," Carter mumbled. He was feeling very emotional and was unable to say much.

Bentley looked at Carter and then back at Susan. "Okay, give us some names, and we will go to work."

Carter couldn't help but wish that Gina was with them right now, helping to find out who hated her cousin enough to set her up for a crime she had not committed. He promised himself that he would do all he could to find the evidence to clear Susan. It would be doing Gina a great favor as well. And since there was nothing more he could do for Gina at this point, he would give his best effort to Susan's case. He knew Bentley would as well.

***

Gina was doing the best she could to help herself and Sammy survive and return home. She was committed, despite the odds stacked against them. She had faith in God, and she placed her trust totally in Him. She prayed continually as they hiked up the next ridge.

When they finally reached its summit just an hour before sunset, she felt huge relief at what lay before them. It was more forest, but she couldn't see any mountains ahead of them. It was mostly a gentle downward trend. That was most welcome.

Sammy, who was looking like he could drop, smiled. "We can do forest. It's mountains that are hard."

He was right. "Let's get into the trees and then find a small clearing to camp in for the night," she said.

They soon found a place that looked like it would do, and they quickly gathered firewood and started a small fire. They both had sore feet and hands from the arduous climbs they'd accomplished that day. Sammy had a blister on his right foot. Gina applied some ointment to it, and then put a Band-Aid on it. She also applied some salve to a small cut she'd gotten earlier and put a Band-Aid on that as well. "I'm sure glad we have these two first aid kits with us," she said as she closed the one she'd been using and laid it next to their rifle. Another long night lay ahead, but she prayed that tomorrow would be a better day, *a much better day.*

They slept fairly well that night due to sheer exhaustion. They started off again shortly after seven in the morning. Gina set a course heading much the same direction that they'd been going until they'd been forced to turn away from the waterfall and climb the mountain. She couldn't say exactly why, but she just had a feeling that she needed to lead Sammy in that direction.

They walked for several hours before they came to a small stream. She felt like they needed to cross it, but she didn't want them to get wet feet if they could help it. They filled their water bottles and then walked slowly down the stream. It finally narrowed and got deeper. "We can jump it here," she told Sammy.

With her help, he made it across. For her, it was easy. They set off again, but Gina stumbled over a root and fell hard. She cried out in pain. She knew, even without looking, that she had a broken arm and probably a badly sprained ankle. Despite trying not to, she cried long and hard while Sammy sat helplessly on the ground beside her, holding her good hand. After a few minutes, she took some Tylenol and tore another of the shirts she'd carried from the crash. With Sammy's help, she was able to put her arm in a sling.

"Thanks, Sammy. I'm sorry I was so clumsy, but we've got to keep going. I can't believe I didn't get hurt climbing mountains, but then I do this to myself when we finally reach mostly flat ground. Help me get the blankets on my back and we'll go again." She didn't know how she could keep going now. The pain was terrible. In fact, it was so bad that she threw up. "I'm sorry. I'll be okay now." She doubted what she said but was fiercely determined to think positively.

"I'll carry the rifle. But before we start walking again, would you let me say a prayer for you?" Sammy asked.

"Of course, that would be great, Sammy," she replied despite the intense pain she was experiencing.

Sammy bowed his head and stood next to her and held onto her good arm. "Heavenly Father," he began in a voice choked with emotion. "I love Gina. Thank you for making her my best friend in the whole world. Please help her not to hurt. I'll help her all I can. But please help her to be okay. In the name of Jesus Christ, Amen."

Sammy leaned against her and sobbed. She cried again, but it was more for the love she felt for this amazing child than for her pain.

Finally, he said, "I guess we'd better go, Gina."

They set off, but she found that her ankle and foot were hurting so much that it was all she could do to walk. She knew that she was in a bad way and that the two of them were in serious trouble. She kept thinking about Sammy's prayer and tried to have faith in his faith. Sammy truly had a great amount of faith for one so young.

About three in the afternoon, as they were moving very slowly through thick trees again, a gunshot rang through the air. She grabbed Sammy with her good hand, her left one, and pulled him to the ground with her. She couldn't imagine who could be out in this forest besides them. But someone was, and whoever it was had a rifle.

She waited for several minutes before Sammy stood up and then helped her get to her feet. They proceeded cautiously ahead. He was packing the rifle with one hand and supporting her as much as he could with the other one. It was all she could do to carry the blanket with their supplies. They had only gone maybe a hundred feet when they could see a meadow through the few trees still ahead of them. In the very center of the meadow was a tall man dressed in camouflage pants, shirt, and hat with tall black boots on his feet. His black hair hung long down his back, and a thick black beard covered his face. He was cleaning a deer, a small buck. She found herself filled with a combination of fear and hope. Sammy mostly had fear. He held tightly to her arm. Gina could hear him sobbing with fear.

The man stood up straight and looked right toward where they were standing just a few feet back in the trees. "Come on out, kids. I won't hurt you. You look like you need help."

"I'm hurt, and we're lost," Gina managed to say.

"My name's Jeremy. I'm a doctor," he said as he wiped his bloody knife on the hide of the deer and then his hands on the tall meadow grass. Gina stood frozen. The man walked toward them. When he reached them, he spoke in a gentle voice, a deep voice that held no hint of malice.

"What's your name, young lady?" he asked.

"I'm Gina Rogers."

"What is your name, young fella?" he asked as he knelt in front of Sammy.

Not a sound came out of Sammy's mouth even though his lips were moving. Gina knew what had happened; Sammy had lost his voice again. The man named Jeremy stood up, towering over Gina. "Can't he talk or does he not want to?" he asked, his deep voice soft and gentle.

"He can't speak when he's scared badly," Gina said as she began to feel faint. "His name is Sammy." She'd no sooner said Sammy's name than she suddenly felt herself sinking. The giant's arms caught her before she hit the ground. And then blackness enfolded her.

Chapter 29

SAMMY STARED AT HIS BELOVED GINA AS THE GIANT MAN HELD HER in his arms. "Come on, Sammy," Jeremy said. "I'll help your sister. I may not look like it, but I really am a doctor. She needs the bones in her arms set properly, and then she needs lots of rest. Will you help me by carrying your rifle over there and laying it by mine? Leave the blankets. After I take care of Gina, I'll come back for the deer and your stuff and the rifles," he said.

Sammy stood where he was.

"I have a nice cabin and lots of food about a mile from here," the big man said. "You can walk that much farther, can't you?"

Sammy nodded. One thing that he knew for sure, he was going to stay close to Gina. He wouldn't let this big man take her out of his sight. So he made his legs move, and then he walked beside the giant who had told them he was a doctor. They crossed the meadow and entered the trees on the other side. It was all Sammy could do to keep up with the man named Jeremy. His legs were long, but Sammy wasn't about to fall behind.

Jeremy kept looking at him. "I'm sorry I'm making you move so fast, but your sister needs medical attention, and I can give it to her. I am not lying when I tell you I am a doctor. I have some medical supplies at my cabin."

"Thank you," Sammy said.

The tall man smiled down at him without losing stride. "You must not be afraid anymore. You can talk now. I'm impressed," Jeremy said.

"We're almost there. My dog will come out to meet us, but don't be afraid of him. He's large, but he's very gentle. He keeps me company."

"I like dogs," Sammy said between breaths. He no longer felt any fear for this giant of a man, so his voice had, indeed, returned.

"I like them too, especially my Blacky. Does your sister?"

"I don't know if she does. She's not my sister; she's my cousin and my best friend. I'd be dead if it hadn't been for her. I love her very much. Please make her get better." The words were flowing from Sammy's mouth now that he could tell that he and Gina had found a friend. He thought of the prayer he'd said when Gina broke her arm and injured her foot. His prayer was being answered. Heavenly Father was blessing them. They were safe with this man. He could feel it.

A few minutes later, a nice cabin set beneath a stand of tall pine trees came into view. "We will take her inside and put her on my bed. You can come in too."

As Jeremy had told him, a large black dog came bounding around the cabin, dodging tree trunks as it ran. It skidded to a stop and sniffed at Sammy. Sammy bravely reached out and touched its head. The dog wagged its tail and licked Sammy's grimy hand.

"Would you open the door please, Sammy?" Jeremy asked as they approached the front of the cabin.

He ran ahead and opened the door and waited while Jeremy carried Gina inside. This was a really nice cabin. It was nothing like Harry's. This one was clean and neat. There wasn't much furniture, only a couple of rustic chairs and a small table that matched them. There was another door to the right. "That door too, please," Jeremy said, nodding toward it.

Sammy opened it and stepped back while Jeremy carried Gina in and gently laid her on a wooden bed that had what Sammy thought was a pile of bear skins on it. He covered her with a thin blanket. Then he grabbed a bag from a shelf near the head of the bed and pulled a small white bottle from it. He shook a pill from the bottle and gently put it in Gina's mouth. He stood and watched her for a few minutes.

Finally, he turned to Sammy. "The pill has dissolved. It will help her sleep and not feel the pain. Stay by her while I hurry and get the deer and rifles and your supplies. I will let her rest before I tend to her broken arm and see if I can tell what the problem with her foot is."

With that, he headed out of the room. "You stay, Blacky," he said to the large black dog. "I won't be long, Sammy. You can look around if you want, but if you do, make sure you check on your friend every few minutes." Then he left the cabin at a run.

There was only one chair in the room. It was a close match for the two in the main room. Sammy slid it beside the bed and then sat and watched Gina. She was breathing evenly and looked peaceful. There was a clock on the wall. It read ten minutes after six. This had been a long day. He and Gina had left their last camp at just a little after seven that morning. He had no idea how far he and Gina had walked, but it had to have been a very long ways.

After a few minutes, he got up and wandered out of the room like the big man had told him he could. Blacky stayed right with him. There were two more doors. He opened one of them. It led into a room filled with what Sammy thought must be food, but everything was in some kind of wrapping, so he couldn't tell for sure. There were wooden shelves, and they were full. He was sure that Doctor Jeremy, as he had begun to think of him, had a large supply of food in here.

The other door led to the outside where there was a large, partially enclosed deck. Firewood was stacked to the ceiling. There was another chair out there that looked like the ones inside. And there was another table. An axe and a large saw hung on the wall next to the large stack of firewood. There were more leather boots next to the wall by the door. Some leather coats hung on nails on the wall above the boots. There were a couple of hats there too. They looked like warm ones.

At the opposite end of the deck, tools hung on the wall. There were hammers and screwdrivers and other things he didn't recognize. He eventually became aware of shutters that when closed would make the deck into a closed room. Another door led to the outside. A few feet beyond that was a large log shed of some kind and a corral and what Sammy assumed must be a barn. He'd never seen an outhouse before, but one small building was built directly beneath one of the large trees, and he knew what it was from pictures he'd seen. Trees towered over all the buildings, which in Sammy's bright mind meant that they couldn't easily be spotted from the air—if at all. Farther from the cabin and other building were trees much taller than the ones the homestead was built beneath.

He didn't see any animals, only Blacky, who followed Sammy, almost like he was protecting him. He walked through trees that had their limbs trimmed to the tops of the log buildings. He went all the way around the house. Sammy noticed a strange thing. There were no vehicles that he could see. There was no place to park one because of the trees. Nor was there a road anywhere that he could see. Sammy was puzzled about that.

He eventually went back inside to check on Gina. She was still asleep. He once again sat beside her and watched her with both concern and love. He offered a silent prayer, asking Heavenly Father to help her get better soon so they could go home. And he thanked God for Doctor Jeremy. The dog sat beside him, his big head on Sammy's lap. He petted the dog's head.

After a few more minutes, Blacky got to his feet and whined. Then he headed for the door. Sammy opened it and could see Jeremy approaching through the pines, carrying the deer, the two rifles and the blankets that contained their supplies. The dog ran to him dancing around him like he hadn't seen him for ages. "Good dog," Jeremy said. Then to Sammy, who stood in the doorway, he asked, "How is Gina? Is she still asleep?"

"Yes, and she looks okay to me, Doctor Jeremy," Sammy said. "But I know when she wakes up, she will be hurting. I'm glad you're a doctor. I'm glad you found us. If you hadn't, we would have never seen your place because it is well hidden. We would have walked right on past it." He choked up and wiped some tears from his eyes. "She would have died, and I would have been all alone. I would have died too."

"God was watching over you. I can take care of her, Sammy. And I will make sure she gets better. And you may call me Jeremy," he said with a smile.

"But to me you are Doctor Jeremy, okay?"

"Whatever you like, Sammy," the big man said with a gentle smile. "Please put these rifles on the table. I'll set your blankets and whatever they have in them here by the door. Then I need to take this deer and hang it in my barn. Maybe tomorrow you can help me skin it and cut it up."

"Okay," Sammy said. "That would be fun."

He did as Jeremy asked him to and took both rifles and laid them on the wooden table in the end of the room nearest the fireplace. Then he studied that end of the room closer. There was no stove, just the large fireplace, which was made out of rock. He wondered why Jeremy didn't have a stove. He thought about the fact that he hadn't seen a truck or even a road. He decided he would ask Doctor Jeremy later. He was sure the gentle giant had a good reason, but he couldn't imagine what it might be.

In a few minutes, Jeremy came back inside carrying two large wooden buckets filled with water. He placed them next to the fireplace and then hung a black iron pot of some kind on a hook in the fireplace, filled it with water from one of the buckets, and then added wood to the smoldering fire. Soon it was blazing, and Jeremy said, "Okay, Sammy, let's go see how Gina is doing while the water heats."

"Why is she sleeping so long?" Sammy asked.

"I told you before that the pill I gave her would help her sleep so she wouldn't feel any pain for a while," Jeremy said.

"Oh yes. So was it a sleeping pill?" Sammy asked.

"Yes, sort of. It was a sedative that dissolves easily in the mouth. That was to make her sleep more soundly and a little longer. It should wear off soon, but before she wakes up, I need to set the bone in her arm. It would be best if she is still sleeping when I do that so that she won't feel it. Do you want to watch me and make sure I do it right?"

"I can't tell if you do it right. I don't know anything about doctor stuff. I trust you, Doctor Jeremy. But I will watch," Sammy said.

The big man took hold of Gina's arm and felt up and down it with his long, slender fingers. "I know what I need to do," he said. With that, he gently moved the arm one way and then the other before suddenly pulling hard on her hand while holding tightly above the break. Sammy heard a gentle snap, and then Doctor Jeremy smiled.

"There, Sammy. The broken bone went back into place nicely. There are two bones in our arms, but only one of hers broke. That was very fortunate. I'm glad it wasn't a worse break. Next, we need to make a splint so that it will stay in place while it heals."

"How long will that take?" Sammy asked.

"Probably five weeks or so," Doctor Jeremy said. "Next I need to check her foot and ankle." He repeated what he'd done when he'd checked her arm. With his long fingers, he felt all over her foot and then her ankle. "I don't know how she walked on this foot. There is a broken bone right above her toes and two of her toes are also broken."

"What do you do for that?" Sammy asked.

"That's a great question, Sammy," he said. "It doesn't appear that any bones are out of alignment; they are just badly cracked. So what we have to do is put a tight bandage on her foot, and then she can't walk on it for several weeks. The bones will heal just fine if she's careful."

"How can she get around then?" Sammy asked.

Doctor Jeremy smiled. "I guess you and me will have to make her some crutches."

"Do you know how to do that?" Sammy asked innocently.

"That's easy, Sammy. See these chairs, the bed, and the table, and for that matter, the cabin and outbuildings? I made all of it with wood I got from the forest. I didn't use any trees here where my homestead is to build with except the ones I needed to cut down where I was going to put the buildings."

"I bet your homestead can't be seen from airplanes."

Jeremy smiled. "That's what I intended. You are a very perceptive young man. With your help, I can easily make crutches for her."

"When can we do that?" Sammy asked.

"That will wait until tomorrow. She must stay in bed tonight. If she needs to use the outhouse, we'll need to help her. Did you see the outhouse?" Jeremy asked.

"I have never seen one before, but I knew what it was because of pictures I've seen," Sammy said with a grin.

"You can use it whenever you need to. We'll help Gina when she needs to go out there. I don't want her to put any weight on her foot. She's lucky she didn't do a lot of damage to it by walking on it after she tripped."

"If she is on your bed, where will you sleep? That's your bed."

"Same place as you. We will lay some hides on the floor and sleep on them. You've been sleeping on the ground, haven't you?"

"Yes, of course," Sammy responded. "It wasn't too bad."

"I think the water is about hot now. We need to clean her foot very carefully before we wrap it. We'll clean both her feet. Tomorrow, you can have a bath."

"Where do you get your water from?" Sammy asked.

"There's a spring of water out behind my barn. It runs year-round. The stream that flows from it goes into a nice meadow not far to the west," Jeremy explained. "I'll show you in the morning. We have enough water for tonight. I have a third full bucket of water on the deck. It's for drinking and has a lid on it."

"Where did you get the buckets? I've never seen any like this before," Sammy said as he pointed to the buckets Jeremy had carried inside.

"I made them just like I made all my furniture. I sealed the cracks with pine gum so they wouldn't leak. Let's get some of that water now, Sammy, and I'll wash Gina's arms and her feet. I'll use some sticks to make a splint for her arm once we get it clean. And we'll use some soft tanned skins to wrap her foot to make it stable," Jeremy said.

Chapter 30

Carter and Bentley uncovered some information that had been expertly hidden in records on Susan's computer at work. They sort of hacked into it, but Susan knew the passwords they needed. They had found enough to show she was not the embezzler. She'd told him that the detective had not even looked at her computer, so she didn't know how he was able to find anything to use to accuse her.

Bentley had explained that he probably relied on what others from the office had told him. The detective that had been assigned to the case was a young, somewhat inexperienced officer by the name of Rand Oakley.

He met Carter and Bentley at Susan Bingham's apartment. "What are you men doing interfering in my case?" he asked when he had been invited in.

Susan was having none of it. "My attorney hired them to find out what really happened since you failed to do anything but blame me."

"I have the evidence that proves you took the money. I have yet to find where you've hidden it, but I will," the young, short, stocky detective said.

"I didn't hide anything, and I didn't embezzle anything," she said hotly.

"Sorry, lady, but I can prove you did. I have witnesses."

Carter and Bentley looked knowingly at each other. "And we can prove she didn't," Bentley said. "And we can do it without using lying witnesses. You need to learn how to do your job. It only took us a few hours to find where you messed up."

"I know who you guys are. You're PIs. And I'm guessing you don't have any idea what you're doing," Detective Rand Oakley said.

"Slow down there, Officer Oakley," Bentley said.

"It's *Detective* Oakley," Rand said angrily.

"You need to do some detecting, then. The reason we asked you to come over was so we could show you what we found that you should have if you had any idea what you were doing. By the way, I'm Detective Bentley Radford, and this is my partner, Detective Carter Keefe," Bentley said. "Now I think we need to start over. Come into Susan's kitchen where we have a laptop set up. We'll walk you through what we found that you missed, what your so-called witnesses lied to you about."

"I didn't miss anything, and no one lied to me," Detective Oakley said. "I'll be going now."

"I don't think you should do that, because if you do, we'll get your chief in here. He is not going to be happy when he sees what we discovered and how badly you messed up," Bentley said just as Carter's phone rang.

"It's Detective Parker," Carter said to Bentley.

"From Duchesne County? This case is none of his business. And you can tell him I said so," Rand snapped.

Carter was already accepting the call and stepping away as Bentley said, "He is not involved in this. Your problem, Officer Oakley, is that you have a bad habit of jumping to conclusions. That's what has got you in trouble with this case of yours."

"You are wrong all the way around," Oakley said. "I'll ask you once more to call me *Detective* Oakley."

"I have a better idea," Bentley said. "I'll call your chief right now unless you look at the evidence we found and help you see what you should have found had you bothered to look for it."

"I'm not looking at anything," Oakley said. "It's not possible for you to have found anything from here in the thief's apartment. I don't know who you think you're fooling. You are not fooling me. I have a solid case against this embezzler, and I will prove it in court."

Bentley took out his phone, went to his contacts, and found the chief's number. He was about to call it when Oakley said, "What are you doing?"

"I'm calling your boss. Chief Nat Combs knows me well. I've helped him on a couple matters. I have a feeling that when he gets here and looks at what you are refusing to look at that he will be making you *Officer* Oakley again," Bentley said. "Or he may even terminate you. He will be very angry with your failure to do your job on this case."

"You're bluffing. You got nothing. My case is solid. Miss Bingham will be going to prison before I'm through," Oakley said.

Just then, Carter said, "Bentley, you've got to hear this. It's about Harry and Larry Jones's younger brother." He looked pointedly at the Vernal detective. "Harry Jones is the man who kidnapped Susan's cousin, Gina Rogers."

Oakley had a blank look on his face. Susan went white.

"What's happening?" Bentley asked.

"He was released a couple days ago from prison. He called Sheriff Goldman just a few minutes ago and said he had some important information for Detective Parker. So, the sheriff transferred the call to Hank. This guy, Barry Jones, told Hank that he was going to get even with me and you and Hank for letting his big brother get killed," Carter said.

"Did he specify how he would get even?" Bentley asked.

"He said it would be two for two. Two of us would die to make up for Harry's and Elliot's deaths," Carter responded. "He told Hank that he was giving us fair warning, but that we wouldn't see it coming. He would make sure two of us died. And he added that I would be one of the two for making the police in St. George put his other big brother in prison on 'totally bogus' charges."

Bentley chuckled. "I wonder how he knew that Harry and Elliot were dead and that Larry had been arrested."

"I guess we will have to figure it out. But first, why don't we finish with Officer Oakley so that the charges against Susan can be dismissed," Carter suggested.

"One more time, Officer, I'm asking you to look at what we found before you force me to call Nat," Bentley said. "And yes, Nat and I are on a first-name basis. Let's go in the kitchen and we can take care of your concerns over this case, and you won't have to face the wrath of your boss."

"I'm not concerned, but you guys ought to be. It sounds like someone is out to get you. I'm not surprised at that," the cocky young detective said as he ran his hands through his dark-red hair. "You probably have it coming."

"How can you say that?" Susan practically screamed. "My cousin is missing. These men are working hard to get her back home. Their lives are threatened now because they're doing their jobs. You are disgraceful. I didn't embezzle anything, and you would know that if you weren't so arrogant and lazy. They found the proof, and you are too thickheaded to even look at it. Please, Detective Radford, call Chief Combs."

Bentley already had him on the line. Everyone in the room heard him say, "Chief Combs, it is very important that you come to the apartment of Miss Susan Bingham. Detective Oakley is here now, and he is refusing to look at the evidence that Detective Keefe and I have found that exonerates Miss Bingham."

Bentley listened for a moment, and then he said, "Thanks, Nat. We'll see you in a few minutes."

"You faked that call," Detective Oakley said. "You can't fool me. I'm out of here."

"Your chief is not happy. He told me to tell you to wait for him to come. So, I'm telling you to wait," Bentley said.

"And I'm telling you to stuff it. I hope that guy that's after you guys finds you! You are disgraceful," Oakley said, his green eyes flashing with anger. With that, he walked out, slamming Susan's door behind him.

"Susan, I did not fake that call. But there is one thing I did that I didn't tell you I was doing."

"What's that, Detective?"

Bentley pulled a small recorder from his pocket. "I started this recording as soon as Oakley came in the door. He has no idea what he has done to himself. I am going to insist that Chief Combs listens to this. He's a good man, and I know that he will deal with his officer appropriately."

As soon as Chief Nat Combs arrived, he looked at the evidence that the two capable PIs had found. He agreed that Susan was totally exonerated. "I promise you, Susan," Chief Combs said, "that I will get the charge against you dismissed first thing in the morning. I'll show the prosecutor what these men found and ask him to dismiss the charges. He will have no choice but to do that. Then I will assign an experienced detective to figure out who actually stole the money. From what I just read, I have a pretty good idea who it is, and so do you and these men. But I'll let a detective prove that."

"We could do it, Nat, but we are only paid to exonerate her, and we have done that," Bentley said.

"My people will take it from here. You men have done a great job. Susan, do you have a printer that Bentley can use to print this information out for me?" the chief asked, and then he hesitated. "Or better yet, Bentley, would you email those documents to me? It's not Susan's problem to help. She's been wrongly accused," Chief Combs said. "I'm sorry, Miss Bingham. I want to make this right. How can I do that?"

"You could help me keep my job. I was suspended after Detective Oakley arrested me," she said.

"I will do that if I can," Nat said, then he turned back to Bentley. "I see Carter is working on sending all of that to me. While we're waiting, I think you had another concern you wanted to talk to me about."

Once again, Bentley pulled his little recorder out of his jacket pocket. "I started this recording when Rand came in. It will tell you everything that took place. He has made some serious errors in judgment, to say the least."

"Okay, let's hear it."

The chief of police's face was red with anger by the time the recording ended. "I will need that if you can email it to me too. I will not tolerate that kind of behavior in my department. Rand Oakley will no longer be employed by my department after tomorrow morning."

Chapter 31

Darkness had set in by the time Gina woke up. But the room was lit by a large candle. The main room also had a candle burning. She was groggy and in pain. She looked to the side of the bed, where Sammy was sitting. "You're awake," he said. "I have a lot to tell you. So does Doctor Jeremy."

She tried to sit up but couldn't. Jeremy came in and said, "I'll help you up if you need to get up, but you can't put any weight on your foot."

"Is it sprained?" she asked.

"No, there are some broken bones in your foot. I've got it secured now so that it can heal. With Sammy's help, I also made a wooden splint for your arm. I popped the broken bone back in place while you were sleeping," he said.

***

The chief walked to the door a few minutes later, armed with the evidence that his detective had failed to find and further failed to even look at and the recording that had been made while his officer so blatantly shamed himself. He opened the door and then turned back and said, "You men be careful. You are clearly in danger. And do what you can to save Miss Bingham's cousin." Then he left.

Susan thanked them over and over again.

"I will let your attorney know what we found out," Bentley said.

Carter grinned. "I already emailed him the same things that I emailed to Chief Combs. If he wants it, I suppose we can also give him a copy of the recording you made while the officer was here."

Carter opened the door to go out and saw the glint of the sun reflected off an object in a man's hand. The man stood behind an old pickup truck.

Carter dove to the floor as a shot was fired. But he'd been too late. Blood poured from his stomach. Bentley saw the old pickup speeding away. He would have liked to chase it, but Carter needed his immediate attention.

"Call 911!" he shouted to Susan as he dropped to the floor beside his young partner.

Susan already had her phone to her ear. She started to speak to the dispatcher as Bentley ripped open Carter's shirt. He applied pressure to his stomach to stop the bleeding. Carter was groaning with pain, but he made no effort to move. As soon as Susan's 911 call was completed, she joined Bentley beside Carter. "Get me some towels," Bentley said.

She did that, and handed them to Bentley as Chief Nat Combs rushed through the open door. "I was the closest officer," he said. "But more are coming. An ambulance has been dispatched."

"Thanks," Bentley said. "We've got to save Carter."

"Did you happen to see who did this?" Nat asked.

"Yes, but only a short glimpse," Bentley said as he continued to apply pressure to the wound, using one of the towels Susan had handed him. "He was driving a faded blue pickup. An older model. Either a Chevy or GMC. It has Colorado plates. No doubt in my mind that it was Barry Jones, age about thirty-five around six feet tall. He was released from prison in Colorado a couple days ago."

"I'll get it on the air right now," Chief Combs said and rushed from the door to his truck just as a couple of uniformed officers jumped from their parked patrol car and sprinted to the apartment.

Bentley stayed right where he was at, speaking softly to Carter. "You'll be okay. Help is on the way."

Carter didn't respond except to blink his eyes. Bentley knew he was conscious, which gave him a lot of hope. As he continued applying pressure, he silently prayed for his partner. He was using a third blood-soaked towel now.

An ambulance arrived after a couple minutes, and Bentley turned Carter's care over to the EMTs. Chief Combs came back in. "No sign of the blue truck yet. But I wouldn't think he could have gone far. We are calling out all available officers in my department and the sheriff's department. Hopefully we'll catch him."

Bentley wiped his hands on another clean towel and then followed Susan into the kitchen where he washed his hands in the sink. He had blood on his pants and shirt, but he wasn't concerned about that. He was only concerned about Carter.

He called Hank Parker. When the detective answered his cell phone, Bentley said, "Carter's been shot. It's bad. He'll be on his way to the hospital here in Vernal as soon as the EMTs have him stabilized. I think the shooter was Barry Jones."

"Oh, Bentley, I'm so sorry. I'm going to head to Vernal. Tell me what Jones was driving, if you know," Hank said.

Bentley described the truck to Hank. "I'll be at the hospital when you get here."

"You must have been on a case over there," Hank said.

"Gina's cousin, Susan Bingham, was arrested for embezzlement. She didn't do it, and we found the proof. I'll tell you more about it later. They are loading Carter on a stretcher right now. I'll be at the hospital."

He ended the call and turned to Chief Combs. "I'm going to follow the ambulance to the hospital."

***

Gina was fascinated with Jeremy's cabin and outbuildings. He'd carried her outside to the outhouse and then back in and placed her gently on one of the two chairs at the table in the main room. He had something cooking in a frying pan he had set on a screen over the hot coals in the fireplace. "I hope you kids don't mind my cooking. It's been years since I cooked for anyone besides myself."

"We've been eating fish that Gina caught and filleted," Sammy said. "We roasted them over a campfire. It tasted good, but I'm ready for something else."

"I'm impressed," Jeremy said. "I don't have a lot of variety in my diet, but I stay full and healthy. While dinner cooks, why don't you two kids tell me how you ended up having to fend for yourselves out in this vast and dangerous wilderness."

Jeremy listened to every word they spoke as they told him of their terrible ordeal, starting with their kidnapping and everything that happened after that. They paused their storytelling so they could eat their dinner of venison liver, fried mushrooms, some green leafy vegetable, and wild raspberries. It tasted good to both of them.

"I live off the land," Jeremy said with a smile. "Now finish your story."

They did, and Jeremy exclaimed, "Wow! You two are blessed to be alive. But you also proved that you could take care of yourselves in terrible circumstances. I am impressed."

"This is a wonderful place you have here," Gina said. "You must have quite a story to tell, yourself."

"Oh, I don't think you kids would be interested in why I live out here," he said.

"We do want to know about you. Don't we, Sammy?" Gina said as she winced with pain.

"Well, I guess I can tell you. But first, I need to lay you on the bed again and give you something for pain," Jeremy said with concern on his bearded face.

"We still have some Tylenol in the first aid kit we took from my father's plane. It's wrapped up in those blankets," Gina said.

"I have some too, and something stronger that I brought with me into the wilderness. Let's get you comfortable, and then I'll tell you a little about myself, if you really want to hear it," Jeremy said.

A few minutes later, Jeremy told the two young people his story. "I was a successful surgeon in a big hospital in Denver. But I was blamed for the death of a patient by her family. I was blameless in her death. The family, who are prominent and wealthy people, persisted. I was investigated and cleared. The patient's death had nothing to do with her surgery. She had a serious health problem that her family had not been told about. It was proven, but that made no difference to those people. One man, the dead girl's brother, threatened me several times."

"That's awful," Gina said, her head turned toward Jeremy.

"Anger and hatred, even when totally misplaced, can be destructive to innocent people, such as me," he said. "They got so much publicity that my reputation was ruined. Patients refused to let me operate on them. The administration met with me and told me that I was hurting their hospital by not resigning, even though they admitted that I was totally blameless. The family of the dead woman was a large donor to the hospital, and so I was told that for the good of the hospital, I should resign. I had a lot of supporters, but their voices were drowned out by powerful and wealthy friends of the dead woman and her brother's ugly threats. I resigned and applied at other hospitals, but the damage was done, so I finally gave up. My wife left me, even though she knew I was blameless. She said she simply couldn't take the shame. We had no children, so I was alone."

"Why didn't you sue them?" Gina asked.

Jeremy sadly shook his head. "I didn't have the appetite for that. They sued me, but they had nothing to go on, and a judge threw the case out. I moved away from Denver and tried to make a living doing woodwork, which has always been a hobby of mine. I did okay at that, but my enemies found out what I was doing and began to let the people know that I was a dishonest man and they should not buy my work. They even demanded that my medical license be revoked, but that didn't happen because of the proof that I had done nothing medically wrong. So, I am still licensed to practice medicine." Jeremy smiled at his rapt audience of two. "So, you are safe with me caring for you."

They both had tears in their eyes. "I trust you," Gina said. "Thank you for helping me."

"You're welcome," Jeremy said.

"So why did you come here?" little Sammy asked.

"I craved freedom from the influence and threats of my enemies. I sold all my investments, withdrew my money from the banks. Made my ex-wife a generous settlement and left civilization, the very civilization which had been so *uncivilized* to me. My money is hidden in secure places here in the forest where no one could ever find it."

"So you just drove out here and started over?" Gina asked.

"No, I didn't drive. I bought a couple of strong mules and packed what I thought I'd need and simply made myself vanish into the forest. No one knows where I went."

"How did you buy this land?" Gina asked.

He chuckled. "I didn't. I don't own it, but no one knows where I am, and my little homestead is hidden by the trees. I didn't want to be found, and I remained hidden until you two innocent kids found me."

"We didn't find you; you found us," Gina said, her voice breaking.

"I guess you're right. But I'm glad I did. Now, you look like you need to rest. Let me help you out to the outhouse again, and then Sammy and I will let you sleep," he told her.

"Have you never gone back out of the forest?" Sammy asked.

"I have occasionally taken my mules and gone after more supplies. I have a lot of wheat, sugar, salt, beans, ammunition, and other things I felt I would need. Those big mules packed a lot, and so I am set for a long time. On one of the trips, I bought a puppy. Blacky has been my faithful companion for the past three years," Jeremy said. "Now I insist, Gina. Let me help you to the outhouse, and then you can wash your hands and face and rest. Your body has a lot of healing to do."

"Doctor Jeremy, where are your mules?" Sammy asked. "I didn't see them when I was outside."

"They died, and I buried them," he said. "They were old when I bought them. I will buy another one when I go in again. That will be when I help you two go home. But I can't carry both of you, and there is a river to cross. Gina, you must heal first so you can walk. I'm sorry that you will have to wait, but there is no choice."

Tears welled up in Sammy's eyes. "I miss my mom and dad," he said.

"So do I," Gina said. "But I can see that I must be patient."

"I could go in alone and get a mule, but that would mean having to leave you two here alone, and I can't do that," he said.

"I would be afraid without you," Sammy said.

"You two are brave. I have never known such courage as you have. Okay, Gina, let me carry you to the outhouse. Tomorrow, Sammy and I will make you some nice crutches. Even with your broken arm, you will be able to get around a little bit using just one of the crutches," Jeremy said.

"I will help you too," Sammy said. "I love you, Gina. And I love you too, Doctor Jeremy."

Gina saw the big man wipe tears from his eyes. She knew that she could trust him, and she would. She wished there was a way to let her family know she was alive and taken care of. And she wished she could let Carter know. She missed him terribly. She hoped he was okay.

Chapter 32

CARTER WAS NOT OKAY—FAR FROM IT. A TEAM OF DOCTORS WORKED for hours to repair the damage a would-be killer had inflicted on him. He awoke, and for a moment, he wondered where he was. But it only took him a minute to realize he was in a hospital bed.

"You're awake, Carter," a sweet voice said to him. He turned his head and was surprised to see Maya at his bedside. Her eyes were red from crying.

"Why are you here?" he asked.

"Two reasons, Carter. First, because Gina would want me to be, since she can't be here."

"What is the other reason?" he asked.

"Hank and Bentley and my dad want me to be here while the police look for the horrible man who shot you. There are two policemen outside the door to your room. They will be there until they catch him."

"You don't have to be here," Carter said. He suddenly convulsed with pain. He couldn't speak for a moment. Finally, he made a great effort. "Did you say I was shot?"

"You don't remember?" she asked.

"I don't," he said. Again, he waited for some pain to pass. "Who shot me?"

"Detective Parker told me that it was a younger brother of the man who kidnapped Gina and the man you helped the police in St. George catch and put in jail," she explained.

"Harry and Larry—them, I remember. Wait, I am remembering a little now. They have a brother, Barry," Carter said.

"Yes. He's the one who shot you."

Carter concentrated for a moment. "I remember a little now. Bentley and I helped Gina's cousin, Susan, who had been falsely accused of a serious crime. I walked to the door." He closed his eyes. "That was when I was shot, wasn't it?"

"Yes, it was," Maya said.

"Maya, I'm remembering more. Hank and Bentley are both in danger."

"Yes, they are."

"So are you," he said, gritting his teeth against the intense pain in his belly.

"That's why I'm here. The police are protecting both of us. You are in a lot of pain, aren't you?"

"What time is it?" Carter asked.

She looked at the clock on the wall. "It's four o'clock in the morning. The doctors operated on you for about eight hours."

"Maya, tell me the truth. Am I going to die?"

She laid a hand on one of his arms. "No, you are not. I promise you that. I'm going to ring for a nurse. You need more pain medicine."

"I'm worried about Gina and Sammy," he said, fighting the pain.

"I'm worried too," Maya said.

"I keep praying that they are safe," he said. "I hate knowing they are still not found."

"We have to have hope and faith," Maya said with a choke in her voice.

"I'm trying," Carter said as another wave of intense pain struck him.

A nurse entered the room, and Maya stepped back before saying, "He's in a lot of pain."

***

Carter was not the only one in pain. The pain pills Doctor Jeremy had given Gina had worn off. Her arm and her foot were both throbbing. But she didn't want to disturb Jeremy. She knew he was sleeping beside Sammy on bear hides in the main room. The door between them was open, and she knew they would hear her if she called out. But she chose not to.

She would endure the pain until Jeremy woke up. So instead of disturbing him, she called on her Heavenly Father, for He was always there. She prayed for her pain to be tolerable.

Gina remembered swearing Maya to secrecy just before she had been kidnapped. She'd told her that she was falling in love with Carter, but that eighteen was too young to fall in love. She knew what she felt, though, and her feelings for Carter never left her.

She didn't know what would happen about the fact that she'd missed graduating from high school. She supposed that something would work out once she got home. But that was, at best, weeks away. She knew that if Jeremy could get her and Sammy out of the forest and the mountains to a town that he would. She believed him when he told her why he couldn't do that. She simply had to wait, be patient, and be grateful that she was alive.

Jeremy stepped into the room. "You are probably in a lot of pain again, aren't you?"

"I am," she said. "But I didn't want to disturb you."

"Gina," he said with a stern tone to his voice, "You are my patient now. There is nothing more important to me than helping you get well. When you are in too much pain, you don't heal well. So please, don't ever neglect to tell me when you need me."

"Thank you," she said. "You are a blessing to me. I would have died if you hadn't found me."

"Yes, you would have, but I can tell that you are a spiritual girl. I know you must pray a lot. I believe in God too. And I am comforted by Him whenever I think about the injustice that was done to me," he said. "I also want you to know that you and Sammy are a blessing to me. I thank God that I could help you. I just wish I could get both of you reunited with your families soon. But you must understand that I can only get you out of this place when you can walk again. I'm sorry. There are many, many difficult miles between us and any civilization. I'm sure you understand how rugged this area is."

"Yes, we do," she said. "I do pray, and so does Sammy."

Jeremy left for a moment and came back with a couple more pain pills and a cup of water. He helped her take them by gently lifting her head so she could drink. He let her down again and stood by, watching her.

After a moment, he said, "I never knew why I brought so many medical supplies with me to this place. I have never been sick, and I didn't think I'd need the things I brought for myself. Now I know. God knew you would be coming to me and that you would need my help. Gina, I believe in miracles. The fact that you and Sammy survived the plane crash and that those evil men who abducted you died is a miracle."

"Yes, it is," she agreed. "And you finding us is a miracle."

Jeremy studied her a moment longer in the dim light from the small candle. After a moment, he said, "You are a beautiful young lady. I think that there is a young man who is in love with you. Let me guess, Carter Keefe is more to you than just a private investigator who is looking for you."

"Yes, he is the most wonderful man in the world. I don't know how he feels, but I know that I love him."

She closed her eyes for a moment. Jeremy continued to stand there by her bed, a giant of a man who towered above her. "You're worried about him, aren't you?" he asked perceptively.

"Yes, I am worried about him. I don't like that he is worrying about me."

"He'll be okay. Somehow, I feel that he loves you as much as you love him. Now, I'll let you go back to sleep." With that, Jeremy touched her forehead ever so lightly, turned, and left the room.

Gina fell asleep in a few minutes, feeling some relief after the talk she'd had with Jeremy.

Chapter 33

Barry Jones felt quite certain that the bullet he'd fired at the young man who had started to leave the apartment had killed him. He knew the moment he saw him that he was Carter Keefe, one of the detectives responsible for Harry's death. He also knew that it was because of him that Larry had been arrested and thrown in jail. Keefe had paid for his treachery. Now Barry needed to destroy one of the other detectives. He didn't care which one, but one of them had to die. Two for two was just, in his mind.

He also needed to do one more thing before he left this area. He wanted a woman to live with, a young one. Barry had done his research. The girl that Harry and Elliot had kidnapped was Gina Rogers. She may have survived the plane crash, but there was no way she could still be alive in the forest and mountains where the crash had occurred. If he thought she was, he'd wait until she was found, and then he'd take her. Elliot would like that, he thought. It only seemed right to his perverse mind.

However, since he was certain that she would never be found, he would love to have the pretty girl who was Gina's best friend. Yes, Maya Warwick would make a fine companion for him. He would find a way to catch her and make her his very own. But he would not let himself be killed like Elliot had. He licked his lips as he sat in the stolen truck where he'd been trying to sleep.

He'd been lucky when he figured out that the two PIs were working a case involving a girl by the name of Susan. Ordinarily, he would not have felt like it was luck when he was almost hit by an unmarked police car. The driver of that car pulled him over and blamed him for nearly hitting him. The guy had said his name was Detective Oakley, and he'd already had a bad day because of a couple of PIs who had interfered in a case he was working.

Detective Oakley had said that he would teach Keefe and Radford a lesson. He'd said he didn't have time to write a ticket right now, that he had things to do. Barry had asked him where the two PIs were at. The cop had asked him why he wanted to know. Barry had told him that he was going to take care of those two when he found them.

"How do you plan to take care of them?" Oakley had asked.

Barry had answered, "In a way that will make it so they won't bother you anymore. Tell me where they're at."

The officer had given him an address. "Good luck, Mr. Jones. Those men are nothing but trouble."

Barry had responded by saying, "You have no idea how much trouble those men have caused me. I'll make them wish they hadn't messed with my family."

He still couldn't believe his luck. The officer had said cheerfully, "Have a good day," then winked at him before turning to his police car and driving off.

***

Detective Rand Oakley sat in his patrol car on a road a long way outside of the city. He'd thrown up twice. He knew that he'd made a terrible mistake. The two PIs were wrong about Susan. She was a thief. They were worthless, but they didn't deserve to die. He wasn't that kind of person. At least, he hadn't thought that he was.

He'd followed the white car and stopped when it did, a hundred feet or so behind it. He had no idea that the man had meant to do more than just scare the PIs. He'd been shocked when the guy had shot Detective Keefe as he was leaving Susan's place. He was almost certain the PI had died. And Rand knew that part of the blame was his.

He finally put his car in gear and drove home. He hoped he hadn't been seen leaving Susan's neighborhood. As hard as it was for him to admit, he'd made a mistake. He should have written a citation to the guy in the white car. But then, he reasoned, it might have been him who was shot. He went into his apartment and pulled out a bottle of whiskey he'd bought a couple days ago but hadn't touched yet. He proceeded to erase his feeling of guilt by drinking the whiskey.

***

The next morning, a phone call from Chief Nat Combs's secretary summoned Detective Oakley to the department to meet with the chief. His head was aching terribly, and he felt sick all over. He'd had way too much whiskey. He told the secretary that he wasn't feeling well, that he would see the chief the next day. Her response shook him. She said that the chief wanted him to come in right then. She hung up on him, and he sat with his head in his hands, wondering what the chief wanted.

Surely, he reasoned, he hadn't been seen near Susan's apartment when the stupid guy in the white car had killed Detective Keefe. He was worried. He didn't know what else it could be. He knew in his mind that he was right about Susan's guilt, so it couldn't be that. So, what could it be?

He cleaned up as best he could, used mouthwash to try to hide the smell of stale alcohol on his breath, and went out to his patrol car. When he arrived at the police station, the chief's secretary told him to go right in, that the chief was expecting him. She didn't even look up at him.

Rand entered Chief Combs's office. "Come sit down, Rand," the chief said.

He did as he was told. The chief stared at him for a minute or more without saying a thing. Finally, he asked, "Did you drive here?"

"Yes, sir, I did," Rand said, wondering what kind of question that was.

He soon found out. "You have been drinking, Rand," he said. "I'm going to have you escorted to the jail for a breath test. You'd better not be over .05. Go wait outside my office."

Rand was worried now. He was sure that he had drunk so much that the alcohol would not all be out of his system. A uniformed officer drove him to the jail a moment later and advised him of his rights regarding the test. Then he administered it.

Once the test was finished, he was driven back to the police department where he was escorted into the chief's office. Once again, he sat down and the chief said, "I got the results from your breath test. Once again, I'm asking if you drove here to the department from your apartment."

Rand was getting mad. "You know I did. But I only came in because you told me to. I tried to get the secretary to let me come in tomorrow, but she told me you wanted me right away."

"That's right, I did," Chief Combs said. "But you knew better than to drive while under the influence. I'm placing you under arrest for driving while under the influence of alcohol. Another officer will take over on that as soon as we are finished here."

"Why did you make me come in?" Rand asked angrily. "I haven't done anything wrong."

Chief Combs shook his head, and anger shot from in his eyes. "You most definitely have. The PIs have irrefutable evidence that Susan Bingham did not commit the crime you arrested her for."

"That's not right," Rand said angrily. "I have a good case."

"You don't have a case at all. Now, let's talk about what you and the PIs talked about."

"I told them they were wrong, and they are," Rand said.

"Is that all that you said?" the chief asked.

"Pretty much," he responded.

Chief Combs pulled his phone from his pocket and waved it in front of Rand. "Detective Bentley recorded everything that was said while you were there. And that's not all. I had the neighborhood canvased. We have two witnesses that saw you follow a white car back to Miss Bingham's house and stop a short distance back. Then you drove off as soon as the driver of that white car shot one of the detectives. It gets worse for you. One of Miss Bingham's neighbors saw you talking to the man who shot the PI a short time before the shooting. He followed you and watched you park near Susan's apartment. Would you like to explain what you said to the man who shot Detective Keefe?"

Rand knew he was in huge trouble. "I want to talk to a lawyer," he said in a choked voice.

"That's a good idea. You're going to need one. But you are going to tell us who you were talking to at some point. Charges are being drawn up by the city attorney. You'll have those charges read to you later. For now, I am notifying you that you are fired. You no longer work for the Vernal City Police Department. Now, get out of my office. An officer is waiting to take you into custody and seize your badge, ID, and weapon, as well as the keys to your patrol car."

Rand's legs turned to jelly. He staggered to the door and opened it. Before he stepped out, Chief Combs said, "You'd better pray that Detective Keefe doesn't die."

***

Chief Combs visited Carter at the hospital that afternoon. "How are you feeling?" he asked.

"I've been better," Carter said with a smile. "It could have been worse."

"Yes, it could have," the chief agreed. "We hope to catch that guy before he tries to do more damage."

"It was Barry Jones," Carter said with a grimace. "I remember now that I caught a glimpse of his face at the same time I saw the sun reflect off his pistol. I'd studied pictures of him, and anyway, he looks a lot like his older brothers."

"We have officers all over Utah and Colorado looking for him," the chief said.

"I wish I could help. I wonder how he knew where we were at," Carter said.

"That's one of the reasons I came to see you, Detective. He was told where to find you by my former officer, Rand Oakley."

"Former?"

"Yes, I fired him this morning. He's in jail with a very high bond. I had no idea he would ever do something like that."

"How did he know Barry Jones?"

"It seems that it was all a matter of luck of sorts. At least, the shooter probably thought it was luck. Anyway, a witness saw them talking. Rand admitted to one of my detectives that Barry had nearly hit him with his car. He pulled him over, and apparently the two got to talking. Rand told him where you were at, and he followed him to Miss Bingham's apartment. He was seen there by two others besides the witness who saw the two of them talking. Rand is being charged as an accessory to the attempt on your life."

Carter stared at the chief for a moment before speaking. "Why would he do that?" he finally asked.

"He admitted that he was angry with you and your partner for trying to prove he was wrong about Miss Bingham. When he was interviewed, with an attorney representing him, he said he had no idea that Barry meant to kill you. He thought he was just going to do something to scare you."

"We've got to catch him. He sounds like he has a screw loose. He's dangerous," Carter observed.

"We will have a couple of officers at your door. You aren't going anywhere for a while. You need time to heal."

"I know you're right. Thanks for coming to see me."

"You are very welcome, Detective. You rest and leave the hunt for Barry Jones to the rest of us."

Chapter 34

BARRY JONES WAS HIDING OUT IN COLORADO, AND HE WAS ANGRY. He'd learned from a news report on the radio that the PI he'd shot was still alive. That would change. He would wait until a few days had passed, and then he'd return to Utah and finish the job he'd started. In addition, he would snatch the pretty Warwick girl. He hadn't planned beyond that, but he would after he had taken his revenge against the officers and had the girl with him.

In his mind, he believed that he would never be caught. His time in prison had taught him some things. He knew how to avoid capture. He was invincible. Or so he thought.

***

The days passed slowly for Gina. The crutches Jeremy had made for her helped her get around. It was awkward because she could only use one arm with the other one in a splint. The man she loved was never far from her mind. She hoped he was doing okay, and that he wasn't worrying too much about her. She wished there was a way to let him know that she was safe and being cared for by a doctor.

She enjoyed sitting on the deck watching Sammy play with Blacky while Jeremy worked. She was amazed at how hard Jeremy worked. He cut wood and stacked it beneath the trees and in a shed and some on the deck. She helped him cook meals and enjoyed stories he told of wildlife he'd hunted. Sometimes he told her about cases he handled as a surgeon.

"Jeremy, it's sad that people no longer have you to care for them. Do you miss it?" she asked one evening as they were making dinner.

"Yes, I miss it," he said. "But I have a good life here. I'll be honest with you, though. I'll miss you and Sammy when you are no longer with me." He smiled at her. "I didn't realize how lonely I was. You two have been a balm to my lonely soul."

"You are such a good man," she said.

Sammy, who had been sitting at the table drawing, said, "I miss my family, but I will miss you as much as I do them when we are able to go home. And I'll miss you, Gina."

"We'll have great memories, and I'll always be able to remember the two of you with the pictures you have drawn for me. You are an amazing artist, Sammy. You will bless lots of lives with your art," Jeremy said sincerely.

They spent many contented hours in the evenings. They learned a lot from Jeremy. But despite how much Gina enjoyed Jeremy's company, she missed her family more with each passing day. She missed Carter too. She thought of him constantly and prayed for him.

***

A full month had passed since Carter had been shot. He was feeling fairly strong and was able to work with Bentley on several minor cases that came their way. They had not seen or heard from Barry Jones since that fateful day. Carter was constantly vigilant, as were Hank and Bentley. They all worried that Barry would return in the near future, and Carter was quite certain that when he came back, he would be disguised and hard to recognize.

Carter had attended church that Sunday morning. Gina's family, Maya and her family, Bentley and his wife and nephew, and Hank and his family were all there that day. Maya's family had invited them all to dinner that afternoon. Gina's mother had already offered to help her prepare the dinner.

They all enjoyed the time together, but Gina was on everyone's mind. They all still held out hope that she and Sammy would be found and returned to them. But it was getting harder every day. Reality was that it wasn't likely for her and Sammy to still be alive after this long in the wilderness. But not one of the group of close friends was willing to give up hope.

Carter had been in touch with the police in St. George and Hurricane on a regular basis since he'd been injured. He got a call on his cell phone as they were all visiting in the Warwicks' living room.

"It's Chief Childers," he said before accepting the call and stepping from the room.

"I'm glad you're healing," Chief Childers said after the two had chatted for a while. "My question now is this: Are you strong enough to travel? We need you in court on Wednesday. I know that only gives you a short time to come down here."

"I can make it," Carter said.

"Good, I was going to call you tomorrow. I'm sorry to bother you today with it being Sunday and all. I wasn't sure you were needed, but the prosecutor's office has been working hard on the cases against Larry. I got a call from the lead prosecutor just minutes ago. He said they just decided they had to have you and asked me to call you," Chief Childers said. He then explained that it was Larry's defense attorney who caused a problem that morning.

"He's been a real jerk," Childers said. "He has been like this for days now, and he doesn't care who he inconveniences. In fact, he seems to delight in it. Again, I'm sorry to bother you on Sunday, but I wanted to give you as much lead time as possible." The two men talked for a while about what the defense attorney was up to and what Carter would need to testify about.

"It's fine. I'll be able to come. I'm doing a lot better," Carter said.

After the call, he returned to the living room. All eyes were on him as he walked in. "What did he need?" Bentley asked.

"There is a hearing for Larry Jones on Wednesday morning," Carter said. "The chief hated to bother me on Sunday, but apparently the defense attorney is trying to irritate the prosecutor. Chief Childers wanted to give me as much time as possible to go through my notes. He could have called tomorrow, but since they had all been inconvenienced by the prosecutor, he decided to let me know today. I'll drive down tomorrow afternoon so I can meet with them on Tuesday."

"Are you sure you are up to that?" Gina's mother asked.

"I can do it. I'm feeling pretty good," he responded.

"I'm going with you," Maya announced. "I can do a lot of the driving."

"That's a good idea," her father said. "What time do you plan to leave in the morning?"

"Probably about nine," Carter said.

"I'll be ready," Maya said.

"I was going to volunteer, but if Maya is going with you, I won't need to," Bentley said.

***

Carter and Maya were not the only ones planning to travel on Monday. Barry Jones was going to drive to Duchesne the next day. He'd waited long enough, and the longer he'd waited, the angrier he'd become. He would get his revenge and grab the girl . He would not be stopped. He looked different now than he did. His hair was longer and bleached blond. He also had a beard that was bleached blond. He had stolen a pickup from the long-term parking lot at the airport in Denver. He didn't think it would be missed for several days.

So he struck out for the little town of Duchesne, Utah. He had a mission of vengeance to complete, and he was determined to do so. He drove the speed limit and made sure he obeyed all the traffic laws. He didn't want to give any hotshot cop a reason to pull him over. He'd gotten lucky with the cop in Vernal, but he didn't delude himself. That would never happen again.

***

Maya asked Carter what the defense attorney in St. George had cooked up.

"I'm not sure. I think it has something to do with me being a private investigator and not a police officer," he responded.

"You didn't arrest anyone or talk to Larry on the phone when he set up the drop. And you didn't go to the drop," she said. "What you did was help them, wasn't it?"

"That's right. I think what I'm going to need to testify about is what, exactly, I did do. I did nothing illegal. I did what the officers asked me to do."

"You are pretty good with computers," she said. "You have the right to investigate anything or anyone as long as you don't hack into sites the public isn't supposed to get into. Am I right?"

"Yes, you are exactly right," Carter responded. He looked over at her and grinned. "I could if I wanted to."

"Wait, you know how to hack into things you shouldn't?" she asked with a scowl.

"I could," he said.

"Carter, you didn't hack to find anything in Larry's case, did you?" she asked.

"I didn't," he said. He grinned at her again. "If I did, I know how to cover my tracks. I wouldn't get caught. But no, I got all the information legally."

"You had me worried for a minute," she said with a sigh. "Are you feeling okay? Do you need me to drive for a while?"

"Yes, I do, actually" he said. "We'll stop at the next exit, and you can take over."

Ten minutes later, Maya was driving, and Carter had the passenger seat back as far as it would go and he tried to go to sleep. He eventually dozed off. When he woke up, it was because his phone was ringing. Since it was synced to his truck, the sound came through his speakers.

He powered his seat up. "Hello, Chief Childers."

"Hello, Detective Keefe," the chief responded. "Are you on your way?"

"We're almost at Richfield," he said.

"We?" Chief Childers asked. "Who do you have with you?"

"Maya Warwick is with me again. She's driving right now."

"Will you call me when you get close to Hurricane? I want to talk with you for a little while. I want to make sure I understand what you can testify to. When we meet with the prosecutor tomorrow, we need to be able to let him know exactly what to expect from your testimony and mine."

"No problem," Carter said.

"Excellent. Tell Miss Warwick hi for me."

Maya spoke up. "I can hear you. Carter's phone is synced to his truck. Hi to you too."

"I'm glad you could come down with him," Chief Childers said. "I was worried about him driving with his injuries. I wondered if his partner might come with him."

"He would have, but he didn't need to since I wanted to come with him again," Maya said.

"I guess your friend and Sammy Anders are still missing."

"I'm afraid so," Maya said. "We've all been so worried."

"So are Sammy's parents. I talk to them frequently.

"We are trying hard to have faith. We are not giving up hope. Wherever they are right now, I am praying that they are okay," Carter said. That was all he could say, but he got a knot in his stomach thinking about it.

Chapter 35

GINA WAS ABLE TO USE HER ARM A LITTLE BIT. JEREMY HAD TOLD HER earlier that it was healing faster than he could have hoped. She was able to get around well now using both crutches. And her foot didn't hurt very much as long as she was careful not to put any weight on it.

All three of them were sitting out on the deck watching rain pour down. It had been raining for three straight hours. "This isn't as bad as the day we were under the cliff," Gina said with a grin.

"It should stop soon," Jeremy told the kids.

"I feel safe here with it raining like this," she said.

"We were scared that day," Sammy said. "But it is kind of fun watching it rain and seeing the lightning and hearing the thunder. I feel safe too."

"Lightning won't hit your trees, will it?" Gina asked as a particularly bright flash of lightning lit up the sky and thunder sounded terribly loud.

"I took some precautions when I selected the site to build my cabin. I wanted to be able to hide it and all my buildings under trees, but if you haven't noticed, there are some much taller trees surrounding my homestead. If lightning gets too close, it will most likely strike one of those taller trees," Jeremy said. "I haven't had any problems so far, and there have been a lot of storms as bad as this one or worse."

After another hour, the storm moved out and the sun began to shine.

"That was a nice storm," Jeremy said. "It's been fun watching and listening to it with you two and Blacky for company. It doesn't seem to bother him. When I first got him, he was scared of the thunder, but he's used to it now."

***

Barry Jones had located the Warwick house where the girl he planned to kidnap lived. He'd also found where Detective Sergeant Hank Parker and his family lived. He already knew where Detective Carter Keefe's apartment was, but he hadn't driven past it in a month. As he drove by, he noted that Carter's truck was nowhere to be seen.

He'd been successful in finding approximately where Detective Radford lived. It was in a remote area of the county west of Duchesne. It was going to be more difficult to find, but Barry knew that with his higher-than-normal intelligence, it would not be much of a problem.

He parked the stolen truck in an abandoned trailer park. He was trying to decide in which order to take care of his tasks. Grabbing the girl, Maya, would have to be last. He needed the detectives out of the way before he snatched her from her house in the middle of the night. He would need to leave town immediately upon putting her in his pickup with him.

Originally, he planned to take out two of the three detectives. His reasoning was that he'd lost two family members because of them. But now it was three for three since his Uncle Larry was in jail and would probably go to prison. Having experienced prison life, Barry considered that to be a fate nearly as bad as death. He'd hated being in prison, and that was why all three now had to go.

He assumed that Carter Keefe was still in the hospital. For all he knew, the young PI might not live. He'd find out if he was still alive after he'd found and eliminated the other two. So now, which should he find first, the deputy or the other PI? He decided after thinking for long enough to consume a bottle of beer. Bentley Radford would be next. His reasoning was that he would be an easy mark since he lived out in the sticks.

He knew about where to go, so he headed there. He assumed he could find a neighbor who would point him in the right direction. He drove out of town on the highway and turned off where he believed the road was that would eventually lead him to the detective's home. He hadn't realized how many roads branched off the road he'd turned onto from the highway. He chose one at random only to discover that it branched off as well. It was all really quite confusing.

Luck intervened. A white van passed him. He knew exactly what it was when he saw Fed Ex printed on the side. It was delivering packages, and he reasoned the driver would know where most people lived in the area. He turned around and followed the van until it turned into a long driveway with a house at the end.

Barry waited, and in a few minutes, it was on its way out. He pulled out his phone and looked at as if he was studying something on it. When the Fed Ex truck reached him, he waved at the driver, indicating he needed help. The driver stopped and leaned from his open door. "You lost, mister?" he asked with a grin. "It's an easy thing to do out here. Are you looking for someone?"

"Yes, a friend of mine lives somewhere in these parts. I have something for him. I was about to call him and ask for directions," Barry lied.

"What's your friend's name?"

"Bentley Radford."

"Yeah, hard place to find," the driver said. "Let me draw you a little map on some notebook paper. The Radfords live at the end of the road they are on. No one else is close to them."

"That would be helpful. I'm embarrassed. Bentley gave me directions, but I didn't write them down." In a couple of minutes, he had a map in hand. "Thanks. This will help," Barry said. "I'm from Wyoming and don't get down this way much." He hoped that if he gave the wrong state, the driver would pass that detail on, if he were questioned.

"Good luck. Tell Bentley hello for me. I deliver to him occasionally. He's a nice guy. His wife is a pretty woman and real nice. The kid who lives with them seems like a good kid." With that, the Fed Ex driver left, leaving a trail of dust behind him.

Ten minutes later, Barry pulled up to a heavy steel gate with no way to drive around it. He cursed. Apparently the Radfords didn't like people visiting.

***

When Bentley got the notice on his phone that someone was at the gate, he quickly accessed the gate camera on his phone. The image was of a fairly new model of pickup with a man in the driver seat. He enlarged the picture. The man did not look familiar, with a blond beard and blond hair. *Wait,* he thought. The shape of the face was right for Barry Jones!

Bentley knew exactly what was up. Barry was coming after him. He called to his wife and nephew. "You guys stay in the house but grab your guns. We have an unwelcome visitor at the gate. I'm going to try to get around him. Call Hank Parker and tell him that Barry Jones is here. He's driving a decent pickup. It looks like it could be green. Stolen, I'm sure."

By the time Bentley had finished his instructions to them, he was armed with a rifle and sidearm and was going out the back door. He locked it behind him and began to circle around toward the gate, knowing Jones could not see him. He moved quickly. This was the man who had nearly killed his partner, Carter Keefe. He wanted to capture him without giving the man a chance to shoot at him.

***

Barry felt like Radford had set a trap. He was almost certain that there was a camera somewhere near, even though he couldn't see one. He put the truck in reverse and backed around so quickly that he hit a tree on the side of the road. Even though it damaged the truck, it didn't stop him. He just put the transmission in drive and completed the turn. He sped down the road. He heard the report of a rifle shot. He felt it strike his truck. He jammed the accelerator to the floor just as another shot was fired. He felt as well as heard a back tire blow.

Barry ducked. Radford was apparently a good shot. The next round could go through his head. But no third shot sounded. He kept driving despite knowing that a back tire was blown. He made no effort to go back the way he'd come. He started making random turns. He assumed that he would eventually make his way back to the highway, but before he did, he needed to steal another vehicle since Radford had seen this one.

***

Bentley knew he'd hit the truck twice. The first round hit the tailgate and probably penetrated the back seat. Despite the dust Jones was kicking up, he could see clearly where to shoot through his scope. His second shot blew out the left rear tire. He knew that he could hit the driver, but that was not his intention. He did not attempt to fire again.

He accepted a call from Detective Sergeant Hank Parker when it came through. "Are you okay, Bentley?"

"I'm fine. Barry got away, but he can't go far. I took out his left rear tire."

"I'm on my way, and so are at least three other officers. Make sure your wife and nephew are safe."

"They are. I'm going to get my truck and head after him. He can't be going very fast."

"Be careful. This man already shot your partner. We don't want him to get you too," Hank cautioned.

Bentley ran back to the house, told his wife what he was doing, and reminded her to make sure she and his nephew didn't leave the cabin. "Keep the doors locked. He's gone, but I don't want you to take any chances. I'm going after him."

Bentley jumped in his truck and sped to the gate. He opened it remotely and then shut it behind him after he sped through. He followed the thin trail of dust that was being thrown up by the crippled pickup. Bentley couldn't imagine that it was going very fast.

There was always the possibility of Jones attempting to ambush him. That's what he would do if the situation were reversed. So, he kept a sharp eye out. As long as there was a trail of dust, he wasn't too concerned because that meant the would-be killer was still trying to get away. The dust became heavier. Bentley was closing in on Jones.

He became ever more alert. Jones had taken several turns. He was, it seemed, trying to simply get away. But there was no way he could go far. The blown tire had disintegrated. Jones was driving on the rim now. Bentley negotiated a turn that he knew was followed by a long straight stretch. He had long ago familiarized himself with the area and knew every turn and every road as well as all the lanes that led to homes. He knew which homes were lived in year-round and which were only occasionally in use.

Barry Jones's damaged pickup was now in sight. Bentley was closing in fast. He was especially alert, thinking that Jones might decide to stop and start shooting. And that's exactly what he did. The pickup slid sideways, and Barry was out of it before it had come to a complete stop. He had a rifle. But he'd shot Carter with a pistol.

Bentley was not surprised. He hit his brakes just as Jones began to shoot. His windshield disintegrated as he slid to a stop and bailed from his truck, his rifle in his hand. The next shot hit Bentley's truck right in the front, and his radiator began spewing steam. Bentley didn't fire until he'd scampered behind a large juniper tree. A bullet struck the tree in front of him.

He peeked around the tree at ground level and fired a shot that kicked up dust inches behind Barry, who was fleeing on foot. Where the gangster had stopped there was a lane to the right. Bentley knew who owned the property. They only occasionally visited their cabin.

Bentley fired another round and Jones, who was zigzagging back and forth, went down face first. He was only down for a few seconds before he got back up, fired a quick shot at Bentley which wasn't even close. Jones was limping as Bentley got him in his scope again, but before he could fire, the landowner came running up the lane with a rifle. He was directly in Bentley's line of fire.

He had no choice but to hold his fire. Jones fired at the landowner who went down in a heap on the ground. The cabin was only about a hundred feet away from where the man went down. Jones kept going, limping but still moving at a good pace. Bentley's concern now was for the landowner. He prayed the man was alive as he ran toward him.

A white jeep was parked in front of the cabin. Jones jumped in it. Apparently, the landowner had left his key in the jeep, because Jones started it and drove around the house. Bentley groaned, because he knew there was another lane out that way. He dropped beside the landowner and assessed the injury to him. He'd been shot in the right thigh, and it was bleeding badly.

Bentley's phone was ringing. He put one hand on the injured man's wound, dropped his rifle, and accepted the call with his free hand. "Hank, there's a man down. He's bleeding badly." He described the location and then said, "Jones is leaving the property to the south in a white Jeep. My truck is disabled. I shot Jones in the left leg. I don't think it's more than a flesh wound."

Chapter 36

Hank made sure the other officers knew the shooter's location and the fact that he was now in a white jeep. No one was close to the location. As soon as he'd done that, he called for an ambulance for the injured landowner. He was frustrated, angry, and worried. This fourth Jones man was a bad one, reckless and deadly.

Knowing Bentley was busy giving aid to the injured man, Hank called Bentley's wife, made sure she and the boy were okay, and said, "Kamryn, Bentley is fine but he's giving aid to a man who Jones shot. Jones is driving a white stolen jeep now. I can't imagine that he will go back to your place, but we can't be sure, so be very careful."

"Okay," Kamryn said. "Cedric and I will be vigilant."

"If Jones happens to come there, call me, and shoot the guy if you feel threatened," Hank said. "Bentley's truck is disabled. I'm assuming Jones got a bullet or two in it." He terminated the call and got back on the radio, checking on the location of the other officers.

So far, no one had seen the stolen white jeep. It was likely that Barry went west, and if so, there would be no officers to see him for there were none in that direction for fifty miles—more officers from Wasatch County were asked to come east, toward Duchesne, but he didn't know if that was happening or not. From Hank's experience with past cases, it was unlikely that Barry Jones would keep that jeep for long. Someone else would lose a car, and he prayed that when that happened, there were not further injuries or, especially, loss of life.

Hank's priority was to get to Bentley's location. He knew he could be there long before an ambulance from Duchesne could. He might be able to assist Bentley in giving aid to the poor guy who had been shot. He had another thought. Bentley's pickup and Barry's stolen one both needed to be towed. So, as he sped toward where Bentley was at, he asked the dispatcher to send two wreckers.

Shortly after he had accomplished that he reached Bentley's truck. It was blocking most of the road, and he had to drive around it. He handled it okay, but he wasn't sure the ambulance could. A short distance ahead, the stolen pickup was also blocking most of the road. Once again, he was able to get around it, but an ambulance probably couldn't.

He drove on to where Bentley was still on the lane to the injured man's cabin. A third person was there, a woman. Bentley assumed it was the injured landowner's wife. That proved to be correct. She was wringing her hands and wanting to help Bentley nurse her husband. Bentley said, "Please go get a couple of wet towels and a couple of dry ones."

She scurried away to do his bidding. "How is he?" Hank asked as soon as the man's wife was out of earshot.

"It could have been much worse. I think it may have barely missed an artery. That would have been a disaster, but I've been able to pretty much stop the bleeding," Bentley said as he continued to apply pressure. "There's a first aid kit in my truck."

"I have one, and my truck is right here," Hank said. He retrieved it and began to help Bentley. The victim's wife returned with the towels as requested. She knelt next to her husband's head and put a hand on his forehead. He was unconscious but she spoke quietly and lovingly to him anyway. Hank was touched by her love and concern.

"We have an ambulance on the way," Hank said. "I've directed it to come in the back way because both the shooter's truck and Detective Radford's are blocking the road that way." He waved to the north. "I was barely able to get around it myself. There are wreckers coming for both trucks."

***

Barry Jones was angrier than he'd ever been in his life, and that was saying something because he had a terrible temper and had lost control of it countless times. He'd tried his best to shoot Detective Radford, but the PI was too fast and had been able to keep out of the way of the bullets. He swore that he'd get him yet. And he'd get the other two detectives.

He finally reached the highway. He was certain this jeep he was driving was being looked for by the worthless cops. So, he stopped in the middle of the road and, using his pistol, forced the driver of a very nice Ford Expedition to stop. He forced the driver out by threatening to shoot him. Then he jumped in and drove to the west. He would drive in that direction and stay west somewhere for the night. But he'd return in the next couple of days. He was not to be denied the revenge he sought.

He had ignored the pain from the lucky shot the PI had made. It had hit him in the lower leg, his calf. He had yet to look at it. He was aware that it had bled some, but he was tough. He wouldn't worry about it. He thought it was probably just a scratch.

***

Maya stayed with Carter as he met with the police chief of Hurricane and later with some officers from St. George. He wasn't needed in the courtroom until one o'clock. He and Maya went to lunch, where they talked about what Carter had learned in a phone call from Bentley early that morning.

"He's lucky he didn't get shot!" she exclaimed.

"He knows he wounded Barry Jones, but he got away. He and Hank both believe he will try again. I've got to be extra careful when we get back. He's a very dangerous man," Carter said.

"I hope he gets caught before we get back tomorrow."

"I agree, but I'm not going to count on it," Carter said. "I wonder how Gina is. Even though it's been many weeks, I still can't quit thinking about her."

"Neither can I," Maya agreed.

Carter had traveled to St. George because of Larry Jones's difficult attorney. He sat in the courtroom with Maya next to him without ever being called to the stand to testify. He was prepared and looking forward to it. The defense counsel and the prosecutor approached the judge's bench. They conferred for a moment, and then the judge granted a short recess.

When the recess was called, Carter and Maya went into the hallway where Chief Childers and one of the St. George detectives joined them. "I apologize, but it looks like you've wasted a trip, Detective. The defense attorney says his client wants a plea deal. So, they are working one out. We'll know in the next hour if it happens, but I believe it will."

"I hope he doesn't get off too easy," Carter said.

"I don't think he will. Let's see what happens in the next hour. Then, if it does settle, you will be free to leave," the chief said. An hour later, that is what they did. The hearing was over, and the case was also over. Larry Jones would be going to prison, but not for as long as he probably deserved.

Carter and Maya went to dinner with the police chief, who insisted on paying. "If it hadn't been for you, Larry would have gotten away with everything. Thanks for your effort. And of course, your rooms are on my department."

They went to some rooms in a nice hotel, hoping to get some good rest. Carter was in a lot of pain, because sitting in the courtroom for all those hours had not been good for him. What he needed now was to take some pain meds and get a good night's sleep before they headed back to Duchesne the following morning.

***

Barry Jones was in a lot of pain. The gunshot wound that the PI had inflicted on him was worse than he'd thought. He'd gotten a motel room in Heber City where he'd cleaned the wound the best he could. Then he'd thrown the ruined jeans in the trash and took a shower. He'd then gone out and found a place to buy a couple of prepackaged ham and cheese sandwiches as well as Tylenol and Hydrogen Peroxide. He'd taken four pills and doused the Hydrogen Peroxide on the wound before eating half of a sandwich. He couldn't eat more than that. He had eventually fallen asleep.

It was dark by the time he crawled painfully from the bed after lying there for over an hour thinking about what he should do. He hated to put off shooting the detectives, but he decided that he would come back in a few weeks and get the job done then. However, he fully intended to grab Maya so he would have some pretty female companionship. He planned that for late that night. It would simply be a matter of picking the lock on a door and going in and grabbing her from her bed at gunpoint.

If anyone tried to stop him it would be too bad for them. He would not be denied that pretty girl. In his mind, she was his. No one could stop him from taking her. Before he could go to Duchesne, he had to find something to drive. He would leave the latest stolen car in the parking lot behind the hotel.

His plan made, Barry Jones took a bunch more of the Tylenol, ate the rest of the first sandwich, and prepared to wait an hour or two before stealing another car and making the seventy-mile drive to Duchesne.

***

With Maya out of town, Dale Warwick didn't worry as much about Barry Jones. In fact, knowing that Bentley Radford had hit him in the leg with a bullet, he was hopeful that Jones would be laid up somewhere. He'd spoken with Detective Sergeant Hank Parker at around seven. Hank had informed him that officers were checking every medical facility for miles around.

The gangster had last been seen shortly after the shootout with Bentley by a man whose car Jones had stolen at gunpoint about twenty miles west of Duchesne. He'd driven west in the theft victim's car after leaving the stolen jeep in the middle of the highway. The stolen car had not been seen since.

Dale and Natalie had talked on the phone with Maya around nine. She'd informed them that the case against Larry Jones had been settled, so Carter had not had to testify in the hearing. She and Carter planned to head home after breakfast the next morning.

The Warwicks had gone to bed about eleven and were sleeping when Dale woke up and thought he heard his front door squeak. He'd been going to fix that for some time but had not yet gotten around to it. The fact that it squeaked in the middle of the night prompted Dale to grab the 9mm he had on the bed stand and roll quietly out of bed.

His movement woke Natalie who started to say something when he whispered, "Shh. There's someone in the house. Get in the bathroom and lock the door," he whispered. "Take your phone and call 911."

Natalie did as Dale asked while he slipped to the bedroom door with his pistol in one hand and his phone in the other. He slipped the phone into the pocket of his pajamas. He stopped without opening the door and listened. He and his wife were the only ones in the house since Maya was gone, and the three older children were all living elsewhere. Her little brother was at a friend's house for the night. No one else should be in the house.

Dale heard nothing at first, but after a moment he heard what sounded like a shuffling of feet in the living room. He opened the door ever so slowly and stood on the far side of it against the wall. Again, he didn't hear anything for a short while. Then, once more, he heard the shuffling. The intruder entered the hallway.

The Warwick's house was two stories with only the master bedroom on the main floor. Three others were upstairs. The stairway was at the end of the hallway that led to the master bedroom. The shuffling stopped there. Then the intruder started slowly up the steps. Dale slipped into the hallway and moved silently toward the stairway. He stopped and stood against the wall at the bottom of the stairs and listened.

The intruder reached the top of the stairs. A dim nightlight at the top gave out just enough light so that Dale could see the intruder's body, dressed all in black, move toward the first bedroom up there. Maya's room. The intruder stopped at the door, and then he slowly opened it.

From Dale's vantage point at the bottom of the stairs the figure was little more than a dark silhouette. Had Maya been home, Dale would have already taken action to stop the intruder. As it was, he simply waited. A cop should be there soon. At least he hoped so. Other than windows in each of the bedrooms, the only exit from the upstairs was the stairway where Dale waited, barefoot and in dark blue pajamas. He hoped he wouldn't be easily seen when the man in black came back out of Maya's room.

Sounds of things being tossed around came from the open doorway of Maya's room. Muttered curses could be heard. Dale was almost certain that he knew who the intruder was. It had to be Barry Jones. Dale was torn. Should he hurry quietly up the stairs and confront the guy in Maya's room? Or should he wait down here and confront him when he started down the stairs? He hoped he wouldn't have to wait long until a cop came. Then he could go to the door and let the officer in and the two of them could confront Jones.

He didn't have to decide about going up the stairs because the intruder came out of Maya's bedroom. In a moment, he could be seen quite clearly in the glow of the little nightlight. Dale stood with his back against the wall across the hall from the stairway. He pointed his pistol at the dark figure and waited to see what he would do.

To his dismay, Jones, if that was who the intruder was, pulled a pistol from his pocket. Without warning, he fired down the stairs. He'd spotted Dale despite the darkness of the house. The bullet hit the wall behind Dale. He crouched low as he fired a round up the stairs. Flames came out of the intruder's pistol at the same time that Dale felt a tug at his right leg.

Dale fired again at the intruder as he was sinking to the floor. He heard the intruder curse and crash against the wall. Then he watched as the shadowy intruder slowly sank to the floor. Still, the man in black fired another shot down the stairway, but by then, Dale had dragged himself toward his bedroom and the bullet struck the wall where he'd been only moments before. He knew his left leg was in bad shape. It felt like the bullet had struck a bone. It was bound to be bleeding badly.

He managed to keep a grip on his pistol as he leaned back against the wall. The dark figure got back on his feet and started back toward Maya's bedroom. Dale almost fired but stopped himself short. The man was just a shadowy figure at that point. The door to Maya's room shut. Hopefully Jones was trapped now in the girl's bedroom.

If only a cop would get here. He'd no sooner had that thought than he heard the front door open. Jones, if he was the intruder, had not locked it behind him, which was not surprising. How he'd unlocked it was a mystery to Dale, but he hurt too badly to worry about that now. He spoke softly to the officer. “He’s in Maya’s room. I’m shot.”

“Dale, it’s me, Hank. I’ll call for an ambulance. More officers are on the way. I was the closest.”

Just then there was a crash of breaking glass. “He’s going out the window,” Dale said weakly. Just then Natalie rushed from the bedroom to Dale’s side. She dropped beside him. “It’s my left leg,” he said, and then he blacked out.

Chapter 37

Hank saw that Natalie was at Dale's side. Dale turned on the flashlight he held, found a light switch and flooded the hallway with light. "I've called an ambulance. I think the shooter jumped out the window of Maya's room."

"I'll take care of Dale. You go outside and catch him," Natalie said. She was already pressing a palm against his leg where the bullet had gone in.

Hank hated to leave Dale and Natalie just in case the intruder had broken the window only to try to make it appear that he'd gone out. He got on his portable radio and instructed an officer to go around to the back. "I'm staying inside," he continued. "Be careful, the guy's armed and dangerous."

Hank got a reply from an officer. As soon as he was sure the outside was covered, he headed for the stairs. He bounded up and then, after reaching the top, he stood beside Maya's door with his back to the wall and reached for the doorknob. He eased it open. A bullet flew past him. He dropped to the floor and shoved the door the rest of the way open.

Barry Jones was bleeding from at least two wounds. He was at the window. He shot wildly in Hank's direction and then dropped through the window to the ground below. Hank rushed over and looked out. Barry was on the ground, not moving. A deputy was approaching him with a gun drawn. It was dark outside, but there was enough light from a nearby streetlight to make it possible for the deputy to tell if Barry tried anything.

"I'm coming down," Hank called out to the officer and ran for the stairs, hurried down, and glanced to where Natalie and Sheriff Goldman were kneeling beside Dale. He could see that the sheriff was now applying pressure to the wound. Hank rushed out the front door and around the house.

Two deputies were now standing beside where the intruder was crumpled on the ground, his face facing the house. Hank joined them. He shined his light on the face of the man. It was definitely Barry Jones. His handgun lay on the ground five feet away. Barry wasn't moving. One of the deputies told Hank that Jones was alive.

"See if you can do anything for him," Hank said. "I'm going back inside. Dale Warwick has been shot."

An ambulance arrived shortly after Hank had joined Sheriff Goldman and Natalie Warwick. Dale's eyes fluttered open. "Did he get away"? Dale asked in a weak voice.

"No, we've got him outside. You did well, Dale."

Three EMTs came running in. "There's an injured man outside too. A couple of deputies are with him. One of you might want to help. Another ambulance will be needed but this man here is our first priority."

Sheriff Goldman moved away from Dale as two of the EMTs took over and the third one headed for the front door at a jog. "I already told dispatch to send one. How bad is Jones? It is Barry Jones, isn't it?" the sheriff asked.

"It is Barry. He's in a real bad way," Hank said.

"He was after Maya," Natalie said as she too made room for the EMTs to care for her husband. "Thank goodness she went with Carter to St. George."

***

Maya awoke to the ringing of her cell phone which she'd placed on the nightstand beside her. She groggily picked it up and looked at the screen. Her mother was calling. "Hi Mom, what's the matter?"

"Your dad will be okay, but he's at the hospital," her mother said calmly.

Maya was instantly anything but calm. “It’s the middle of the night. What happened to him?” she shouted.

“He was shot in the leg by Barry Jones who came to the house to take you by force. Thank goodness you are in St. George,” Natalie said. “Your dad shot him as well. Twice, I’m told. He jumped out of your window. For Jones, it was that or he would have been shot by Hank Parker. He’s no longer a threat.”

Maya felt faint. “Is he dead?” she asked as she sank down on her bed, holding her phone above her.

“No, but he’s busted up badly. He’s been shot three times. Your dad got him twice, but he has a badly infected wound on his calf from where Bentley shot him before,” Natalie said calmly.

Maya’s heart was racing a mile a minute, and she had broken out in sweat. Her hand was shaking. “Where are you, Mom?” she asked.

“I’m on the way to the hospital,” she said.

“Mom, you shouldn’t be driving,” she said.

“I’m not, Maya. Sister Rogers is taking me in her car.”

“It’s late. Make sure she doesn’t get too tired.”

“She’s wide awake, and so am I,” Natalie said. “I would like you to wake Carter and come home as soon as you can.”

“Okay. He’s in a room two doors down from mine. I’ll call him,” Maya said. She was finally calming down. “Let me know how dad is when you get to the hospital.”

“I will dear,” her mother said. “You and Carter will need to take turns driving.”

“I know. I’ll do as much of the driving as he needs me to.”

***

Carter’s phone woke him from a sound sleep. He’d been dreaming about Gina, which he did quite often. He wondered if the call was to tell him she had been found. He answered the phone without looking at the screen.

“Carter, it’s me, Maya. We need to head home as soon as we can be ready.”

Maya sounded fairly calm. She wasn’t talking rapidly like she usually did when she was excited or upset. “Please tell me that Gina has been found and is okay,” Carter said.

"I'm afraid it's not that. Barry Jones tried to find me and take me from my house," she said.

"It's good you are down here, but tell me what else is going on, Maya."

Now her voice became less calm. "Dad is going to be okay," she said and then gave Carter a short version of what had occurred.

Carter said, "This is awful, Maya. Well, awful about your dad, but it's great news about Barry Jones. I'll meet you at your door in five minutes, if that's enough time for you to be ready to go."

"I'll be ready," she said as Carter looked at the time on his phone. It was about 4:30. He hoped they would be awake enough to drive.

He started out as the first driver after agreeing with Maya that they would need to take turns since they didn't want either one of them to get too tired. They were nearly at Cedar City. Carter said, "Should we eat now or wait until we get to Beaver?"

"Beaver," Maya replied.

"Sounds good," he said just as his phone rang. Since it was synced, they could both hear whoever the caller was.

It was Bentley. "It's been quite a night here. I'm glad you guys were out of town," he said.

"I wish we were back in Duchesne," Carter said. "Maya is anxious to see her father."

"That's one of the reasons I'm calling. He is in surgery, but they say he will recover okay. The bullet broke a bone, so that has to be repaired. An orthopedic surgeon is taking care of that now."

"I'm glad he wasn't hurt worse," Maya said with a catch in her voice.

"We all are," Bentley agreed.

"What's the other reason you're calling?" Carter asked.

"It's about the guy that shot you," Bentley said. "The wound from the bullet I hit him with is badly infected. He has a lot of other problems, such as broken bones from jumping from Maya's window. He also has two gunshot wounds from where Maya's dad shot him. As dark as it was in the house, it's hard to believe he hit him twice. Barry got him once, but he shot a lot more at him and then more at Hank. But the doctors tell us that the infection will probably kill him. It's spread all through his leg.

"If it's that bad, how did he manage to keep going?" Maya asked.

"Hatred, I guess. You guys drive carefully. I'll see you later," Bentley concluded.

Bentley called them three hours later. "Maya, your dad is out of surgery and resting. Your mother is with him in his room. She'd like you to come straight to the hospital if you guys can still drive safely by then."

"We'll be okay," Carter said.

"One other thing," Bentley said. "Barry Jones died a few minutes ago."

"I know I shouldn't say this, but I'm glad. Now if only Gina and Sammy would be found. I know that's not likely after this much time, but I'm not giving up hope," Carter said.

"I'm not either," Maya added. "All we can do now is pray for a miracle. President Nelson said in one of his talks that we should pray for miracles and then expect them. I've sure been praying for one."

"I have too," Carter added. "I wish I could say I expect a miracle, but I sure hope for one."

Chapter 38

A COUPLE MORE WEEKS PASSED, AND GINA WAS FEELING QUITE GOOD. She was using her arm and was able to put a little weight on her foot. Neither one of them hurt too much. As they were eating breakfast one morning Jeremy said. "Gina, there's no way you can walk out of here yet. It would be too much. But let me ask you both something."

"What?" Gina and Sammy asked in almost perfect unison.

"Would you still be afraid to stay here alone for three or four days?" Jeremy asked.

"Why would we need to be alone?" Gina asked.

"How bad do you guys want to get home?"

"You know we want to get home as soon as we possibly can," Gina said.

"I really miss my mom and dad," Sammy said.

"If you guys could stay here and take care of Blacky for three days, maybe four, I could hike into a town, buy a mule and bring him back."

"Do you mean we could ride him through the forest to go home?" Sammy asked.

"Yes, that's what I have in mind. Would you be willing?"

Gina had been thinking about it very seriously. "Sammy, we were okay alone in the forest for all those days. I think we would be okay here, don't you?"

"I feel safe with you, Gina. And with Blacky I would feel even safer," Sammy said.

"Is it okay with you guys then? I promise that I'll hurry."

Sammy looked at Gina and nodded. She said, "Yes, we'll be fine."

"I'll fix a pack for myself and leave right after we finish the breakfast dishes," Jeremy said.

"We'll do the dishes," Gina said. "The sooner you leave the sooner you'll be back."

A half hour later, Jeremy hugged the two of them "You know, it will be lonely here for me after you two are gone. But I'll just have to get used to it again, won't I?"

"I love you, Doctor Jeremy. Thanks for saving our lives," Sammy said.

"You'll leave me some of the pictures you've drawn to remember you by, won't you?"

"Of course I will."

"Jeremy," Gina said. "You saved our lives, but you also helped me to heal. I can never thank you enough. Like Sammy, I love you."

"And I love both of you. I'll be on my way now."

They watched him as he disappeared from view, and then they went back in the cabin and proceeded to clean up from breakfast. Gina was so excited she nearly burst. She would be seeing Carter in a few days. And her parents and younger brother, too, she thought. And she'd see her best friend, Maya. She tried to imagine how surprised and happy they would all be. They might have thought she and Sammy were dead, but they had survived, thanks to Jeremy and to Heavenly Father.

***

Jeremy was motivated, so he made good time on the long, arduous trek to a small Colorado city where he had purchased supplies before. He walked to the same ranch where he had bought his first mules. They had a nice big black mule that was super gentle, well broke to both a saddle and a packsaddle. He wasn't young, but at twenty, there were a lot of years left in him. He hadn't been able to bring a packsaddle with him, so he bought an old but serviceable one at the ranch.

He led the mule with the packsaddle strapped on his back to the nearby town, where he began to buy supplies. He stepped out of a grocery store when he saw a man across the street that looked like Anders Fowler, the brother of the woman whose death he had been falsely accused of causing. Anders was a hateful, angry man. He hoped Anders hadn't recognized him, if it was Anders, because he didn't want a confrontation with the guy.

The man across the street stepped into a small shop. As soon as he was out of sight, Jeremy took his purchases to where he'd tied his new mule and loaded them on his back. He wanted a few more items, so he went back into town but to a different street than the one where he'd seen the man he believed was Anders. He kept looking for the man but didn't see him.

He wanted to get something special for Gina and Sammy. So he bought them both a new pair of shoes and a pair of pants and shirts he thought would fit them. He bought a couple of packages of cookies and some candy. He also bought Gina an iPhone. She wouldn't be able to use it until he left her and Sammy at the town in two or three days. Then they could both call and surprise their families. He had to smile at the thought of the wonderful surprise it would be.

He had already talked to them about the fact that they could not tell anyone his name or attempt to describe where he lived. They'd both understood and agreed to what he wanted, or what he needed.

He bought some more items he could use at the homestead. He also bought wheat, flour, sugar, salt, and dried beans. He added a small supply of macaroni and spaghetti. He also purchased a fifty-pound sack of potatoes. That was a luxury but he would enjoy having potatoes occasionally. Finally, he loaded the mule with everything. It was heavy but the mule was strong and healthy. He knew it would not be a problem for the mule.

He looked around before heading to the nearby forest. He hadn't seen Anders Fowler, or the man he thought was him, since that one time. Before leading the big black mule into the forest, he looked around once again. Then he set off at a steady pace for his distant homestead.

***

Good to his word, Jeremy walked into the homestead leading a large black mule in the early afternoon of the fourth day since he'd left. Gina and Sammy started to leave the house to greet him. But when they stepped onto the deck, Gina saw something that threw terror into her heart. She put a restraining hand on Sammy as she cried out, "Jeremy, look out! There's a man with a gun behind you!"

Gina had only got the first words out when Jeremy dropped the mule's lead rope, jumped to one side and drew his pistol. A shot rang out, then a second. The man behind Jeremy missed and the bullet struck a tree just a few feet from Sammy and Gina. Jeremy did not miss. The man dropped to the ground, his pistol falling away from him.

Blacky roared like an angry bear and tore past the kids and Jeremy and grabbed the man on the ground by the throat. "No, Blacky!" Jeremy shouted.

The big black dog let go of the shooter, but he stood over him, growling menacingly. Jeremy was jogging back to where the dog stood guard. He patted Blacky's head. "Good dog," he said.

Gina had been unable to restrain herself. To Sammy she said, "You stay here." Then she ran to Jeremy.

He was staring at the man on the ground. Jeremy's swift shot had been true. Blood covered his chest. And his throat was torn where Blacky had seized him with his powerful jaws.

"Is . . . is . . . he dead?" Gina stammered.

Jeremy looked down at her and shook his head. "No, but even though I'm a doctor I can't save him. His injuries are way too severe."

The man on the ground stirred. "You . . . killed . . . my . . . sister."

"Jeremy dropped to the ground beside the dying man. "I had nothing to do with your sister's death, Anders. It was proven, but you, in your blind hatred, continued to blame me for something I didn't do. I'm truly sorry about your sister," Jeremy said sadly. "You and your family destroyed my career as a surgeon, and I was a good one."

Once again the man on the ground spoke as bloody froth sprayed from his mouth. "I . . . knew . . . you . . . must . . . have . . . a . . . place . . . out . . . here. It . . . should . . . be . . . mine. You . . . owe . . . me." The man's eyes closed, a ragged breath shook his body and then he was still.

"I must bury him before I take you two out of the forest so you can join your families," Jeremy said softly as tears poured from his eyes and ran down into his black beard. "Anders's family just couldn't accept the truth, but I had no idea Anders's hatred was so out of control. I thought I saw a man that looked like him in town. I guess it was him."

Gina hugged her big friend and then looked down at the dead man. He was a small, muscular man with short brown hair. A backpack was wedged under his body. She tore her eyes from the grizzly sight. "I'm sorry, Jeremy. You are the best. I love you."

"I love you too, Doctor Jeremy." Sammy, unnoticed by Gina, had quietly joined them.

"His name is Anders Fowler," Jeremy said after lifting Sammy from the ground in his strong arms. He held him tight in a loving embrace. "I thought I saw Anders in the town near the ranch where I bought the mule. I didn't see him again, so I decided it must not have been him."

"He followed you here," Gina said. It was not a question.

"He must have done so, because no one could ever find this place any other way. If Blacky had been with me he would have known and tipped me off, but I'm glad he was here with you guys," Jeremy said as he wiped his eyes and put Sammy back on the ground.

"Let's catch the mule and take the pack off him, and then I'll put him in the barn. I'll go out there somewhere and dig a grave later this afternoon. After he's buried, we'll unpack the supplies I bought. I'll begin taking you two back to civilization tomorrow, which is quite some distance from here Oh, how I will miss you both."

"We will miss you too, won't we Sammy?" Gina said.

"Yes," Sammy said as he choked back a sob.

"Jeremy, do you think his family will realize he came here? Will they come after you too?" Gina asked as she helped Jeremy undo the straps that held the large pack on the mule's back.

"No, he was the one who kept them all stirred up. He never would even look at the evidence like a few members of the family eventually did. He was an evil man by nature. I'm sure they'll wonder what happened to him, but there is no way I can take his body back. It would only cause me more trouble, and I don't need more trouble," Jeremy said. "Let's lead the mule to the deck and unload the supplies he carried here for me. I love this place I built."

They were walking toward where the big mule stood a few feet from the cabin. "But it will sure seem lonely when you two are no longer here with me. You are my family now and I love you both deeply."

When Sammy and Gina both insisted that they come with him to bury the body, Jeremy said. "I hate to expose you to that."

Gina put her hands on her hips and said, "We know all about dead bodies. We had to carry supplies from the back of the plane over Elliot."

"I guess you won't be too shocked then when we load him on the mule and carry him a couple of miles from the homestead," he said. He grabbed two shovels and they loaded the dead man on the mule and trekked through the dense forest for a couple of miles. It reminded Gina of the trek he and Sammy had made those days after the crash.

The ground was rocky but soft due to the recent rain. They worked hard at digging the grave. Jeremy did most of it, but Gina and Sammy took turns digging. They dug until the hole was about three feet deep. Then they rolled the dead man, his pack and his gun into the hole and spent the next hour shoveling the rock and dirt back in.

Chapter 39

Sammy squealed when Jeremy pulled cookies and candy from the supplies the mule had carried for him. "These are for dessert, but you may each have a cookie and a piece of chocolate before dinner. We are going to fry potatoes and some slices of venison to eat."

"I haven't had potatoes for a long time," Sammy said as he licked his lips in anticipation. "I like candy and cookies too." The boy was grinning.

The next morning was a sad occasion and a happy one. Gina was excited to be going home at last and couldn't wait to see Carter. But leaving this place was hard. She and Sammy had made a lot of fond memories here.

"I have something else for you, Gina," Jeremy said. He presented her with a brand-new iPhone. I don't want you to turn this on until I am on my way back here. The code to open it is 4321. Of course, you can change that and add your picture to open it with. I'm sure you know all about such things."

"Thank you, Jeremy," she said as she flung herself into his strong arms. "You are such a wonderful man."

"I'm glad you think so," he said.

Jeremy put an old riding saddle on the mule. He put both the young people on, added a pack behind the saddle with some supplies for the trip. He also carried a backpack and had his six-shooter strapped to his side. Gina already knew that he was an excellent shot with the big revolver. He'd shown that when Anders Fowler had tried to shoot him

The three of them camped before they reached the edge of the forest and the towns beyond. They sat around a small campfire and visited like the good friends they had become. When they laid on blankets that night, Gina felt secure, something she had not felt on those nights she and Sammy had camped while lost and afraid. She had Jeremy to thank for that. She would never forget him and his kindness. He was a wonderful man who had been badly mistreated. But he did not pass that mistreatment on to others. He showed genuine love and support. Meeting and knowing him made all the horrors Gina had endured worth it.

The next morning, they had a small breakfast and then continued on their way. Gina insisted on walking beside Jeremy for a short distance. He kept asking how she was feeling, and she said she was doing okay. "When it gets uncomfortable, I will tell you," she said to him. "If it weren't for you, I would have ended up crippled for life. Thank you, Jeremy, for healing me."

"It was my pleasure," he said. "But you still have a lot of healing to do, so be very careful with your foot and arm, too."

They spent another night in the forest. The next day they eventually came to a road, the first one they'd seen since leaving the homestead two days and many miles back "We will cross this road," Jeremy said, "and go through the forest on the other side. When we get through there, I will leave you and start my return trip. I don't know that any of Anders's family will be in this town looking for him, but I can't take that chance."

"I will miss you," Gina said.

"I will miss you as well. I'll miss you too, Sammy," he said as he looked at the boy who was still on the mule. "Gina, you will need to do some walking as you go into town. I don't want you to overdo."

They reached the point where they needed to separate in another hour. They stood together inside the trees, out of sight of the highway Gina and Sammy needed to cross. Beyond it there were homes. She felt a churning in her gut as they said their goodbyes. Just before Jeremy let them go to the highway, he said, "Gina, I need to have you make a promise to me."

"Anything you ask," she said, and she meant it.

"Don't change the number on the phone I gave you. Do you promise?" he asked with a smile on that big, bearded face of his.

"I promise, but why?" she asked.

"Because I know that number by heart and when I get into town once or twice a year, I would like to be able to call and talk to you, to see how you are doing and to let you know that I will never forget you," Jeremy said.

"Wow! You would do that for me?" she asked.

"Yes, I would. You and Sammy are the only friends I have left in the world. You are my family. When I talk to you, I would hope that you would have a way to call Sammy and tell him what we talked about. In fact, if you keep in touch with him, you can tell me how he is doing and how his family is."

"I would love that, Jeremy," she said.

"Again, you can tell people you love, but only them, about how we came to know each other. And don't tell anyone but your family my name. Do you promise?" he asked.

"Yes, you have my word." Then she grinned. "Of course, I can't give them your last name because you never told us."

He smiled. "I was just being careful. That way no one could ever force you to tell. If you said my first name it would probably not do me any damage, but it is best that you don't know my last name. Thank you for promising me. I know that you will keep your word."

"I won't tell anyone your name either and I won't show anyone pictures of you. But I will keep one for myself and give one to Gina, if that is okay," Sammy said.

"You promise me that, Sammy?" the gentle giant asked.

"I promise," Sammy said. "I love you Doctor Jeremy, but I will never say your name again except to my family."

There were tears shed by all three. And there were hugs. Finally, Jeremy said, "I will watch until you are safely across the highway, and then I will return to my home. Oh, one last thing. I hope that it works out well for you and Carter."

The two formerly lost and missing young people walked to the edge of the road. They waited for traffic to clear and then they hurried to the other side. They both turned back. They could just barely see their giant of a friend inside the tree line. They both waved at him. He waved back, and then they watched until they could see him no more.

"Well, Sammy, it's just the two of us. Do you remember your mother's phone number?" she asked.

"I remember hers and my father's," he said.

She turned the phone on, entered the password and it opened. "There is only one bar here. We will wait until we have a good signal. Then we'll call our parents."

"And Carter," Sammy said.

"Yes, and Carter," she agreed. Then, limping noticeably, Gina led Sammy toward the town.

Chapter 40

Carter and Bentley were eating lunch at a local café in Roosevelt. They were working on a case that they'd accepted the day before. It looked like it was a simple case and they hoped to finish it up that afternoon and have a report ready for their client the next morning.

It was late in June. They had received the case on Thursday. They would work on the report together at Bentley's home in the hills. His wife had asked Carter to stay for dinner, which he gladly agreed to. His own cooking wasn't great.

Carter's phone rang as he was lifting a bite of salad to his mouth. He put the fork down and pulled his phone from the holder he now wore on his belt. He lifted it to his face and looked at the screen. "I don't know this number. Should I answer it? It could be a call to sell me something I don't need or want."

"Or it could be a potential client, even though for someone to call your phone is most unusual," Bentley said. "Answer it and see what it feels like."

It had rung several times by then. He hurried and accepted the call. "Hello, this is Carter," he said.

"Carter, it's Gina," he heard. His face went white, and his hand started to shake.

"What is it?" Bentley asked.

He didn't answer Bentley. Instead, he asked, "Gina, is that really you?"

"Yes," the caller said, and Carter noticed his partner's jaw drop.

"Of course it's me, silly. I just got this phone. I was afraid you wouldn't accept the call because you didn't recognize the number." The caller chuckled.

Oh yes, it was Gina Rogers. He knew that chuckle. He loved that chuckle. "Gina, are you safe?"

"Of course I'm safe," Gina said. "So is Sammy. I wouldn't be calling you if we weren't safe. We just crossed a busy highway, but we waited for a break in the traffic, and then we ran across. I held his hand the whole way."

Carter was stunned. He suddenly found it hard to speak as his emotions plummeted out of control. Tears poured down his cheeks. He even sobbed.

"Carter, are you there?"

"Y . . . yes. I'm in shock is all."

"Are you crying?" she asked.

"Of course I'm crying," he said. "What do you expect me to do?"

"To cry, and now I'm about to. Carter, I need to remind you of something."

"What?" he asked as he tried to control his brain which seemed a bit out of order.

"You owe me dinner and a movie. I got kidnapped before we got to go out like you'd asked me to, and I had agreed to."

"Well, let's do it. I sure don't want to be indebted to such a pretty girl," he said.

"Do you think I'm pretty?" she asked with a tease in her voice.

"I think you are gorgeous," he said.

"But you don't know that," she said. "You can't see how bad I look right now."

"Are you hurt?" he asked as he suddenly felt a twist in his gut.

"Not very much anymore," she said.

"What does that mean," Carter asked.

"It means I was hurt but now I'm almost healed," she said.

"Tell me what happened," he said.

"Not now. Not until I see you,"

"Will you take a selfie and send it to me?"

"You won't like what you see?"

"You don't know that. I will like what I see whatever you look like now."

"Are you sure?" Gina asked.

"Please. I'll wait."

"Okay but just because I li . . . like you," she said.

"I'm waiting," he told her. "Bentley. I am in shock. It's really her."

"You've been telling me that you felt like she was alive. So why are you in shock?"

"Aren't you in shock too?"

"Yes, Carter, I am in shock too."

Carter's phone dinged on an incoming message. He opened it and enlarged the picture she sent. He gasped. She looked rough. Her long blonde hair was a gnarled mess. And her face was dirty. Not only that, but it was darker. Like she'd tanned, he decided. He turned the phone so Bentley could see it too. Bentley shook his head. At least she looks like she's not hurt."

He clicked to the call again. "Yep," he fibbed. "You look gorgeous."

She chuckled. "Thanks for not telling me the truth. But give me a couple hours and I'll look better, I promise," she said. "Carter, I can't reach my parents, either of them."

"They are with Maya's folks at the temple. Their session should be over soon."

"I'll call them in a little while. How are they doing?" Gina asked.

"It's been rough on them, as you can imagine. Maya's folks have been very supportive." He didn't mention that Dale Warwick was on crutches. That bit of news could wait. "Where are you and Sammy at right now?"

She mentioned a town in Colorado. "It's about the size of Roosevelt. Do you know where it's at?" she asked.

"No, but I'll find it," he said.

"Why do you need to find it?" she asked.

"Because I'm coming to get you and Sammy," he said as Bentley nodded in agreement.

"Sammy and I need to get a motel room and clean up," she said.

"But don't you need money for that?" he asked

"I have some. A kind man gave us money, and I took some from Elliot's and Harry's wallets when they died. I figured they owed me that."

He had lots of questions, but they could wait until they were in the truck with him. He told her that he would be heading that way in about twenty minutes. The call ended. "I'm sorry, Bentley," he said. "I need to go."

"I will finish this case and type the report. You go get your girl and Sammy. Let me know how they survived all these weeks."

Carter was more excited than he'd ever been in his life. He loved Gina. And Maya had told him that Gina loved him. He prayed as he drove. Unlike the earnest prayers concerning her being found, he was praying now in humble gratitude to a loving Heavenly Father for protecting Gina, the love of his life.

***

Jim Rogers turned his phone on as he and his wife and the Warwicks left the Vernal temple. He'd found some peace as he'd prayed for Gina as he sat in the celestial room. But he was still worried sick over her. He'd prayed that day for a miracle. He and Sue desperately needed a miracle. There had been so many weeks pass since Gina had been taken from them.

Dale Warwick was using his crutches. He was healing from the bullet that had shattered the bone in his leg. It would be a while before Dale could drive. Jim and Sue had brought their car to the temple that day. The two couples were slowly making their way through the parking lot when Jim's phone rang. "That didn't take long to have a call come in. I just turned my phone on and it's ringing already."

Jim glanced at the screen and said, "Some spam call, it looks like."

"Jim, answer it anyway," Sue said.

"Why?" Jim asked.

"I don't know why, just do it," she insisted.

Jim shrugged his shoulders. He hit the accept button, lifted the phone to his ear, and said, "Hello."

"Daddy! It's me. It's Gina."

Jim stopped in his tracks as he felt the blood drain from his face. For a moment he couldn't speak for the shock.

"Jim, you don't look good. Who is it?" Sue asked.

Jim didn't answer Sue, but he finally found his voice and spoke into the phone. "Sweetheart, is that really you?"

"Of course it's me," Gina said. "Don't you recognize my voice?"

"Yes, Gina, I recognize your voice. I am in shock. We just left the temple where I prayed for a miracle."

"I am your miracle, Daddy," the much-loved voice of his daughter said.

"Let me put this on speaker. Your mother is jerking at my arm."

As he hit the speaker button on his iPhone, Sue was jumping up and down. "It's Gina. Oh my word. It's our daughter. She's alive."

"Yes, Mom, I'm alive and so is Sammy."

"Where are you?" Dale asked as Sue and Maya's mother hugged, tears streaming down their faces.

Gina named a town in Colorado. "I know where that is. We need to take the Warwicks home and then we'll come after you."

"Carter is coming. Call him. He's probably about to Vernal by now. You could ride with him. Please, I can't wait to see you guys. I've missed you so much, and I love you."

***

Carter was driving past the rest area just west of Vernal when his phone rang. He grabbed it, saw it was Jim Rogers, and said, "Hi, Jim."

"We just talked to Gina. She says you are on your way to get her. We'd like to come with you."

"That would be great. Are you still near the temple?"

"We are in the parking area. Nicole will drive our car back to Duchesne if you will pick us up and let us ride with you," Jim responded.

"I'll be there in a few minutes. I'm just coming into Vernal. Can you believe it? It's a miracle."

"It is that," Jim agreed.

Chapter 41

Maya was sitting on her bed doing what she did a lot these days. She was sobbing. She was afraid she would never see her best friend again. She was so sad, but it was not all for her. She was sad for Carter. She'd gotten to know him well on their trips to St. George. He was a wonderful guy. He loved Gina. He needed Gina. If only Gina was okay. But she feared that she wasn't.

When her phone rang she picked it up without even looking at the screen, choked back a sob and said, "Hello."

"How's my best friend?" she heard Gina ask.

"Gina!" she screamed. "You are alive." Her tears flowed freely now. But they were tears of indescribable joy.

"Of course I'm alive. How could I call if I wasn't?"

The girls laughed and cried together. Gina told her just the barest sketch of where she was and how she'd ended up there. Maya also recognized a miracle when she saw one, and this was a miracle.

***

Ophelia Anders was walking around the neighborhood. Her heart was heavy. She and Samuel had lost Sammy, but they'd regained their health. Samuel was at work now. She was aching for him to be home soon. She needed him so badly since Sammy had been taken. And she knew he needed her.

She had her phone tucked in the back pocket of her jeans. She hated to call him at work, but she needed to hear his voice right now. But before she could dial her phone rang. She didn't recognize the number so she rejected the call. She wished spam calls could be stopped. The only voice she wanted to hear right now was Samuel's. The unknown caller was persistent. She accepted it and said, "I don't need whatever you are selling," she said.

Before she could end the call, a small voice on the phone said, "Mommy. I need you."

Nicole felt herself fainting and she slowly sank to the sidewalk. Could it really be?

She fought off the faintness and finally said into the phone, "Sammy. Is it really you?"

"Yes mommy," the voice of her beloved son said. "I miss you and daddy."

"Daddy is at work," Nicole said. "We both miss you, Sammy."

For a moment, her son didn't speak. When he did, he said "I'm coming home. Gina and I are safe."

After speaking tearfully to her son for several minutes, Nicole called Samuel at work. "Dear, we need to go to Duchesne. Sammy is safe and he is going to go there with Gina."

"What! Nicole, are you serious? Is our son really safe?"

"Yes. Watch for a number you don't recognize. It will be Sammy," she said.

"It's ringing right now, I'll take it," Samuel said. "I'll talk to you shortly."

Chapter 42

One year later

GINA WAS A BEAUTIFUL BRIDE. SHE STOOD BESIDE HER NEW HUSBAND, glowing. They were outside the Vernal Utah Temple, where she and Carter had been married a few minutes earlier. Pictures were taken outside the temple. The entire Rogers family was there. So were the Warwicks and the Bentleys. And to Gina's joy, Sammy Anders and his parents had come all the way from St. George to be there for this special day.

Sammy Anders was beaming in a new blue suit. He turned to Maya, who was at his side. He said, "Isn't she pretty?"

"She certainly is," a deep voice said behind Sammy and Maya.

Sammy spun, squealing in delight. "Doctor Jeremy," he cried and jumped into the giant's outstretched arms.

Gina, who had been looking at her husband as a picture flashed, heard Sammy and looked over to where he and Maya were standing. She cried, "It's Jeremy!" Then she ran from the steps she'd been standing on and flew toward the giant who had saved her life. Jeremy held Sammy in one long arm and wrapped the other one around Gina.

"I didn't expect to see you here," Gina said with glee.

"You told me a few months ago when and where you and your young man were getting married. So Blacky, the mule, and I, made a trip to town. I rented a truck and took off immediately. Remember, you two are my only family."

When Jeremy released Gina from her hug, she shouted, "Hey, everybody, this is the wonderful man who saved my life and Sammy's! Come meet him."

About the Author

Clair M. Poulson was born and raised in Duchesne, Utah. His father was a rancher and farmer, his mother a librarian. Clair has always been an avid reader, having found his love for books as a very young boy.

He has served for over fifty years in the criminal justice system. Twenty years were spent in law enforcement, ending his police career with eight years as the Duchesne County Sheriff. For thirty-one years Clair worked as a justice court judge for Duchesne County and is now retired from the court. He is also a veteran of the US Army where he was a military policeman. Clair has been personally involved in the investigation of murders and other violent crimes in his career. He has served on various boards and councils during his professional career, including the Justice Court Board of Judges, Utah Commission on Criminal and Juvenile Justice, Utah Judicial Council, Utah Peace Officer Standards and Training Council, an FBI advisory board, and others.

In addition to his criminal justice work, Clair has farmed and ranched all of his life. He has raised many kinds of animals. He is also involved in the grocery store business with his oldest son and other family members.

Clair has served in many capacities in The Church of Jesus Christ of Latter-day Saints, including as a full-time missionary (California Mission), bishop, counselor to two bishops, Young Men president, high councilor, stake mission president, scoutmaster, high priest group leader, Sunday School teacher, and young single adult advisor.

Clair is married to Ruth, and together, they have five children, all of whom are married: Alan (Vicena) Poulson, Kelly Ann (Wade) Hatch, Amanda (Ben) Semadeni, Wade (Brooke) Poulson, and Mary (Tyler) Hicken. They have twenty-six grandchildren who they both cherish and love to spend quality time with. They also have seven great-grandchildren. Clair and Ruth met while both were students at Snow College and were married in the Manti Temple in 1969.

Clair has always loved telling his children, and later his grandchildren, make-up stories. His vast experience in life and his love of literature has always contributed to both his telling stories to children and his writing of adventure and suspense novels.